THRILL KILLERS

THRILL KILLERS

Clifford L. Linedecker

PaperJacks LTD.

TORONTO   NEW YORK

AN ORIGINAL

PaperJacks

THRILL KILLERS

PaperJacks LTD

330 STEELCASE RD. E., MARKHAM, ONT. L3R 2M1
210 FIFTH AVE., NEW YORK, N.Y. 10010

PaperJacks edition published March 1988

ISBN 0-7701-0650-1
Printed in the USA

PREFACE

Stretching from the tension-filled streets of overcrowded metropolitan areas to the once quiet and safe outposts of rural America, there is growing terror afoot about a certain type of killer.

He is a mystery to many psychologists and criminologists and a frustrating nightmare to law-enforcement officials. He has many faces, varied backgrounds, and an intelligence level that literally runs the length of the I.Q. scale. We neither fully understand him nor know his motivations. In all too many instances — perhaps literally hundreds — we don't even know *who* he is. Yet he has made such a terrifying impact on us that his actions have earned him his own special title, and he has become something of a dark chamber celebrity to a population fascinated by the bizarre. He is the Serial Killer who, generally during aimless travels (sometimes in a relatively small geographic area; sometimes coast to coast), seeks out victims for reasons that range from carnal thrill to the mad response to demands from imagined voices on high.

We have called him Bundy and Berkowitz, Gacy and Henley, Buono and Bianchi, and have celebrated his evil cruelties in screaming newspaper headlines, in books, and on movie and television screens. We have given lurid nicknames — the Green River Killer, the Vampire Murderer — to those of his kind whom we know to be still at large.

And with each new revelation of his crimes, we become increasingly aware that no one is immune to his madness. He has brought a chilling new meaning to the word "random." The Serial Killer acts on the slightest, most casual of motives; his potential victims are everywhere — you, me, the people next door. Because of him we have a new fear of the dark.

And from that fear has been born a public demand that the horror be ended; that law-enforcement agencies somehow magically make our streets and homes safe again. That cannot be done unless more attention is paid to the motives and methods of the Serial Killer: to wage proper battle, one must first understand the enemy.

Though it is believed that some 5,000 Americans die annually at the hands of those the FBI has described as "recreational killers," not much information has been collected that points directly to the cause. The Serial Killer remains the enigma of the criminal world. He is just as likely to be an outwardly charming, intelligent, and financially successful individual as he is to be an obviously deranged drifter from the bottom of the social barrel. He might be a doctor or a lawyer — or an alcoholic ex-con hitchhiking nowhere without a dime in his pocket.

Researchers have provided what amounts to little more than generalized scattershot theories, piecing together thin lines of similarities that seem to run through the personalities of such sadistic murderers. The Serial Killer, they tell us, was born to an unwed mother, likely a prostitute. He was a bed-wetter as a child. He has an elongated second toe. He likely suffered some form of brain damage at an early age. He has a hair lip or some other physical deformity. As a child he endured beatings and torture at the hands of his elders. He is stricken with recurring headaches and hallucinations, blackouts, and seizures. He has a low opinion of himself as well as of his victims. He is lacking in courage.

The Serial Killer, say some analysts, sees his nameless victims as symbolic surrogates for a parent who dealt him dark miseries as a child.

None of these theories is of much use to members of law-enforcement task forces who must sift through sometimes conflicting generalities to find a particular killer. The personality profiles supplied by the experts fit many people who have never had so much as a traffic ticket.

If, then, we are ever to discover who the Serial Killer really is, what triggers his rage, and how he plans and executes his gruesome crimes, we must somehow get to know him. Only in his mind will the answers be found.

This is why the book now in your hand is so important. The insight it provides is the first step toward finding the answers so desperately needed.

— Carlton Stowers
author of
Careless Whispers

ACKNOWLEDGEMENTS

I am indebted to many individuals and organizations for their contributions to the writing and accuracy of this book.

Police officers, prosecuting attorneys and members of their staffs, other courthouse employees, and journalists have all had a hand in its production, from the initial concept to the completed manuscript.

Special thanks, however, are due to the men and women of the Indian River County Sheriff's Department in Vero Beach, Florida, for assistance in obtaining photographs that deal with crimes that occurred in their jurisdiction; to *The Record* newspaper in Hackensack, N.J., and to the Federal Bureau of Investigation for photos as well as for an outpouring of information about serial killers in general, and several killers in particular. All other photographs in the book are courtesy of AP/Wide World Photos, Inc.

Thanks also to my literary agent, Dawson Taylor; and to Laurie Campbell for the many hours she spent assisting me in the preparation of the manuscript.

CONTENTS

INTRODUCTION

Perhaps the most infamous serial murderer of all time was Jack the Ripper. Yet only five victims (some crime historians say there was a sixth and final victim killed by him in February, 1891) are officially attributed to the reign of terror he visited on London prostitutes a century ago.

As shocking and hideous as the murders were, the Ripper's grisly toll pales by comparison to the grim death rosters compiled by today's serial killers. Like John Wayne Gacy who slaughtered at least thirty-three young men and boys and buried most of his victims under his house, most stop only when they are at last imprisoned.

Some, like Jack the Ripper, whose ghastly surgical assaults on prostitutes in London's sleazy East End mysteriously ceased after three terrible months in 1888, may never be apprehended and identified. The notorious "Green River Killer," whose crimes have baffled Seattle police since his first known victim was found in

July 1982, is one of those undiscovered killers. Despite the efforts of a police task force of nearly sixty men and women funded by an annual budget of between $2 million and $2.5 million, after four years the death toll attributed to the Green River Killer had climbed to a staggering forty-six women and girls. Yet, investigators appeared to be no closer to a solution in the case. The baffling slayings seemed to have slowed or stopped, however, and there were some indications that the killer might have moved his operations to Honolulu. Distressingly similar murders of young women were being investigated by police there.

In 1986, victims, usually black prostitutes, were also being stalked by serial killers in Miami and in Los Angeles, where the combined toll exceeded thirty dead by mid-year. In Houston, another mysterious woman-killer had been linked to a series of slayings and disappearances with similarities to the earlier bloodletting of convicted murderer Coral Eugene Watts.

Sadistic and merciless, serial killers usually spread murder and mutilation over a long period of time, and often over a wide geographical area. Henry Lee Lucas, the one-eyed drifter who once confessed to more than 360 murders, is known to have roamed thirty-six states, killing, raping, and stealing. Although he later recanted his confessions to all but three of the homicides, and law-enforcement authorities reluctantly conceded that they had wrongly closed the files on hundreds of murder cases, Lucas has, nevertheless, been convicted of ten slayings. He now faces execution in Texas for one of the murders.

Despite Lucas's tall-tale telling, his transient nature and casual selection of victims — often drifters like himself with no close family ties — helped him to get away with the murders he is known to have committed. Law-enforcement authorities are convinced that the bodies of scores, perhaps hundreds, of murder victims are disposed of and never found because there is no one to miss them and report their disappearances to police.

Some killers, such as Gacy and Los Angeles' notorious "Hillside Stranglers," Kenneth Bianchi and Angelo Buono, can be just as frustratingly elusive and difficult to run down. Because these killers move from one city neighborhood or suburb to another in their search for victims, their crimes are often obscured in the confusing bureaucratic tangle of different police jurisdictions.

The violence, which is sadistic and impersonal, and frequently is directed at targets that have nothing in common, can be baffling and nearly impossible to halt. Many times the slayings are not even recognized as serial murders until the killer is brought to justice and ashen-faced investigators begin to pull rotting bodies from under a house in suburban Chicago, from shallow graves in Florida citrus groves, or from dried-up Texas river beds.

Still other murders, such as those committed by the son of Sam killer, David Berkowitz, and the Love Bite slayer, Ted Bundy, are marked by a unique style, technique, timing, or other pattern that makes them easily identifiable as the work of a serial killer.

One factor that is common to almost all serial murders is the absence of a profit motive. Most, although not all, victims are killed for sex and power.

Serial killers may be sadistic homosexuals who rape, mutilate, and murder because of perverse hatred for others who share their own lifestyle.

Serial killers may be lust-driven heterosexuals who ravish, torture, and kill women and girls, sometimes violating the corpses in obscene acts of necrophilia.

Still other serial killers are cruel pedophiles who sexually abuse and murder children.

These killers may also be genuine lunatics as were Herbert William Mullin and Big Ed Kemper. Mullin murdered at least thirteen men, women, and children in a crazed scheme to offer human sacrifices to the gods and prevent an earthquake along California's San Andreas Fault. Kemper shot and killed his grandparents when he was fifteen, was released from a psychiatric hospital four years later and murdered six University of California coeds, sexually violated the corpses, and ate some of the flesh. He was finally arrested after murdering his mother and her best friend.

Older women, sometimes so frail that they are confined to nursing homes, are increasingly the victims of serial killers. A rape slayer — or slayers — who haunted the same neighborhood of Columbus, Georgia, during 1977 and 1978, murdering seven women aged fifty-nine to eighty-nine, was nicknamed "The Stocking Strangler." Carlton Gary, a career criminal, was eventually convicted of three of the slayings and sentenced to death in each case. Brandon Tholmer, the rock musician who was once suspected of murdering twelve elderly women in the Los Angeles area, was sentenced to life in prison after conviction in 1986 for killing four of the twelve victims. In Paris, thirty-one elderly women were slain between 1984 and mid-1986 by a serial killer dubbed "The Market Murderer." And in London, eight elderly men and women were murdered between April and July 1986, by a killer known as "the Stockwell Strangler."

Serial killers are not solely an American phenomenon. Nevertheless, the problem is more pronounced in the United States than anywhere else in the world, and experts with the U.S. Justice Department estimate that as many as thirty-five serial slayers — those who kill and kill again — are leaving ghastly trails around the country at any one time. Serial killers are believed responsible for a staggeringly large percentage of the nation's 5,000 annual unsolved slayings. Prostitutes, topless dancers, bar girls, teenage runaways, hitchhikers, young homosexuals, and street people without close family ties are favorite targets.

Whatever the reasons for multiple murders, the number of people who commit them is rapidly increasing. During the first fifty years of this century, police and court records point to fewer than a dozen known serial slayers in the United States.

Law-enforcement authorities were obviously unprepared for the current increase in this type of bloodletting. However, valiant efforts are now being made to deal with the frightening criminal phenomenon.

The most promising development is the establishment of the FBI's Behavioral Science Unit based at the Bureau's academy in Quantico, Virginia, where serial killers and other slayers are profiled in order to assist in bringing them to justice and exposing their techniques. The profiling program was started in 1977 by FBI veteran Howard Teten, who taught criminology at the academy. When former students began to contact him to ask questions tied to dead-end investigations, he started to build a file on the cases — and to recognize patterns that emerged.

The psychological profiling team, nicknamed "The Mind Hunters," has been so successful in determining the characteristics and backgrounds of suspects that state and local police agencies are also using the FBI team to run down other types of criminals, including rapists and child molesters. The FBI service, which is free to police who request it, says that about 70 per cent of the individuals convicted of profiled crimes match the information developed by the Mind Hunters.

In a March 5, 1984, *Washington Post* article, Special Agent Roger L. Depue was quoted as remarking: "We believe that in most crime scenes, the killer leaves his signature there. If you're sensitive to what those things are, you can construct a profile of the killer."

But profiles do not catch criminals. It's careful investigative work, helped by informants or a slip-up by the perpetrators, that's usually required to bring them to justice. Wayne Williams, convicted of two of the infamous Atlanta child murders, was correctly profiled by the Mind Hunters. He was not caught, however, until after he tossed a body over a bridge where police were on a stakeout.

The FBI cautions local police officers not to take any profile too literally or to limit their investigations to only those people whose characteristics match those in the Behavioural Science Unit's sketch.

In mid-1985, the FBI began a new approach to taking vicious killers out of circulation, through the establishment of the Violent Criminal Apprehension Program, (VI-CAP). VI-CAP is a centralized information center and analysis system based at the FBI academy, which collects and analyzes reports of all unsolved murders. The program is designed to disclose early serial-killer patterns.

A personality profile compiled by the FBI after interviewing thirty-six serial killers provides some insight into the typical serial slayer. Most are eldest sons, of average or above-average intelligence or street smarts, whose fathers were generally unskilled laborers but were regularly employed. About 70 per cent of the study group had a history of alcohol abuse in their families, and about 33 per cent had a record of family involvement in drug abuse. Most of the murderers were mistreated during childhood and had unhappy or unsatisfactory relationships with their fathers. Sixteen of the thirty-six men profiled reported cold or lukewarm relationships with their mothers.

It was learned that most of the killers indulged themselves in violent and sadistic fantasies. Responding to a request to indicate their primary sexual interests, 81 per cent of the men put pornography at the top of the list.

During my own research, I was amazed at the broad cross section of men, and women, who have become serial killers. The killers are white, black, or Hispanic in approximate proportion to the percentage of their race in the general population. Hong Kong–born Charles Chitat Ng, who is accused in the Calaveras County, California, sex and survivalist slayings, is the only Oriental that I'm aware has been charged or convicted in serial slayings.

Women who become serial slayers usually do so because they have been lured into the murder schemes by dominating male companions. But there are exceptions. The so-called Black Widows, who murder a succession of lovers, husbands, or other family members, usually for insurance money or other types of inheritance, account for one. Nurses who become Death Angels and murder ailing babies, the elderly, or desperately ill patients in apparently misguided efforts to end pain and suffering are another. And there is Christine Falling, whose wretched acts are recounted in Chapter Nine. Females who murder, whether they are serial killers or not, tend to select family members, lovers, or other people they know and with whom they have close relationships.

I, too, found overwhelming evidence of twisted sexual fantasizing, and addiction to pornography in the backgrounds of many of the killers profiled in this book. It seems that the much-maligned U.S. Justice Department commission report on pornography, which concluded that much of the smut sold in the United States is potentially harmful and can lead to violence, may deserve more serious consideration from the conventional press than it has been accorded. Curiously, out of the fifteen cases studied in this book, three serial killers were admirers of — and usually owned several editions of — the classic John Fowles novel *The Collector*. The 1963 work, later made into a movie starring Terrence Stamp and Samantha Eggar, traces the activities of a shy clerk and butterfly collector, who kidnaps a beautiful art student and holds her captive until she becomes sick and dies from lack of medical treatment. Then he stalks a new victim.

Another common trait, which I found and which others have noted, is a tendency for serial killers to be law-enforcement groupies or military buffs. Accused Calaveras County killers Leonard Lake and Charles Ng were both former Marines and ardent survivalists. John Wayne Gacy often trolled for victims in an official looking car with huge spotlights and posed as a plainclothes policeman. Hillside Strangler Kenneth Bianchi had been rejected for employment as a county sheriff's deputy, but worked in several jobs as a security guard. David Berkowitz had also worked as a security guard. Florida sex-slayer David Alan Gore worked as an auxiliary sheriff's deputy until he was fired, then posed as a deputy. Wayne Williams was a freelance photographer who haunted fire, accident, and crime scenes in Atlanta. And Ted Bundy studied to be a lawyer and worked in a program counseling rape victims. The attraction to law-enforcement jobs makes sense when we consider that they offer an excellent opportunity to control other people.

The majority of serial killers also appear to fit in exceptionally well with their peer groups and neighbors. Gacy could be charming. Bundy had no trouble attracting pretty, intelligent women as lovers, and men as friends. And lust-killer Christopher Wilder was a well-liked businessman and neighbor, who dated scores of beautiful women and was welcome among their friends and relatives. Yet, a close look at the background of these "good neighbors" who were eventually unmasked as serial killers, reveals that most of them had histories of brushes with the law or of psychiatric treatment.

Scientists and researchers talk of various genetic

flaws, abusive parents, poverty, pornography, and a host of perceived or suspected causes of violence that might lead individuals to kill and kill again. The sad truth is, no one yet knows why one individual who has suffered brain damage, or has been beaten by an abusive father or humiliated by a prostitute mother, becomes a serial killer, while another person with a similar background or experiences, doesn't.

Let us hope, that with more knowledge we *can* learn why. There's ample room as well as a serious need for study of the hidden causes of violence, not only by psychiatrists, neurologists, pathologists, criminologists, and sociologists but by writers as well. In the meantime, the legal-justice system needs to make every effort to apprehend and permanently remove from society those serial killers who are already going about their deadly work.

Fifteen separate cases, representing about twenty-one different killers working singly, and in teams, have been selected for this book. Some of the killers, for example, Wilder, Williams, Bianchi, and Buono, are internationally infamous. The murderous careers of others, such as cousins David Alan Gore and Fred Waterfield, have been barely noted outside their own immediate geographical area. If Florida and California appear to be slightly overrepresented here, it is because an inordinate number of serial slayings occur in those states. The killers go where the victims are, whether it's the warm beaches of Florida's Gold Coast, Hollywood's kiddie-prostitute-haunted Sunset Strip, or the gay ghetto of San Francisco's Castro District.

To my knowledge, no one has come up with a set number of victims that a specific criminal must murder before he or she is considered to be a serial killer. More important in classifying this particular type of criminal,

I believe, is the probability that the individual would continue killing until stopped by imprisonment or death.

Clifford L. Linedecker
Lantana, Florida
August 1986

CHAPTER I

THE DEATH RANCH MURDERS

LEONARD LAKE AND CHARLES NG

(1983-1985)

It appeared to be a routine shoplifting arrest. How could anyone have suspected the horror that was about to be unveiled? But when a clerk spotted a man leaving a lumberyard with a vice he hadn't paid for, the lid was ripped off a Pandora's box of evil and perversion. Suicide, grisly multiple murders, World War III survivalist fantasies, dark hints of a blood cult, a mad hatter's scheme to abduct perfect sex slaves, and an international brouhaha over custody of an accused serial killer came tumbling out into the open.

The bizarre story began to unfold on a quiet Sunday afternoon, June 2, 1985, in South San Francisco when the clerk told a nearby policeman that a "young Chinese guy with big glasses" had just left the lumberyard with a stolen vice. The lawman later said that he spotted the man loading the vice into the trunk of a car and started after him, but the suspect took to his heels and escaped. However, seated behind the driver's seat of the car was a middle-aged, balding white man with a beard who was taken into custody. It is a federal offense to own or possess a weapon with a silencer, and the police officer had found a .22-caliber automatic pistol with a silencer in a small tote bag in the car's trunk.

At police headquarters the man, who identified himself as Robin Scott Stapley, insisted he had been unaware that the tote bag containing the weapon was in the car. He said he had hired the Chinese man to do some work for him, and knew him only as "Charlie."

When officers advised Stapley that he would be charged with illegal possession of a weapon and held in custody until a routine computer check could be run on him and his car before he was allowed to post bail, the prisoner calmly asked for a drink of water. A few minutes later he popped a capsule into his mouth, gulped it down with water from a paper cup, and then slumped face down on the table in front of him. He appeared to have suffered a sudden heart attack. A short time later, in the emergency room of San Francisco's Kaiser Hospital, he was pronounced brain dead and placed on a life-support system.

The man hadn't suffered a heart attack; he had swallowed a cyanide pill. And his name was not Robin Stapley. A fingerprint check disclosed that he was Leonard Lake, a San Francisco native who had served with the Marine Air Corps for more than six years, including non-combat duty in Da Nang, Vietnam. He had been discharged in 1971, after two years of treatment for psychiatric problems at the Marine Corps base hospital at Camp Pendleton.

After his discharge from the Marines, Lake moved to San Jose, married, and quickly developed a reputation as an ardent survivalist and sex freak. He bought scores of guns, and was an avid reader of paramilitary magazines. Alarmed neighbors complained that he routinely sneaked around the area armed and dressed in military fatigues or combat greens. He also developed a taste for bondage, and liked to photograph sex partners while they were shackled, handcuffed, or restrained in leather harnesses. His wife had divorced him.

A police check disclosed that at the time of Lake's apprehension outside the lumberyard, he was being sought on a fugitive warrant. He had jumped bail following an arrest in 1982 on charges of possession of explosives and illegal automatic weapons. Using the name of a close friend, Charles Gunnar, Lake had been hiding out on a two-and-one-half-acre Calaveras County ranch about 150 miles east of San Francisco in the rugged foothills of the Sierra Nevada. Strangely, Gunnar, who had served as best man at Lake's wedding to his second wife, Claralyn "Cricket" Balazs, on August 13, 1981, had been missing since about the time the bridegroom became a fugitive. Although the second Mrs. Lake had divorced her husband after he got in trouble with the law, she had remained on friendly terms with him and with the young Chinese man who was his frequent companion.

Detectives learned that Lake's Chinese friend was Charles Chitat Ng (pronounced "Ing"), a twenty-four-year-old troublemaker, who was the ne'er-do-well son of wealthy parents in Hong Kong. After Ng had been expelled from school in Hong Kong, his parents had sent him to an expensive private school in England, where it was hoped he would learn discipline, and reform. Instead, he got into more trouble, and was expelled from the school for stealing from another student. According to an uncle he lived with for a time, he had been picked up for allegedly shoplifting from a department store, before leaving for California to live with other relatives and continue his education. But he quickly got into trouble in San Francisco as well and joined the Marines after involvement in a hit-and-run traffic accident.

Ng's bad-boy reputation followed him into the military service, and several of his fellow Marines frankly admitted they were deathly afraid of him. Ng was an expert in the unarmed martial arts, and during barracks talk at the Marine Corps air base at Kaneohe on Oahu, Hawaii, the wiry lance corporal bragged about his toughness and talked darkly about his ability to kill. He also boasted that he was the reincarnation of a Ninja warrior, one of the legendary black-garbed Japanese assassins who terrorized medieval Japan.

In Hawaii, the menacing young non-commissioned officer quickly got into serious trouble when he masterminded a harebrained scheme that led him and two companions to steal a small arsenal of deadly weapons — three grenade launchers, two machine guns, seven pistols, and a night-sighting scope — from Marine quartermasters. Ng admitted planning the caper and, after being ordered to submit to a psychiatric examination, told his attorney that he had "assassinated" someone in California. However, he didn't name the alleged victim or provide other details of the crime.

An attorney later quoted Ng as claiming that while he was stationed at Kaneohe, he had placed cyanide in the mess hall salt shakers, but inexplicably no one had died as a result. Ng also claimed he had tried to kill a staff sergeant by firing a grenade launcher at him, but the grenade didn't explode. Apparently, only Ng knows if the stories are true, or merely the result of idle but gruesome fantasizing and misplaced braggadocio.

While in custody for the armaments theft Ng escaped and fled back to California. There, he contacted Lake through an advertisement in a specialty magazine published for mercenary soldiers and survivalists. Obsessed with guns, the military, and survivalist skills, Lake often said that his life started when he joined the Marines. And as a civilian, he was often seen strutting around in a t-shirt printed with the slogan, "Mercenaries do it for money."

Lake and his second wife were living in Anderson Valley in coastal Mendocino County in 1982 when Ng joined him. Lake was convinced that every teenaged boy should know how to make and use explosives. He and his wife, who worked as a classroom aide at the Anderson Valley High School in Boonville, once offered to instruct pupils how to make and use explosives, faculty members later recalled. Because Anderson Valley was an agricultural community, Lake suggested it would be helpful if the students knew how to blow up tree stumps and use explosives for land-clearing activities, but the principal rejected the proposal.

Lake had gotten into trouble with the law in 1980 when he was arrested for grand theft after stealing weatherizing material from a low-income home building project. He was sentenced to one year's probation. However, the criminal charges that forced Lake undergound were filed after a SWAT team flew into the tiny community of Philo in a dramatic sweep to apprehend the fugitive Ng, who was known there as Richard Charles Lee. The raiding party, fully outfitted in camouflage clothes and carrying high-powered rifles, surrounded the motel that Lake managed, but neither he nor Ng was there. The raiders then moved on to a ranch outside of a town where Lake and his wife were employed as caretakers, and arrested Ng. They also filed charges against Lake, after confiscating a small arsenal of machine guns, silencers, bomb components, and other weapons at the ranch. Civilian charges against Ng were dropped and he was turned over to military authorities in Hawaii. In return for a promise that he would have to serve no more than three years of a fourteen-year sentence, Ng pleaded guilty at a court martial in August 1982, and was sent to the military stockade at the federal prison in Leavenworth, Kansas. After only eighteen months behind bars, he was favored with an early parole. He avoided deportation to Hong

Kong by using his Marine enlistment records which falsely indicated that he was born in Bloomington, Indiana. Not long after his parole he was working as a warehouseman in San Francisco and was back in touch with his old survivalist buddy, Lake.

After Lake's arrest at the lumberyard, the farther the police probed into the strange relationship and activities of the two men, the "curiouser and curiouser" they became. Investigators learned that the young man whose name Lake was using when he was apprehended had been missing for several months. Twenty-six–year-old Robin Scott Stapley, who was one of the founders of the San Diego chapter of the Guardian Angels, seemed simply to have vanished.

A computer check revealed that a couple of months earlier his pickup and camper had been involved in a fender-bender with a tractor-trailer truck in San Francisco. The driver of the Stapley vehicle had given the other driver a false name and address. The trucker told authorities that the other motorist was an Oriental, and the police knew the near-sighted Ng was a notoriously poor driver.

Inspection of the car Lake had been apprehended in provided added cause for concern. The license plate it carried was not the one issued for the vehicle. More ominously, bullet holes and two spent slugs were found inside, and there was dried blood smeared on the front seat. The 1980 Honda Prelude was registered to Paul Cosner, a thirty-nine-year-old San Francisco used-car dealer reported missing seven months earlier. He'd been last seen on the night he had left home to show the car to a prospective buyer who had replied to a newspaper ad, and whom Cosner had referred to as a "weirdo." Although they had barely begun investigating, the authorities had already come across three missing men who had been connected with Lake or Ng. As police probed deeper, they began to realize that there was much more involved than the activities of a pair of rather clumsy thieves.

When a couple of San Francisco officers paid a call on Calaveras County Sheriff Claude Ballard, the detectives learned that Lake had constructed a large cinderblock bunker into a hillside on the ranch and covered it with tons of dirt. It would be his shelter, in the event of a nuclear holocaust, which he insisted to acquaintances was inevitable. He believed that only a chosen few would survive, and he meant to be among that select group.

As Sheriff Ballard and his deputies added even more names of people who had dropped from sight in recent months, ominously, the number of mystery disappearances grew.

Lonnie Bond and his girlfriend, Brenda O'Connor, a couple who had moved to California sometime earlier from the small town of Coldwater in Southern Michigan, had vanished with their infant son, Lonnie, Jr., and a housemate — Robin Scott Stapley. The couple had lived in San Diego for a while, but moved to Calaveras County because they thought it would be safer than the big city. Stapley was known to have been living with them in their green A-frame home a bare seventy yards northeast of the Lake house. The parents of the young woman, Richard and Sharon O'Connor, said Brenda had told friends that Lake had invited Lonnie and her over to watch pornographic movies and that she was afraid of him.

"She also said she thought she had seen him burying a woman's body," Mrs. O'Connor revealed, in an Associated Press interview.

Friends insisted that the couple hadn't mentioned having plans to leave their home. But shortly after their sudden disappearance, a man identifying himself only as "Gunnar" tried to sell their furniture. He had claimed that Bond had said he and his girlfriend were moving away and gave him the furniture in payment for a loan. The would-be furniture salesman wasn't Gunnar, however, but Lake.

Sheriff's deputies were also investigating the disappearance of a couple who had been camping at Schaad Lake, a popular fishing spot about a mile from the ranch hideaway. Other campers said the pair went for a walk in the woods and never returned, although most of their camping gear, including food, was left behind.

Sheriff Ballard obtained a search warrant, and accompanied by the San Francisco officers and some of his deputies, drove to the secluded ranch. One of the first things they saw after passing through a heavy iron gate was a pickup truck parked near the house. A sign on the truck advised: "If you love something, set it free. If it doesn't come back, hunt it down and kill it." The ruthless slogan aptly presaged the horror that was about to be discovered.

From the outside, the two-story clapboard house seemed to be typical of others in the rustic California Mother Lode country that had once drawn hordes of adventurers with the promise of gold. More recently the region had attracted a special breed of farmers who sought riches by surreptitiously cultivating fields of jealously guarded marijuana plants.

Inside, a house of horror was revealed. The living room, littered as it was with gun racks, video equipment, and stacks of pornographic books and magazines, attested to the interests of the owner, but the bedroom offered more of a surprise. A huge double bed dominated the room, with eye bolts secured to the ceiling above it and along the walls. Shackles and chains were found dumped into a box. It appeared that the occupant had decidedly kinky sexual tastes.

However, a closer inspection of the premises, which included a look at the interior of the bunker, indicated that activities more sinister than playful games of bondage had taken place. The law-enforcement team uncovered strong circumstantial evidence of rape, perverted forms of sexual abuse, and murder.

The main room of the bunker was filled with survival gear that included food, water, candles, medical supplies, and several automatic rifles and ammunition.

But a check of a closet-sized room filled with frilly feminine lingerie and equipped with a two-way mirror, revealed a trap door that led to a basement room outfitted with a bed. One wall was covered with photos of girls and young women in provocative poses, some naked or scantily clad. One of the girls had been photographed in a field of marijuana. There were I-bolts attached to the bed, by which someone could be spread-eagled to the mattress. A series of brown stains that looked suspiciously like blood to the trained lawmen was splattered over the ceiling.

A San Francisco policewoman advised her partner that the expensive video gear in the living room was similar to equipment believed stolen from the apartment of a family which had recently disappeared mysteriously from the city. Harvey and Deborah Dubs, and their sixteen-month-old son, Sean, had dropped from sight without notifying family, friends, or employers that they were leaving. Dubs, a twenty-nine–year–old printer and freelance video producer, vanished with his family after placing a classified ad to sell some of his film equipment. His employers reported he had not picked up his last paycheck. Neighbors told investigators that a young Chinese man had moved the furniture out of the Dubs' apartment shortly after the family was last seen.

If any doubts had remained that Lake, and possibly Ng, were involved in at least some of these disappearances, they were dispelled by a discovery on a hillside a few yards away from the ranch buildings.

Deputies stumbled upon the burned and scorched fragments of a large number of bones and several teeth that were unquestionably human.

Much later, local historians would ruefully comment that Calaveras County got its name from the Spanish word "calaveras" which means "skulls." A Spanish officer, Lieutenant Gabriel Morago, coined the county's name in 1850 because he had found so many Indian skulls along the river banks.

The team of law-enforcement officers was concerned with more immediate history, however, and with the more recent dead. Calaveras County Coroner Terry Parker was summoned to the ranch, and police technicians were called in to gather up the bones or bone fragments after cataloguing their exact location. Before Parker and the technicians arrived, other deputies unearthed two badly decomposed bodies from a trench on the property.

By running a comparison check on the serial numbers, the San Francisco policewoman was able to confirm that the video equipment in the house had indeed come from the Dubs' apartment. Authorities in the city had also checked Ng's basement apartment and determined that, after outrunning the policeman in the lumberyard parking lot, he had stopped there to retrieve some personal items before fleeing again.

At the ranch the team of investigators was continuing to uncover one horror after another. Two handwritten diaries were found, which Lake had developed into a chilling five-hundred–page record of kidnapping, sexual abuse, torture, murder, and finally, the cremation of his innocent victims. The diaries told of "Operation Miranda," which detailed his sick fantasy of surviving the inevitable nuclear holocaust in a concrete bunker stocked with food, weapons, and female sex slaves. Lake was fascinated by John Fowles' novel The Collector, in which the first kidnap victim is named Miranda.

According to other entries in the meticulously kept diaries, some of the men who had had the misfortune to fall into Lake's clutches may have been sent into the rugged Sierra Forest and, like game animals, been hunted down with high-powered weapons. Notations in the journals indicated that Lake could have been inspired to hunt human prey by R. E. Connell's short story "A Most Dangerous Game."

Lake started one of the journals by penning the observation: "Death is in my pocket and fantasy my goal."

In another entry, he observed that, "The perfect woman is totally controlled. A woman who does exactly what she is told and nothing else. There is no sexual problem with a submissive woman. There are no frustrations, only pleasure and contentment."

Elsewhere in the journals he wrote: "Women are like books. You put them on the shelf and take them down when you need them. You train them to do what you want," and in another entry, "God meant women for cooking, cleaning house and sex. And when they are not in use, they should be locked up."

In the diaries he recalled that he had known only one female who met his requirements for offering total satisfaction. "She's a whore, drugger and fool," he wrote. "Still, I enjoy using her, and seemingly she enjoys being used."

As shocking as the journal scribblings were, a stack of color videotapes found in a cabinet revealed even more graphically the extent of the orgy of lust and murder unleashed at the ranch.

In one of the tapes, Lake was shown talking about holing up in a bunker to survive a nuclear explosion and providing himself with sex slaves so that he could continue the human race. He talked in detail about the weapons he planned to stock and described individual sex acts that he planned to commit with female captives.

In the first portion of another tape, a terrified young

woman, who appeared to be in her teens, is shown bound to a straight-backed chair. Lake warns her: "if you don't cooperate with us, if you don't agree this evening, right now to cooperate with us, we'll probably put a round through your head and take you out and bury you in the same area we buried Mike."

According to investigators' statements, and a transcript of the videotape filed with the Calaveras County Superior Court, the helpless girl was shown being untied a short time later and ordered by her captors to undress. "If you don't go along with us, we'll probably take you to bed, tie you down, rape you, shoot you and bury you. Sorry lady, time's up! Make your choice. . . . It's not much of a choice unless you've got a death wish." She was forced to strip, shower with the Asian man investigators claim is Ng, and pose for nude photos.

Later in the same tape, Lake and the Asian man are seen tormenting and sexually abusing their neighbor, Brenda O'Connor, whom they had also tied to a chair. As she pleaded for her baby, her husband, and a friend, all of whom had visited Lake for dinner, the Asian leaned over her with a bayonet and cut off her blouse and brassiere. He tossed the clothes into a wood-burning stove. Then she was untied, and like the young woman shown earlier in the tape, was forced to finish disrobing before being placed in leg-irons, made to bathe, and forced to submit to sexual abuse.

"By cooperating with us, that means you will stay here as our prisoner, you will work for us, you will wash for us, you will fuck for us. Or you can say no . . . in which case we'll tie you to the bed, we'll rape you, and then we'll take you outside and shoot you. Your choice!" Lake told his captive.

Several different women, including some of those tied to the chair, were shown in the tapes and in still photographs found in the bunker, being subjected to rape, sodomy, and a variety of other degrading sexual acts. The agonized form of one of the women that flashed on the screen was recognized by the San Francisco policewoman. The bound victim was thirty-three–year–old Deborah Dubs.

The morning after Sheriff Ballard had led the original band of law-enforcement officers to the ranch, it was jammed with an army of investigators. Among the newcomers were several agents from California's State Department of Justice. Mobile crime labs were parked on the property, and an anxious host of print and electronic-media journalists were ringing the compound, clamoring for information about the atrocities carried out at the remote Calaveras County hideaway. It was developing into one of the biggest crime stories in California since the notorious Manson Family murders and the kidnap and search for newspaper heiress Patty Hearst and her crazed Symbionese Liberation Army captors.

"It's like a horror film," Sheriff Ballard told assembled journalists. "Vicious, vicious, vicious."

In San Francisco, detectives linked two more missing people to Ng. Twenty-three–year–old Michael Sean Carroll, of Milpitas, and his eighteen–year–old girlfriend, Kathleen E. Allen, a San Jose high-school senior and supermarket bagger, had been reported missing. The teen had confided to a co-worker that a man she knew had told her that her boyfriend had been shot. She said he promised to take her to Lake Tahoe on the California-Arizona border to meet her injured sweetheart. But she had arranged with her employers to mail her last check to the ranch near Wilseyville.

The missing high-school girl was identified by investigators as the frightened teenager being tormented by Lake and his companion on the early portion of one videotape. Lake's threat to kill and bury her like

"Mike" was believed to be a reference to Michael Carroll, who had served time with Ng in the military stockade at Leavenworth.

Even though most of the bones scattered on the hillside were chips and pieces no more than three inches long, police technicians, working with painstaking care to preserve evidence, gathered more then forty-five pounds of remains from the area. The teeth of two or more children were included. Lawmen also gathered up driver's licenses issued to Ng's friend, Carroll, and to Miss Allen, missing San Francisco used-car dealer Paul Cosner's automobile registration, a t-shirt with the Guardian Angels emblem on it believed to belong to Stapley, albums filled with more than a hundred photos of young girls ranging in age from about twelve to early twenties, and other items linking the occupants of the ranch house to missing people. More than a thousand items of evidence were sent to the California state crime laboratory for evaluation.

Two more bodies were dug up from the red clay, and the surprised investigators learned that analysis of the skulls showed that the badly decomposed corpses had been those of blacks. They then discovered from people who knew Ng that he was openly racist and hated blacks and Hispanics. Investigators also learned that a short time earlier he had hired two black men, reputedly to do some work at the ranch.

Dogs from the sheriff's canine unit brought to the site led searchers to two more bodies. Dirt was moved a few inches at a time, and teams of lawmen followed behind in the sweltering 100-degree heat, inspecting the loose soil for additional human remains. Technicians from California's State Department of Justice also scanned the grounds with infrared detection devices designed to register the presence of bone and tissue.

Searchers working near the bunker found a power saw and a pair of tree trimmers smeared with blood.

Police theorized that they were used to cut up the bodies before the pieces were stuffed into metal drums — also found at the site — for cremation in a small incinerator. The scorched bones had been pulverized with a shovel.

On Thursday, four days after Lake swallowed the deadly cyanide capsule, doctors ordered his life-support system removed. He stopped breathing a short time later. He was cremated, but his brain was preserved for use in research to help scientists study the causes of violent behavior and learn what drives some people to kill.

By the time Lake's death had been confirmed, the search team had located six distinguishable bodies on the property and forensic anthropologists were sorting through the burned bone chips, attempting to determine how many more victims they had on their hands, as well as the sex, race, and approximate age and physical characteristics, including size. The date and location of each item of human remains recovered were logged, with descriptions of all other evidence found, in a state computer.

Authorities released fifteen of the twenty-one photographs of young women found in the bunker to the news media in an effort to learn their identities and to determine if any of them were among the presumed murder victims. The other six women had already been identified and those who were located were interviewed in order to develop leads on additional victims of Lake's sadistic fantasies. Two years later, all of the women except one, who appears to be an attractive Oriental in her late teens or early twenties, had been located alive. At this writing her identity and whereabouts are still unknown.

The discovery of a crude map at the ranch led to the dispatch of search teams to coastal Mendocino County and other sparsely populated and forested areas of north-central California to look for additional gravesites. The map was apparently drawn while Lake was living in Mendocino County, and several marks carried the notation "buried treasure." Authorities reasoned that the "treasure" just might be bodies.

No bodies were uncovered by the search team in Mendocino County, but police dogs found the grave of a man and a woman in a heavily wooded area about a mile from the cabin and bunker in Calaveras County. They had been shot with a small-caliber weapon and buried in sleeping bags. They were believed to be the missing campers.

While the grim search for bodies was continuing at the ranch, investigators had traced Ng to Chicago. A San Francisco gun dealer told police that Ng had telephoned him from there, asking him to forward to Chicago an automatic pistol left at the businessman's shop for repair. Ng reputedly asked the dealer to ship the handgun to him under the name "Mike Kimoto." The shop owner informed him that it was against federal law to ship a handgun across state lines to an individual, but that it could be shipped to a Chicago dealer and picked up there. Ng reportedly became angry, told the gun dealer to forget it, and threatened to return to San Francisco and kill him if he reported the conversation to police.

Chicago police were notified that the fugitive was thought to be in their city, and they learned that a man using the name Mike Kimoto had been staying in a hotel. But he was gone when police arrived there. Nine days after the incident in the San Francisco parking lot, the FBI officially joined in the manhunt and issued a warrant for Ng's arrest on federal fugitive charges. Bail was established at $1 million. The Bureau notified the Paris-based international police agency, Interpol, to be on the lookout for the fugitive. Federal agents warned that Ng was an expert in demolition and booby traps, as well as the unarmed martial arts, and that he was thought to be armed.

Suspecting that Ng might try to make his way to Toronto, Canada, which has a large Chinese population and where it would be easier for him to blend into the community and escape detection, investigators informed Canadian authorities.

Two weeks after the grim investigation began, State Attorney General John Van de Kamp had assumed overall charge and was heading an on-the-scene operation that involved some sixty people from six counties, five cities and towns, the California State Department of Justice, and federal agencies. He called a press conference and informed journalists that the remains of nine people had been recovered in or near the ranch. Because of the advanced stages of decomposition, positive identifications hadn't yet been made.

However, Kathleen Allen, Brenda O'Connor, and Deborah Dubs had been identified on the videotapes, and it was presumed that they, and those with them, had been killed.

"We have definitely established that at least twenty-six persons known to Ng and Lake have been reported missing," Van de Kamp announced. "How many more there may be, we have no idea at this time and it is likely we may never positively identify all the victims because a large number were cremated and their bones were crushed into small pieces."

Van de Kamp added that Ng's active involvement in at least some of the crimes was documented in Lake's diaries and in the videotapes. "Unless we can locate Ng and get him to talk, the chances are slim that we'll ever know everything that went on out there," he continued. "It has become a case so overwhelming, so enormous and so gruesome that our computer system hasn't been able to keep up with it."

The Calaveras County murders were not only shaping into one of the most grisly cases in the annals of American crime, but into one of the strangest and most grotesquely convoluted studies in criminal behavior as well.

There appeared to be little doubt that Lake's friend, Gunnar, a theater worker from nearby Morgan Hill, was one of the victims. But police learned that Lake's younger brother may have been slain in the runaway murder spree, as well. Donald Lake's mother reported him as missing to police in San Bruno, California, in July 1983, after he left to visit his older brother and look for work as a carpenter in Humboldt County. The brothers didn't get along well, and Leonard had been known to describe his thirty-two–year–old brother as a "leech" and to observe that their mother would be better off without him.

One of the more complete skeletons, discovered buried under an old chicken coop about fifty yards from the house, was eventually identified as being that of Randy Jacobson, a long-haired, thirty-four–year–old drifter. Jacobson, whose friends described him as a gentle flower child left over from the 1960s hippie period, appeared to have been selected for death for the same reason that several other male victims had been: he had had a good-looking female companion who attracted Lake's attention.

Jacobson's girlfriend told investigators that they met Lake in the spring of 1984, when he was using the name "Alan Drey." She said Lake tried unsuccessfully to date her. Then he asked her to become the caretaker of a marijuana plantation he claimed he had in coastal Humboldt County in northern California. Again, she refused.

She said the last time she saw her boyfriend, whom she nicknamed "Cosmic Angel," because he was "so handsome and beautiful," was in October 1984 when he told her he was going to sell Lake his 1981 Ford van. When Lake was arrested in San Francisco, he was carrying a twenty-four-hour bank card belonging to Jacobson. After authorities notified Jacobson's friends that his body had been found at the death ranch, the *San Francisco Chronicle* reported that they held a memorial service in a soup kitchen.

Detectives later pointed out that the date of Jacobson's disappearance coincided with a cryptic entry in one of Lake's journals, referring to "PPIII." They believed the letters "PP" referred to the Pink Palace, a rooming house in the Haight-Ashbury district where Jacobson stayed that had acquired its colorful name because it had once been painted hot pink.

Additional coded notations referring to "PPI" and "PPII" are believed by investigators to have referred to two other victims of the serial slayings lured from the same rooming house. Twenty-six-year-old Cheryl Okoro and thirty-eight-year-old Maurice Wock both disappeared from the neighborhood at nearly the same time that Jacobson vanished.

Wock, who was black, was described as a hippy-type character who had many friends but seldom ventured outside his cell-like room. He was a fine guitar player who idolized the late rock guitarist Jimi Hendrix, and shortly before he disappeared had been talking of moving to the country "to get his head together."

A sister-in-law of Mrs. Okoro, who was from Grand Rapids, Michigan, said she warned the woman during a long-distance telephone call not to run off with Lake. The relative said Mrs. Okoro identified Lake by name and called him "my old man" when she talked of going with him to a farm. A sister of the missing woman was quoted in the *San Francisco Chronicle* as saying that Cheryl, "who had never been very stable," loved money and the fast life, and earned cash by marrying illegal aliens. Cheryl's name had been on the mailbox at the ranch when authorities drove through the gate with the search warrant.

Police also began to seek a link between remains found at the ranch and the disappearance of thirty-year-old Jeffrey Askren, an amateur photographer from Sunnyvale whose car was found abandoned near Lake's cabin, and of Jeff Gerald and Cliff Parenteau, San Francisco men who had worked at the warehouse with Ng. The Hong Kong–born fugitive was known to hang around after work with the two movers at the Rockin' Robin bar where he sipped rum and Coke. A bartender there said the last time she saw twenty-four–year–old Parenteau was right after he won $400 in a Superbowl football pool at work and he said he was going to the country with Ng to spend the money. Twenty-five–year–old Gerald, who played drums evenings with a small band, vanished after telling a friend he was going to help Ng move to Stockton.

Ng was named on murder charges and other counts, for the slaying of a popular San Francisco disc jockey during a botched robbery attempt in July 1984. Thirty-seven–year–old Donald Giuletti was shot three times in the head with a .22-caliber handgun in the study of his home by a young Asian man after placing a classified ad in a sex tabloid offering free oral sex for "straight" males. Giuletti's roommate had been shot and wounded. According to legal documents filed in the growing serial murder case, Lake's ex-wife, Claralyn Balazs, later told police that Ng had claimed he shot two homosexuals in San Francisco.

Authorities theorized that a few of the earliest victims of the bloodbath were relatives, friends, and neighbors, selected because they trusted their killer or killers and were easy to lure to their deaths. The women were chosen because they were sexually attractive, and the men because the women were their mates or because their money or identification was desired. Some of the males may have been lured to the ranch to work, then murdered when their labor was no longer needed.

As efforts to unravel the tapestry of terror progressed, bizarre stories began to surface, linking the slaughter at the Wilseyville ranch to strange blood cults and lurid sacrificial rites. One of Lake's neighbors told a journalist that she spent three days helping him build the cinder-block bunker. As they were eating lunch one day, she said, he suggested that she travel with him to a meeting of some people with whom he was involved.

"He said the group was very small and very confidential and that they believed in life sacrifices, and *if* somebody deserved to die they should be dead," she was quoted as saying in the *San Jose Mercury News*. Wisely, she declined the invitation. "He scared the hell out of me," the woman declared.

Photographs showed Lake wearing robes such as those donned by modern-day witches and other benign pagan cultists, with his then wife and Lancelot — a "unicorn" now with the Ringling Bros. and Barnum & Bailey Circus. Lancelot had been raised and transformed from goat to reputed unicorn with a single horn grafted onto the center of its forehead by naturalists Otter G'Zell and Morning Glory in Mendocino County, where Lake lived in 1982.

The FBI sent five hundred posters displaying a photograph, description, and psychological profile of Ng, developed by their Behavioral Unit, to law-enforcement agencies in Canada. A short time later, Canadian authorities notified the FBI that a man thought to be Ng had been sighted in Chatham, Ontario, across Lake St. Clair from Detroit. A young Chinese man was spotted in a bus-station washroom shaving off his sideburns and eyebrows. Although Ng was expert at disguises with a chameleon-like ability to change his appearance, the witness picked out his picture from a selection of photos shown to him by police.

A Chicago man contacted the FBI to tell them he had driven the fugitive from Chicago to Windsor, Ontario, then on to a motel in Chatham before they parted company. He said he had no idea that his former companion was on the run from authorities until he read about the manhunt in newspapers.

Ng was next reported to have been seen in Sudbury, a bustling city of 100,000, perched on the far northwestern tip of Ontario. The manhunters then turned the focus of their Canadian search from Ontario to around the Vancouver area of British Columbia. They were worried that the fugitive might be trying to reach the Pacific coast again in order to escape to Hong Kong or to another Asian country.

But Ng's clumsy shoplifting habits once again betrayed him. Barely a month after he had fled from the San Francisco parking lot, Ng was spotted in a store in Calgary, Alberta, slipping a bottle of soda pop under his vest.

When Hudson's Bay department-store guards John Doyle and George Forster attempted to arrest him, Ng tried to get away. While Ng was attempting to squirm free from underneath the store guards, two shots were fired from a .22-caliber automatic Ruger pistol Ng had been carrying. Doyle was clipped on a finger by one of the slugs.

The gunman was subdued and taken to police headquarters, where officers sifted through the sheaf of different identification papers he carried. Among the welter of I.D. a California driver's license issued to Charles Chitat Ng was discovered. The thirty-four–day international manhunt was ended at last.

Ng had been hiding out for a week in a dirt and wood lean-to in a 200,000-acre wilderness preserve bordering

the southern edge of Calgary. He was down to his last
ten dollars, a penknife, a few cans of fruit, and some
war novels. Fourteen-year-old Ronald Finlaison later
told Calgary police that he and a school chum stumbled
onto Ng's hideout about a week before the arrest and
knocked on the shelter with a penknife. They said Ng
crawled outside and sent them away, explaining that he
was sleeping.

Canadian authorities notified the FBI that the fugitive
was in custody. He was placed under a twenty-four-
hour suicide watch with video-surveillance equipment in
a maximum-security cell at the Calgary Remand Centre.
Ng had reportedly sworn never to be taken alive, and
there was also concern that he and Lake may have made
a pact to commit suicide if taken into custody.

A team of investigators working the serial-murder
case was quickly put together with officers from the
Calaveras County Sheriff's Department, San Francisco
Police Department, and the California State Depart-
ment of Justice. They flew to Calgary and talked with
Ng for five hours.

Later, the press was informed that Ng had blamed all
the abuse and sexual torture of the women and the
murders, dismemberment, cremation, and burial of
bodies on Lake. Detectives observed that Ng's rush to
blame everything on the dead man hadn't come as a surprise. The statement helped them to begin to put some
of the missing pieces in the puzzling case together,
however. Sometime later, police sources disclosed that
Ng had actually provided important details about the
fate of six San Franciscans — the Dubs family, Cosner,
Gerard, and Parenteau — linking them to the gruesome
activities at the death ranch.

California authorities began extradition proceedings,
which set off an expected legal wrangle between the two
neighboring nations. According to a 1976 U.S.-
Canadian extradition treaty, Canada, which has no

death penalty, is not obliged to return criminal suspects to the United States if the charges provide for execution. Thirty-seven of the fifty U.S. states have a death penalty, including California, although no execution has been carried out there since 1967.

Ng's attorneys have vowed to strongly resist his extradition to face capital murder charges and a possible death penalty.

Ng has nevertheless been named on charges of participating in the murders of Kathleen Allen, Brenda O'Connor, Michael Carroll, Lonnie Bond, Lonnie Bond, Jr., Robin Scott Stapley, Clifford Parenteau, Jeffrey Gerald, Donald Giuletti, Harvey and Deborah Dubs and their son, Sean, and has been named as an accessory in the slaying of Paul Cosner. Some of the murder counts allege special circumstances — including multiple murder — which would make it possible to sentence Ng to death in California's gas chamber if he is convicted. Several other charges have also been filed against him, including attempted murder in the wounding of Giuletti's housemate, kidnapping, and conspiracy to kidnap.

In the meantime, in Calgary, Ng was sentenced to four and one-half years in prison after being found guilty of aggravated assault, robbery, and illegal use of a weapon for the incident at the department store. He was acquitted of a more serious charge of attempted murder.

At this writing, U.S. authorities are continuing in their efforts to cut through the maze of legal roadblocks and extradite Ng, who must be considered innocent of the charges filed against him in California until such time as he might be brought to trial and proven guilty.

CHAPTER 2

THE MIDWEST MURDER SPREE

ALTON COLEMAN AND DEBRA BROWN

(1984)

When her personable acquaintance offered to take Juanita Wheat's young son and daughter to a carnival set up a short distance from their home in a poor black neighborhood of Kenosha, Wisconsin, she agreed easily.

There wasn't much extra money in the family, and the excursion was an unexpected treat for the little boy and girl, who returned tired but excited and full of stories about the outing with their generous adult friend.

So when the engaging young man suggested that her little daughter, Vernita, accompany him on a fifteen-mile cab ride across the Wisconsin state line to his apartment in Waukegan, Illinois, to pick up a stereo, the child's mother gave her consent.

The nine-year-old girl never returned home. And when the frantic mother began to look for her daughter and the friendly high-stepper with the disarming smile whom she knew as Robert Knight, there was no trace of them. Police were able to find their trail only briefly, locating a cab driver who recalled picking them up in front of a bar in Kenosha a few minutes before midnight on May 29, 1984, and dropping them off about a half-hour later, outside a barbeque house in Waukegan's black ghetto.

The next day, while Debra Denise Brown was walking up the steps of the Lake County Courthouse in Waukegan with her boyfriend, Alton Coleman, where he was to appear at a pre-trial hearing on rape charges, he muttered, "I done something wrong."

The cryptic utterance was puzzling, but Debra had lived with her temperamental companion long enough to know that it was best for her not to ask too many questions.

At twenty-eight, Coleman had already compiled a thick police rap sheet listing an impressive array of violent crimes and sex offenses that he had been accused of, although not always convicted of, committing. He had a nasty temper and quick fists, and it seemed that the slightest thing could provoke him to violence. In the dark and cluttered apartment they shared with Coleman's grandmother, in a public-housing development among the rubble-strewn streets and empty lots of Waukegan's black ghetto, Debra had merely to stick her head outside the door without Coleman's permission and he would erupt in a frenzy of violence. He would beat her, slamming her slight hundred-pound body against the wall as he screamed ugly curses and threats.

A few minutes later as Debra cowered inside, whimpering, he would strut out of the apartment and chat with his female neighbors as if nothing had happened. Despite his charm, the women who lived near the apartment knew what was going on and sometimes talked among themselves about how sorry they were for the young girl who was a virtual prisoner of her mean-tempered lover.

It was, therefore, not surprising that Debra didn't question him about what he had done wrong; for almost all of his life, Alton Coleman had been doing things wrong.

As Coleman was preparing for the hearing on rape charges stemming from an alleged assault on a fourteen-year-old girl in the city of North Chicago, the FBI was already looking into his long, sordid record of violence and lawbreaking. Permitted to enter the search for the missing Wisconsin child because it had been established that she had been transported across a state line, in apparent violation of federal laws, FBI agents had taken up the trail. A few hours after Coleman appeared in court with his nineteen-year-old girlfriend, they knocked on the door of an apartment occupied by one of his sisters. But Coleman had been tipped off that they were looking for him and had escaped through a back door into a darkened field.

Investigations had revealed that the character who called himself Robert Knight was really Alton Coleman. But by the time agents had identified him, picked up his trail, and begun making the rounds of his known relatives, he had already made his court appearance and gone underground. On June 1, lawmen questioned Debra. Then she, too, vanished.

A federal grand jury in Milwaukee returned a kidnapping indictment against Coleman and he became the subject of a nationwide manhunt. But as an ex-convict and experienced criminal, he knew how to disappear among the graffiti-smeared buildings and trash-littered lots of the Midwest's black slums. Law-enforcement officers were generally distrusted and disliked in black-ghetto neighborhoods such as those where Coleman was believed to be hiding out. Court-ordered tests, school records, and general observation had disclosed that although he wasn't especially bright, Coleman was streetwise and now he was desperate as well. Known to have used at least five aliases as well as the name on his birth certificate — "Elton Coleman," not the personally preferred "Alton Coleman" — he wouldn't be easy to track down.

Police and court records also revealed that life's lottery had dealt a miserable beginning to Coleman. He was the middle child of three boys and two girls born to a woman who was described as a prostitute in court records and in an FBI profile. She first gave birth when she was fourteen, and died of breast cancer in 1974. Because Coleman's father wasn't there to raise him and since his mother showed no interest in the infant, her mother, Alma Hosea, took over the job.

The old woman, who was seventy-two when her grandson and his girlfriend suddenly moved from her apartment and dropped out of sight, was a protective and loving element in his life. The grandmother later revealed her bitterness at the daughter who had so callously abandoned the child when she told a *Chicago Tribune* reporter: "She threw him away, just like you'd throw away garbage."

Fiercely loyal, she also insisted that he was always well behaved as a child. Court, police, and psychiatric records indicate otherwise. They show that he was an unhappy, bitter youngster without direction, who was lonely and wet his pants so often that other children tagged him with the humiliating nickname "Pissy."

He dropped out of grade school and began to carve out a meager living, never holding down a steady job, although he worked for short periods of time in the kitchen of a nearby veterans' hospital, helped a second-hand furniture dealer, and shoveled snow. Most of the time, he subsisted on fitful winnings as a small-time gambler, when he was lucky. When he was unlucky, he accepted handouts from relatives, friends, neighbors, or anyone else he could sweettalk into giving him food, shelter, and money. Women and naive church-going older folks were his prime marks.

And no one called him "Pissy" anymore. Although

he was of moderate height, five feet, ten inches tall, and weighed only 145 pounds, he was known to carry a knife in his boot. The weapon, along with his hair-trigger temper, helped convince others to refer to him by the new nickname he had acquired, and preferred — "Big Al." He strutted along tough McAlister Avenue in Waukegan, grandly decked out in his favorite outfit — gaudy red pants, a red pullover sweater, and a black cap and hairnet carefully arranged over his Afro hairstyle.

He had also learned to charm women, then to control and use them. He abused most of the women who were close to him, with fierce physical beatings, sexual assaults, or both. By May 1984, when Vernita rode away with him into the night, he had served slightly more than two years in Illinois State Correctional Center at Joliet, and six months in the Lake County (Illinois) Jail. But he had been named in a staggering number of complaints and formal criminal charges, most for sexual offenses. Even in prison he built an evil reputation for aggressive homosexuality and sexual bullying of other inmates.

In 1973 he was charged with raping and kidnapping a Waukegan woman, leading to the prison term on a reduced charge of robbery. He had been free for only a few months when he was charged with raping another Waukegan woman, and was acquitted. In 1980 he was found not guilty of raping a Michigan woman in North Chicago. Both acquittals of rape were returned after he admitted to juries that he had had sex with the women, but insisted that each of them had consented. He was married for about six months, but his teenaged wife left him after arranging for police protection while she moved her belongings out. Much later she would remark that she "couldn't take it no more," and would provide a graphic courtroom description of his fascination with bondage, young girls, and violent sex.

In the summer of 1983, one of Coleman's relatives accused him of sexually abusing her young daughter. In court, however, the little girl's mother changed her story and insisted that he had not molested the child. The judge angrily branded her new account as "completely implausible," and further observed: "I think the woman as she stands here today is terrified by this man." She continued to insist on his innocence, and once again Coleman walked out of court a free man.

He was facing charges of raping the fourteen-year-old daughter of a woman he had met and befriended in a North Chicago restaurant when he allegedly carried Vernita away, then went into hiding.

Unknown to investigators at that time, Coleman had fled along the southern lip of Lake Michigan to Chicago, then with his girlfriend across the Indiana state line to Gary, the grimy, onetime bustling steel city that in more recent years has become notorious for its high unemployment, savage street gangs, and high crime rate.

After settling in a rented basement apartment, Coleman began working the Gary streets, using his charm to befriend his new neighbors, especially the women. One of them, Donna Michelle Williams, was a pushover for his smooth talk and beguiling manner. Tall, with the long legs and slim figure of a model, she was a trusting and religious young woman who was concerned about the spiritual and material welfare of others. She took an immediate interest in the glib, good-looking newcomer to the area, and his quiet, slight companion whom he claimed to have married thirteen months earlier. The outgoing twenty-five-year-old Gary beautician quickly turned the talk with her new friends to her church activities, and was thrilled when they indicated they were interested in attending services with her.

She was looking forward to introducing them to the congregation of the Good News of Jesus Christ

Evangelical Church, where she was an assistant pastor, when Gary was shocked by one of the most heartless and depraved acts of violence in its crime-ridden history.

Two little girls, seven-year-old Tamika Turks and her nine-year-old aunt, were walking to a hot-dog stand in the Glen Park neighborhood when a man and a woman stopped them to chat. The trusting children were lured into a nearby wooded area where the man explained that they were going to play a little game. He took off Tamika's top and slashed it into strips with a pocket knife. Then, with help from the quiet woman he called "Slim," he used the shredded garment and an elastic edging, cut from a bedsheet he had with him, to tie up both girls.

The two adults threw the frightened children onto the ground, and when Tamika started to cry, "Slim" looped the elastic edging around her throat and pulled with one hand, while pressing the other hand over the girl's mouth and nose. While Tamika struggled to breathe, helplessly kicking her feet and waving her arms, the man viciously stomped the child's face and chest with his feet. Once, during the brutal assault, he turned and snarled at the older girl, warning her that if she continued to watch, he would do the same thing to her. When he finally had enough of the cruel stomping, he and his companion carried their victim's broken body deeper into the woods. When they returned, the man threw himself on the terrified survivor and raped and choked her until she passed out.

Later that afternoon, a neighborhood man helping to search for the missing girls found the dazed and bleeding nine-year-old, her clothing dirty and torn, staggering out of the woods. Somehow she had worked free of her bonds. She was rushed to nearby Methodist Hospital for treatment. There, under gentle but persistent questioning, she told of the chance meeting that turned an innocent neighborhood trip by two little girls into a nightmare. It was June 18, only twenty days after another child, Vernita Wheat, had vanished.

After a city-wide search that included use of a helicopter and canine teams, Tamika's pathetic remains were found the next day in a swampy area of the woods. And on the same day, in Waukegan, two men stumbled across the rapidly decomposing remains of Vernita Wheat, trussed up with coaxial cable, in a first-floor apartment in a trash-littered, abandoned building. Autopsies revealed that both children had died of strangulation, and that Vernita had been raped.

FBI spokesmen in Chicago and Milwaukee announced that a special task force had been established to head the manhunt for Coleman and his girl. At the FBI Academy in Quantico, Virginia, members of the Behavioral Science Unit began to prepare a profile on Coleman, detailing his personality traits and habits, to assist police in their search. In Gary, Mayor Richard Hatcher called a press conference and pleaded for the public's help in running down the rapacious kidnappers of the two local children.

It was already too late for another of Gary's unsuspecting citizens. The friendly couple Donna Williams had been so anxious to introduce to her fellow church-goers had apparently already driven away with her. She was last seen by her friends when she left the church in her 1976 model car to pick up the newcomers and bring them to evening services.

A few days later her car was found abandoned in a garbage-littered alley on the southwest side of Detroit. Bogus identification carrying Debra Brown's photo was found in the vehicle. There was no trace of the vehicle's owner, and investigators said they were treating her disappearance as a suspected abduction. Hopes of finding her alive were becoming increasingly slim.

Then, a couple answering the fugitives' description

burst into the suburban Dearborn Heights home of sixty-two–year–old Palmer Jones and his fifty-year-old wife, Maggie, as they were eating breakfast. The intruders bludgeoned the startled homeowners with a club, then drove away with the Jones's late-model car. FBI agents streamed into the Detroit area, and local law-enforcement officers circulated descriptions of the dangerous pair and the stolen car.

A day or two later another Detroit woman and a male friend met an engaging young couple in a park on the southwest side. The city woman invited the strangers to her apartment, but the newcomers were there only a few minutes when the young man turned on his hosts and gave them a savage beating, tied them up, and robbed them of $100 and a car.

Meanwhile, charges against Coleman were piling up. An assistant U.S. district attorney filed federal counts of kidnapping in the Wheat abduction. And the Lake County, Illinois, State's Attorney's Office filed a first-degree–murder count against him for the girl's slaying.

Several other assaults, robberies, and sightings linked to a man and woman answering descriptions of the fugitives were reported to Detroit-area police. A car was stolen at gunpoint from a pair of Detroit men who had given a ride to a couple resembling Coleman and Brown. Although one of the victims was held for several hours, he was eventually released and no one was hurt. When the vehicle was found abandoned in a Detroit suburb, police responded with a late-night door-to-door sweep of neighborhood houses and used dogs to comb a deserted industrial complex. Helicopters were also used in the manhunt without success.

The elusive duo was moving fast, and the next reports of their violent trek through the Midwest placed them about forty miles south of Detroit, just across the Ohio state line, in Toledo. A shaken Detroit woman told police she had been abducted from her home and forced at knifepoint to drive to the bustling industrial city by two people matching descriptions of the renegade lovers. They had released her, frightened but unharmed.

The rapidly shifting search for the suspects had barely moved to Toledo when the corpse of thirty-year-old Virginia Temple and her ten-year-old daughter, Rachelle, were discovered stuffed into a dark basement crawl space in a decaying neighborhood of the city. Both the mother and daughter had been strangled and raped. A search team uncovered the bodies after police were called to the modest two-story house by relatives who had become alarmed after confirming reports by neighbors that four younger girls in the family, all under six years of age, were wandering around alone and unsupervised. One of the older surviving children told police that her mother had permitted a strange man and woman to stay at the house the previous night. A coroner's examination of the bodies indicated that the sexual assaults and double slaying had occurred at that time.

Friends of Mrs. Temple had seen her the previous afternoon in a corner grocery store with a man resembling Coleman. They said she seemed to be nervous and stammered that a babysitter was at home with the children, as her mysterious male companion waited silently a few feet away near the back of the store.

Several other reports of violence involving people resembling the descriptions of Coleman and Brown, including the exchange of gunshots with a bar owner, were filed in quick succession with Toledo police. The minister of a Baptist church said a man he believed to be Coleman asked him for money, and when the stranger was refused, left cursing.

Another pastor said he met a couple he later believed to be Coleman and Brown in a fast-food restaurant and was asked for food and money. He took them home to feed them, and it was at his home they met Mrs. Temple, who was visiting with the clergyman's wife.

Although authorities were unable to verify that Coleman was responsible for all the crimes eyewitness accounts seemed to link him to, there was strong evidence that he was tied to the Temple slayings. And there appeared to be almost no doubt that the ruthless pair had been responsible for a vicious attack on an elderly white Toledo couple, who were robbed of $200 and their car. The man and wife, both in their seventies, were bound, handcuffed, gagged, and left in an upstairs bedroom. Before leaving, the intruder growled: "I've already killed three niggers. Don't make me kill you."

Two other people who were robbed and beaten by a couple believed to be Coleman and Brown said their male attacker claimed that blacks were somehow forcing him to kill other blacks.

Coleman was added to the FBI's list of the nation's ten most-wanted fugitives as a special eleventh member. The extraordinary step had been taken by the nation's law-enforcement agency only nine other times in the thirty-four-year history of the list. An FBI spokesman explained that the list was expanded to include Coleman, "due to the severe and violent nature of the crimes for which he is wanted."

Coleman's ability to win the confidence of strangers was helping him to stay a step ahead of his frustrated pursuers. His practice of abandoning cars no longer than ten or twelve hours after stealing them was also an important factor working in his favor. He and his companion also often switched to public transportation after relocating in a new neighborhood, and rather than cars, Coleman liked to ride around on bicycles, a mode of transportation that seemed innocent and helped him elude the law.

The fugitives may also have avoided capture near the

Temple home because of their ability to melt so easily into the background of impoverished black neighborhoods where crime and hassles with police are reluctantly accepted as an inevitable fact of everyday life. A teenaged boy eventually reported seeing Coleman riding a bicycle with his girlfriend as passenger when a police car appeared some distance behind them. Coleman leaped off his bicycle and ran between some nearby houses to hide, but the youth didn't flag down the squad car or notify other authorities of the bicyclist's suspicious behavior at that time. As a Toledo police detective was later quoted in the *Chicago Tribune* as saying: "The kid didn't think much of that. Around here, it's not unusual to see someone running from police."

A high-ranking Waukegan police official who had known the fugitive since an encounter with him as a juvenile offender, informed the FBI task force that Coleman was known to dress as a woman, especially when he was on the run, and that he was a mean-tempered bisexual who sexually assaulted both male and female victims.

The policeman added that he did not consider Coleman to be a typical serial slayer who murdered for thrills, but a cruel, predatory criminal with a strong sense of survival who killed when he was in a rage or felt threatened.

A psychiatrist who had studied Coleman when he was previously in custody, identified him not as bisexual, but as "pansexual," someone who was excited by sex with anyone — man, woman, or child.

Coleman's companion, Debra Brown, was described as the fifth child in a family of eleven, a high-school dropout, and a natural follower, a woman who was easily led and dominated. Engaged to be married when she met Coleman in a Waukegan bar, she almost immediately broke off with her old boyfriend and moved in with the new man in her life.

The background information about the renegade twosome was valuable, but they were moving too fast during their ghastly spree for the manhunters to get a fix on them. It seemed that they would barely surface in one place before a spate of assaults, robberies, and murders elsewhere signaled that they had moved on.

On July 11, four days after the Toledo mother and daughter were slain, the remains of Donna Williams were discovered in an abandoned slum building in Detroit. She had been strangled with a pair of pantyhose.

On July 13, a suburban Cincinnati housewife, Marlene Waters, was brutally bludgeoned to death and her husband, Harry, was ferociously beaten by a black couple who rode up to their house on gleaming ten-speed bicycles and talked their way inside. The male claimed he had recently been discharged from the military and was interested in buying a camper the victims had offered for sale in a newspaper classified ad.

The couple's daughter returned home to find her parents tied and bludgeoned in the basement of the house. A crowbar, vice-grip pliers, a four-foot wooden candlestick, and a knife were used in the murderous assault. The house had been ransacked, and the family's late-model car was missing. Like others, the self-employed tool sharpener and his Sunday-school-teacher wife had been too kind and trusting to strangers. The sinister trail of violence had now moved more than 230 miles across the state from the lakeshore city hugging the Michigan line to the sprawling factory town hugging the Ohio River border. And for the first time, one of the murder victims was white.

On July 16, Oline Carmical, Jr., a forty-five-year-old political-science professor, was walking to his car in the parking lot of a motel in Lexington, Kentucky, after attending a seminar when he was confronted by two men and a woman and forced inside the vehicle. For the next several hours the Cumberland College, Kentucky, instructor didn't know if he would live or die, as his kidnappers took him on a terrifying ride north across the Ohio River before finally abandoning the car in a Dayton park. He was freed, unhurt, at about 6:00 A.M., after passers-by heard pounding noises coming from the trunk of the car.

Carmical told police that the kidnappers drove for a while after his abduction, then ordered him to get out and telephone his wife with a ransom demand. When he complained that he couldn't get the money so late at night, he was forced into the trunk and driven to Dayton.

A short time later police arrested Thomas Farrell Harris on a kidnapping charge. The Lexington man was accused of helping Coleman and Brown kidnap the professor. The thirty-three-year-old Harris told FBI agents he met up with the fugitives on a Lexington street shortly before the abduction and was "kind of forced" to participate. Harris identified Coleman and Brown from photos and told interrogators that the woman had wanted to get rid of Carmical by driving the car off a cliff with the professor inside. He claimed that he talked the fugitives out of killing their prisoner.

While Carmical's ordeal was ending in Dayton, FBI agents were flooding into Kentucky. The car stolen from the Walters had been found abandoned in a cornfield near a black neighborhood in Lexington. But by that time, their quarry was backtracking — Coleman and Brown had returned to Ohio.

A half-hour after Carmical was freed, an elderly minister and his wife were found beaten in their Dayton home. Investigators learned that the couple had met Coleman and Brown, who were using false identities, about a week earlier. The fugitives moved into the preacher's home for a couple of days, departing on friendly terms when their hosts drove them to Cincinnati, ostensibly to attend a prayer meeting. Less than a week later, the strangers showed up again in Dayton, administered a fierce beating to their former hosts, and stole their stationwagon.

Later that day a nine-year-old in Columbus, Ohio, told her mother that a man and woman had stopped their car as she walked along a street and gruffly ordered her to climb inside. Instead, she ran home and reported the incident. The information was relayed to police, and a description of the pair provided by the child matched those of the fugitives.

The next sightings of the killer pair to be taken seriously by police turned up in Indianapolis, and more than a hundred miles upstate in South Bend, Indiana. An innocent Indianapolis man who, unfortunately, closely resembled Coleman in appearance, was located and apparently accounted for the reports placing the fugitive there. The look-alike lead in South Bend was also determined to be bogus. Some investigators, however, were already speculating that the suspects would be seeking safety outside the Midwest because of the widespread attention their crime spree had drawn to the Great Lakes area. One anonymous telephone tip to the FBI placed Coleman and Brown as far south as Fort Lauderdale, Florida, where they were reportedly seen getting into a taxicab. Like dozens of others, the tip was followed up and found to be an apparent case of mistaken identity.

Residents of black inner-city neighborhoods in the Midwest were terrified, especially in communities where the couple had already struck. Toledo police warned parents to keep their children indoors and under close adult supervision. Applications for the purchase of handguns swelled overnight, and the Toledo chapter of the New Union of Blacks in America offered a $500 reward for information about the couple. An organization spokesman explained that the reward was offered because of the terror among the city's black population.

Dayton Chief of Police Tyree Broomfield urged

residents to take extra precautions, and to temporarily halt garage sales, private car sales, and other similar activities Coleman could use as an excuse to ingratiate himself with potential new victims. Broomfield said that forty-five police departments in a seven-county area that included the cities of Dayton and Cincinnati were cooperating in the massive search of southern Ohio for the fugitives. He pointed out that Coleman was especially skilful at preying on "Christian-minded people," and warned that citizens should be wary of strangers asking for help. He added that Coleman had "a propensity for little girls. Parents of pre-teens should be cautious."

In Waukegan, Coleman's frantic grandmother issued a pathetic tape-recorded appeal, calling on the fugitive killer to surrender.

"Alton, please, in Jesus' name, for God's sake, give yourself up so you can go and get well," she pleaded. "Please, you're killing me. I'm worried to death."

While the massive search was focusing on southern Ohio, a handsome man and his petite companion rode up on bicycles to the home of an elderly couple in Dayton who were having a yard sale. The strangers quickly talked their way inside the house, then turned on their hosts, bound and gagged them, and stole their car. The vehicle was abandoned a few hours later alongside the Economy Car Wash in Indianapolis, formerly operated by Eugene Scott, a devoted churchman and father of eleven children, who was celebrating his seventy-seventh birthday that day.

That evening a pair of motorcyclists discovered the body of the old man sprawled in a ditch in rural Boone County a few miles north of the Indiana capital city. He had been shot four times with a .38-caliber handgun; his hands had been slashed with a knife, indicating he had tried to fight off an attacker; and his right leg was broken. His fourteen-year-old vehicle, which he drove daily to the neighborhood surrounding the car wash to chat with other elderly men, was missing.

As Indiana and Boone County investigators were preparing to notify the FBI of their suspicions that the retired Indianapolis businessman had been a victim of the Midwest's killer team, the bloody seven-week reign of terror came to an abrupt end less than forty miles from where it had begun.

Coleman and his teenage accomplice were taken peacefully into custody on July 20, as they sat in an Evanston, Illinois, park quietly watching a pickup game on a basketball court. A former childhood acquaintance had recognized Coleman as he was walking along the central business area of the Northwestern University college town shortly before noon and tipped off police. Officers traced him to the sunlit park.

Three male officers with guns drawn closed in on Coleman, while two female officers apprehended his companion. Coleman was carrying two blood-smeared knives, one in a pocket and one in a boot. Debra Brown had an unloaded .38-caliber snub-nosed revolver in her purse. Although neither of the fugitives put up physical resistance, Coleman did attempt to use his glib con-man tongue to slither out of trouble. Lightheartedly joking with arresting officers and still insisting that his name was Jones, he was locked in a holding cell at Evanston police headquarters. Even though he tried using bogus identification to convince police that they had made a mistake, had shaved his head of his former bushy Afro and was thin and haggard from his weeks on the run, police knew they had the right man. Formal identification was made at police headquarters by checking fingerprints. Coleman's companion, who had also given a false name, quickly relented and admitted her true identity.

At 5:00 P.M., the Boone County sheriff was notified that Scott's car had been found in Evanston, abandoned about five blocks from the park where the fugitives had been taken into custody. A fingerprint matching Debra Brown's was inside the vehicle.

The manhunt was over, and authorities in five states linked the rapacious pair to at least six slayings in which they either were already charged or were suspects, and to a host of other crimes.

On July 21, the prisoners were transported in separate cars to Chicago's Dirksen Federal Building for bond hearings before U.S. Magistrate Carl Sussman in the Vernita Wheat case. When Coleman, handcuffed and wearing prison blues and slippers, appeared before him, Sussman angrily demanded, "What is a reasonable bond for a man who is charged with abducting and murdering a nine-year-old girl?

"This nation has been under a siege. This nation has been under a reign of terror not knowing when the next victim was going to be taken. I am going to make sure no other victim will be subject to this man . . . . I set bond at $25 million full cash," the jurist declared. Although unprecedented, there appeared to be few in the court who thought the huge cash bond undeserved.

Earlier statements by law-enforcement authorities that Debra Brown had been a virtual prisoner of Coleman had apparently been made in order to lure her into surrendering, but when Coleman's teenaged sweetheart appeared before the magistrate in handcuffs, and with her head bowed, Assistant U.S. Attorney Jeremy Margolis insisted that she had been a willing participant in the crime spree. "She was part of the trail of bloody violence, which took the lives of men, women and, most tragically, children," he declared. "She is not looked at as a slave of Alton Coleman who was doing his bidding." The magistrate set a $20 million cash bond for Brown. Both she and her lover were locked up in Chicago's high-security Metropolitan Correctional Center.

The day before the capture of the nation's most wanted fugitives, the owner of a vacant building in a Cincinnati suburb discovered the partly nude, decomposing corpse of fifteen-year-old Tonnie Storey. The teenager, whose mother had reported her missing nearly two weeks earlier, had been raped and strangled. Her name was added to the list of suspected victims of the Coleman-Brown sex-and-murder rampage.

In Waukegan, police announced that a special hotline was being established to assist state and federal prosecutors from throughout the Great Lakes states and Kentucky who were expected to file charges against the murderous pair. A few days later about fifty representatives from the FBI and sixteen law-enforcement agencies in six states met with Assistant U.S. Attorney Margolis in his Chicago office to compare evidence in the cases and decide in what order they would be scheduled for trial. The couple were suspects in eight murders, numerous abductions, sexual assaults, beatings, and thefts involving both local and federal offenses.

It was decided that Ohio authorities would get first crack at the duo. "We believe prosecution [in Ohio] is most likely to result in the swiftest imposition of the death penalty," U.S. Attorney Dan K. Webb stated. Prosecution of the Walters case in Cincinnati would be strengthened by the presence of an adult eyewitness. And conviction on murder charges tried under Ohio state law permits the death penalty, while federal offenses would more likely lead to prison terms. Webb added, however, that the government would not be satisfied with a single murder conviction.

Still, the first court proceedings in Ohio did not deal with a murder case, but with federal kidnapping charges against the couple for the abduction of the Cumberland college professor. Both Coleman and Brown entered guilty pleas to the kidnapping and were given twenty-year sentences in federal prisons by U.S. District Judge Walter Rice in Dayton. The magistrate then ordered their immediate transfer to Cincinnati for their first murder trials. He had turned down an earlier request by the couple to be wed, but minutes before sentencing they signed legal documents entering them into a common-law marriage.

During separate trials in Cincinnati, both Coleman and his companion were convicted of first-degree murder in the death of Mrs. Walters. Coleman was sentenced to die in Ohio's electric chair, and Debra Brown was sentenced to life imprisonment.

The jury that convicted Coleman was shocked during the penalty phase of the proceedings when his accomplice took the stand and insisted that she, herself, had committed the murder. Her own trial had already been concluded, and she had escaped the death penalty.

"I killed the bitch and I don't give a damn. I had fun out of it," Debra Brown boasted, in what appeared to be a desperate bid to save her lover from the electric chair. She also claimed to have personally murdered several other people during the bloody eight-week crime spree, and said she didn't "give a damn about anyone" except Coleman.

The lovers were also tried separately in Cincinnati in the murder of Tonnie Storey, convicted, and each received death sentences. Debra Brown, who cried when her jury recommended the death penalty, was given an additional prison term on a charge of aggravated robbery. Coleman was found innocent of an added charge of aggravated murder allegedly committed to hide his rape of the girl.

During Coleman's trial for the murder of the Cincinnati teenager, FBI agents testified that he boasted he could have killed the officers who arrested him in Evanston, but didn't because he was mentally exhausted.

Indiana was the next state to get the murderous pair. In the Lake County courthouse in Crown Point, a jury of seven women and five men found Coleman guilty of the murder of little Tamika Turks. He was sentenced to die in Indiana's electric chair at the state penitentiary in Michigan City for the slaying, and to a hundred years in prison for the rape and attempted murder of Tamika's nine-year-old playmate.

Debra Brown went on trial a few days later and was also convicted of murder, and of attemped murder and child-molesting for the attack on Tamika's playmate. She received her second death sentence on the murder charge and consecutive forty-year prison terms on the other two counts. Prior to sentencing, she sent a hand-written note to Lake County Superior Court Judge Richard W. Maroc, apologizing for her role in the crimes. "I'm a more kind and understandable and lovable person than people think I am," she wrote.

Coleman's trial for the kidnap-murder of Vernita Wheat was held in Waukegan, with jurors selected from nearby Rock Island, Illinois, after he claimed that a fair and impartial jury could not be found in Lake County because of the heavy publicity in the case. At his insistence, he was permitted to represent himself, although he was assisted by two court-appointed attorneys. The jury deliberated four hours at the conclusion of the five-day proceedings before returning a finding of guilty of aggravated kidnap and murder.

Coleman allowed his court-appointed attorneys to represent him during the penalty phase of the trial, and told the jurors he was not asking for mercy.

"I'm a dead man. I'm dead already," he claimed. "You are talking to a dead man, not a live man."

The jury deliberated thirty minutes before recommending the death penalty. Lake County Circuit Judge Fred Geiger, who was legally bound by the recommendation, sentenced him to execution by lethal injection.

Prosecutors said they believed Coleman was the only man in the United States under four separate death sentences.

There were no plans to prosecute Coleman or Brown in the remaining four deaths blamed on them in the Midwest murder spree.

CHAPTER 3

THE MAN WHO KILLED MODELS

CHRISTOPHER WILDER

(1984)

It was a promising, sun-drenched Sunday morning on February 26, 1984, when perky twenty-one–year–old Rosario Gonzalez left her family's house for the second day of a two-day job at the Miami Grand Prix.

Promised $400 to pass out aspirin samples during the race, the pixyish young beauty was radiantly happy about her life as a model and her approaching marriage to a young college student, which was only three months away.

Dressed fetchingly in red shorts and a white t-shirt inscribed with the product logo, she was at the company tent by 8:30 A.M. Picking up her sample tray, she worked on Biscayne Boulevard for nearly five hours before returning to the tent to retrieve her purse and begin her lunch break.

She never returned to work that afternoon. And that evening she didn't return to the pleasant home in the suburb of Homestead where she lived with her parents, Blas and Haydee Gonzales, and a sister, eighteen-year-old Lisette. By 9:00 P.M., her parents, who had settled in Dade County, Florida, in 1979 so that their girls could grow up in the sunshine near relatives, were calling police to check accident reports. Then they called the hospitals. "By 3:00 A.M., we were so hysterical, screaming and crying," Rosario's mother later told an Associated Press reporter. "We couldn't even control our emotions long enough to say a prayer. The rest has been torture."

Three days after Rosario's inexplicable failure to return home, or to notify her family of her whereabouts, Miami police joined the search already launched by her parents.

A couple of nights later, William Kenyon and his family, who divided their time between homes in Lockport, N.Y., and prosperous Pompano Beach, a few miles north of Miami, were among the thousands of South Florida residents who watched a late-news telecast that mentioned the search for the missing young woman. For a scant few seconds a photo of Rosario's face was flashed on the screen.

On March 4, barely a week after Rosario vanished from sight, the Kenyons' own vivacious daughter, Elizabeth ("Beth"), also disappeared. Although a teacher of emotionally disturbed children at Coral Gables High School in south Miami, like Rosario, the twenty-three–year–old 1982 Orange Bowl Princess had dabbled in the dazzling world of modeling.

The year in which she reigned over the popular bowl game at the University of Miami, Beth was a finalist in the Miss Florida contest. Lovely, clever, and from a well-to-do family, it seemed that her options in life were almost unlimited. She was also an emotionally stable young woman and, although independent, remained close to her family. She would never have run off on a whim without notifying them or her roommate in Coral Gables of her plans, or without making arrangements with her employers. But there hadn't been a word from her to her parents or to school administrators.

The Kenyons went through a routine agonizingly similar to that which the Gonzalez family had endured a few days earlier. They contacted police agencies and hospitals, and telephoned their daughter's friends in a desperate search for her. Finally, with no more numbers in his daughter's address book to call and no more local hospitals to check, William Kenyon walked into Miami's Metro Dade Public Safety Building and filed a missing-persons report.

By that time, a policeman friend of Beth's, Clifford "Mitch" Fry, who had been assigned by the Coral Gables Police Department to the high school campus, had already started his own private investigation of her disappearance. He had telephoned everyone listed in the personal directory she kept at her apartment, but no one he called could, or would, tell him how he could find her. "Christopher Bernard Wilder" was one of the names in the directory but Wilder never responded to a message left on his telephone-answering machine, puzzling behavior for such a close friend of the missing woman.

A thirty-nine–year–old self-described photographer with a love of fast cars and an eye for comely females, Wilder had dated Beth and was so taken with her beauty and charm that he had asked her to marry him. Although she had refused, the two remained good friends, and Wilder had been a welcome guest in her family's home.

Flamboyant, but charming, the bachelor playboy who often wore a gold chain around his neck and expensive rings was known at local pickup bars as an entertaining companion and generous tipper.

Unknown to Beth's worried family and her concerned policeman friend, Wilder also knew the missing Rosario Gonzalez. And he was a race-car enthusiast who drove to seventh place in the Miami Grand Prix where Rosario was distributing aspirin samples. Another model eventually revealed to investigators that she had met Wilder at the 1982 Miss Florida Pageant. About a month later the other model introduced him to Rosario who had been the winner at the Miss Mannequin Pageant. Rosario's fiancé also confirmed that she had posed for Wilder at least once after he promised that one of the photos would appear on the cover of a romance novel. The picture never did appear on the book, and according to her fiancé, Rosario suspected Wilder of being a phony.

Her suspicions were well founded. Not only was Wilder a phony, but he had come to the attention of authorities in two countries as a dangerous sex criminal with an insatiable desire for beautiful young women and girls.

Born on March 13, 1945, in Australia to an American Navy career man who reached the rank of chief warrant officer, and a Sydney girl whom he had met during World War II, Wilder was the oldest of three sons. The family had moved back and forth between the United States and Australia several times before settling in New South Wales where Wilder's father, who had retired from the Navy, established himself in the construction business.

Three times the family nearly lost its first born. Christopher was so sickly as an infant that he was once given the last rites. A couple of years later he nearly drowned in a swimming pool, but was revived. And when he was three years old he had nearly died, after losing consciousness while on a drive with his parents, but, again, he recovered.

By the time Wilder had reached his teens his troubles were of a far different nature. He was seventeen when he and several buddies were arrested for the gang rape of a girl on an isolated Australian beach. After a few days in jail, Wilder pleaded guilty in juvenile court to a reduced charge of carnal knowledge, and was released with one year's probation that included mandatory counseling. Part of the counseling program included group therapy and electroshock treatments, a painless but often frightening experience.

At twenty-three, he married, but the union lasted only a few days. Police in Australia later told a *Miami Herald* reporter that the short-term bride complained about various forms of sexual abuse and of finding a collection of women's underwear, *Playboy* magazines, and photographs of pretty girls — some wearing only bikini bottoms — in a briefcase he kept in the trunk of his car.

The reporter also noted that, "Early on, there was some suggestion that he was involved in what we call snow dropping, stealing ladies' clothes off clotheslines. The wife found some in her house, clothes that weren't hers."

In November 1969, he talked a naive nineteen-year-old student nurse into posing nude at a beach a few miles from Sydney on the pretense that he could help her get a modeling job. Then he threatened to mail copies of the embarrassing pictures to the hospital where she was training if the nurse refused to have sex with him. The girl notified police, but as she didn't want to testify, there were no formal charges filed. But Wilder knew that his name was in police files and that his sexual hijinks had firmly tagged him as a man local authorities would keep an eye on. So he struck out for the United States, and the sunsplashed beaches of South Florida with their opportunities for surfing, boating — and meeting pretty girls.

He did well in the Sunshine State, setting himself up in electrical contracting and construction businesses. The companies were named Sawtel Construction and Sawtel Electric, after a popular Australian resort town where his parents had retired and where he had trolled the beaches for girls earlier in his life. Three years later, Wilder and a business partner, L. K. "Zeke" Kimbrell, were employing seventy people. Wilder invested much of his profits in real estate, including a posh bachelor pad of his own which he outfitted with an expensive stereo sound system, a jacuzzi, and an indoor-outdoor pool highlighted by a map of Australia outlined in tiles on the bottom. Behind the resort-like home, twin derricks were installed along a canal so he could launch his speedboat. Dozens of beautiful girls whom he met on the beaches or in beachfront bars along the Gold Coast paraded in and out of his house, cruised with him in his speedboat, or went joy-riding in his Cadillac El Dorado and customized Porsche 911. It seemed that he was leading the kind of life which was every bachelor's dream.

Local law-enforcement authorities, however, knew there was a darker side to the Australian-American's busy life, a sinister obsession with the domination and sexual abuse of women and girls.

In March 1971, he was arrested in Pompano Beach for trying to talk girls he met along the oceanfront into posing nude for photographs. He pleaded guilty to a charge of disturbing the peace and was assessed a small fine.

In October 1977, he offered to help find a high-school girl a part-time job as a secretary, then drove her to an isolated area where he threatened to beat her if she didn't perform oral sex. Reluctantly, she complied, and as soon as she was freed, she notified police. Although Wilder admitted the crime to therapists, the statements were not used in court, and a jury acquitted him of sex charges.

On June 21, 1980, he raped a teenaged vacationer from Tennessee after luring her into his pickup truck by claiming to be a representative from a famous modeling agency who would help her launch her career. A police investigation indicated he had weakened her defenses by spiking a pizza he bought her with a drug. He pleaded guilty to reduced charges of attempted sexual battery and was sentenced to five years' probation, with a proviso that he regularly visit a psychologist for therapy.

About that same time an employee in the photo department of a Boynton Beach store opened a package of prints developed from film Wilder had brought in and found pornographic pictures of young women and prepubescent girls. Much later, police would discover that one room in his Boynton Beach home had been professionally outfitted as a photographic studio. Investigators also learned that not all the pretty young models who posed there, often naked or wearing nothing more than high-heeled shoes, had done so willingly. Wilder's photo workshop was equipped with chains, straps, and manacles.

During a visit to his family in Australia, the bearded playboy with the charming "Down Under" accent got into more trouble. Three days after Christmas, in 1982, he was accused of kidnapping two fifteen-year-old girls from a New South Wales beach and taking them to a park where he made them strip, then forced them to pose for pornographic photos. After the first picture-taking session he bound the frightened teenagers, shoved them into a car, and drove them to a motel for more photography. As soon as the girls were released, they notified police. They told investigators that their abductor had introduced himself as a professional photographer and had shown them a business card naming a talent agency in Florida.

Police traced Wilder through the license number of his rented car and charged him the next day with kidnapping and indecent assault. He was scheduled for trial on May 7, and after family members posted $350,000 bail he was allowed to leave the country to take care of what he claimed were pressing business matters at home.

In South Florida only a few of Wilder's friends knew about his latest troubles in Australia. But by the second week of March, there were sinister clues piling up that indicated he might know a lot more about the inexplicable disappearance of Beth Kenyon than he was admitting. Wilder's therapist entertained a fleeting suspicion that he might know something about the disappearance of Rosario Gonzalez, which she had read about in an area newspaper. Aware of his sex-slave fantasies and fascination with John Fowles' novel *The Collector*, she asked Wilder if he knew anything about the missing woman during one of their last counseling sessions. Without batting an eye he replied that he, too, had read about the search for the model, but had had nothing to do with her disappearance.

A few days after the policeman friend of Beth Kenyon left his message on Wilder's answering machine, Kenneth Whittaker, Jr., the private investigator hired by her family, telephoned Wilder and asked if he had seen Beth. He replied that he hadn't, explaining that he had been out of town for a while. At the private eye's request, Wilder telephoned the Kenyons and repeated his assertion that he knew nothing of their daughter's disappearance, but they weren't satisfied with his denial.

A Coral Gables gas-station attendant had been located who had seen Beth the day she disappeared. He said she had been with a bearded, balding, middle-aged man who had paid for her gas. When the attendant was shown a sheaf of photos of men that Beth had dated, he picked out a picture of Wilder as the man he had seen with her.

Still working independently, Fry had also come to the conclusion that Wilder might be connected not only to Beth's disappearance but to Rosario's as well. He took his suspicions, and his information, to the Miami Police Department. In short order, the Metro Dade Public Safety Department, the FBI, and other local police agencies in South Florida were focusing considerable attention on the high-living womanizer.

Wilder did his best to put on a calm front and ignore the policemen and private detectives who were suddenly snooping around his home and business in Boynton Beach. When his partner questioned him, he replied that he was puzzled that the Kenyons and others seemed to think he had had something to do with Beth's disappearance.

On March 13, he purchased an eleven-year-old Chrysler New Yorker. A far cry from the flashy Porsche and Cadillac he tooled around in while hunting for attractive women, it seemed a curious present to treat himself to on his thirty-ninth birthday.

On March 16, an article appeared in the *Miami Herald* reporting that authorities were seeking a race-car driver from Boynton Beach for questioning in the disappearance of two young women. The man wasn't named in the story, but the next day, Wilder missed his appointment with his therapist and didn't show up at work. Two days after the article appeared, Wilder telephoned his partner from Tallahassee, Florida's state capital, then drove back to Boynton Beach. In tears, he told his business partner that police were trying to frame him for Beth's disappearance, and vowed he would not go to jail. That night, he took his three English setters to a Fort Lauderdale kennel that he was part owner of, then drove away into the darkness in his old Chrysler. It was the beginning of a hellish cross-country odyssey of sex, torture, and murder.

In Indian Harbour, a couple of hours' drive north along the east coast of Florida, twenty-one-year-old Theresa "Terry" Anne Wait was seeing her boyfriend off on a trip to Fort Lauderdale for spring break, an annual frolic that attracts college students and other young people from all over the country. She had planned to go with him, but work commitments interfered.

Like Rosario and Beth, Terry was a beauty, and although she was currently working at a t-shirt–printing company, she had given some serious thought to a modeling career. But when she drove away from the home she shared with her mother and stepfather, Indian Harbour Police Captain Don Ferguson, at about noon Sunday, her thoughts were on a shopping trip she had planned with two girlfriends. As neither of her friends could go, she drove to a nearby shopping mall by herself. She never returned home.

Shortly before midnight, the slender, dark-eyed brunette's stepfather found her car parked in the mall, with the blue-jeans and blouse she had worn when she left home locked inside. A clerk in a boutique was located who remembered selling her a blouse. She had been last seen by a mall employee at about 2:30 P.M.

Investigators later learned that about an hour after Terry was last seen at the mall, a man telephoned a service station in nearby Cocoa Beach to ask for a tow. His Chrysler New Yorker was stuck in sand in a stand of trees in a local lovers' lane. The driver, who was middle-aged, bearded, and balding, paid for the tow with a credit card registered in the name of L. K. Kimbrell. The same name was used a short time later when a bearded man checked into a West Cocoa Beach motel.

Two days after Terry Wait's disappearance, a freshman student at Florida State University in Tallahassee was at a shopping mall a few miles from the campus when a man with a camera slung around his neck approached her. He explained that he was a fashion photographer and asked her to pose for him. Excited at the prospect of a professional modeling job, she agreed to return to his car with him to sign some release forms. At the car her companion suddenly turned on the willowy blonde, slammed a fist into her stomach, punched her in the head, and shoved her into the vehicle. Later he zipped her into a sleeping bag.

The terrified nineteen-year-old was driven two hundred miles to Bainbridge, Georgia, where her brutal abductor hoisted her over his shoulder and carried her into a motel room. He dumped her onto a bed, unzipped her from the sleeping bag, stripped her, raped her twice, and forced her to perform oral sex. Then, he attached the ends of an electrical cord to her toes and used a switch to control the current as he repeatedly jolted her with electrical shocks for two agonizing hours.

Even then, her ordeal wasn't over. The sadistic kidnapper had still another toy in his grotesque bag of tricks. He pulled out a tube of superglue, and as the girl lay helplessly on her back with her hands tied and her mouth taped shut, he squeezed beads of the substance onto her eyelids, using a hairdryer to make the glue seal faster. Finally, satisfied that her eyelids were glued together, he ordered her to get up and dance nude in time with the music from an aerobic show he had tuned in on the television. The girl's foot was still wired to the cord.

The glue hadn't closed her eyes as effectively as he thought, however, and she could still see through her lashes. She suddenly jerked the cord from the wall and lurched toward the bathroom. He caught her before she could stumble inside, and they struggled, he smashed her over the head with the hair dryer, slashing her scalp. But she was fighting for her life and managed to slip out of his grasp, run into the bathroom, and slam and lock the door. Then she started to scream and pound on the walls. The kidnapper scooped up a pile of their clothes, zipped up his suitcase, and fled naked out the front door. He raced away from the motel in a 1973 Chrysler sedan.

When the shaken girl related her story to police, the

description she provided of her abductor was remarkably similar to that of the man being sought as a suspect in the disappearances of Rosario Gonzalez and Beth Kenyon. When eventually asked to identify her abductor from among a collection of police photos, the coed selected a picture of Christopher Wilder.

A few hours after the coed's screams had chased her kidnapper from the motel, an electric-company crew working on lines in Florida's rural Polk County discovered the bloated body of a young woman floating face down in a snake-infested creek. Dental records, used to make positive identification of the corpse, proved the search for Terry Wait was over.

News coverage of the tragedy was extensive, and authorities located a woman who told them that on the Sunday afternoon Terry had disappeared, she had seen the girl talking to a balding, bearded man with a camera dangling from around his neck. The FBI initiated a full-fledged search for the suspected sex-slayer, and newspapers, television, and radio across the South carried stories about the manhunt. Wilder was desperate, dangerous, and he was on the run.

On March 23, the same day Terry's parents learned that her body had been found, a lovely twenty-four-year-old nursing student and mother dropped off her daughter at a day-care center in Beaumont, Texas, and drove away to attend classes at nearby Lamar University. That afternoon, Terry Diane Walden didn't return to the nursery school to pick up her four-year-old daughter. Nor did she arrive home to meet her nine-year-old stepdaughter when the girl returned from school.

Other students had seen Mrs. Walden at the university late that Friday morning. And that afternoon, a schoolgirl reported seeing a bearded man driving a white Chrysler along a narrow dirt road through a sprawl of rice fields. There was a woman passenger in the car whose head was slumped against the side window, the girl said. About an hour later she saw the man returning down the same dirt road driving fast and alone.

It was the following Monday before Terry Walden's family learned what had happened to her. A worker checking an isolated canal dam on the west side of the city found her body, fully clothed, floating face down in the water. The dam ran along Walden Road and was on the same dirt trail the cream Chrysler had twice traversed. Mrs. Walden had been stabbed three times in the chest. Marks on her body and a cord found nearby indicated that she had been tightly bound and her mouth taped when she was killed, then untied and dumped in the ditch. Her orange 1981 Cougar was missing.

Terry's grief-stricken husband told investigators that before her disappearance his wife had confided to him that a bearded, middle-aged man had approached her on campus, claiming to be a photographer and asking if she wanted to model. She had told him to leave her alone.

Nearly two weeks later, a Beaumont policeman discovered an abandoned car in the downtown business district. It was the cream-colored 1973 Chrysler purchased by Christopher Wilder on his birthday which the FBI had been looking for. But by the time Wilder's car was found, three more women had been kidnapped, sexually abused, tortured, and murdered in what had become a runaway cross-country killing spree.

In Oklahoma City, a twenty-one-year-old secretary and aspiring model, Suzanne Wendy Logan, was abducted from a shopping center. The next day a fisherman found the attractive woman's half-naked body shoved under a cedar tree along the banks of a reservoir near Manhattan, Kansas, nearly three hundred miles north of where she'd been abducted. Her breasts had been savagely bitten and her back was scored with tiny puncture wounds, apparently made with the sharp tip of a knife. Someone had cut the straight blond hair on her head, shaved her pubic hair, and raped her. She had been stabbed to death with a single vicious thrust from a knife just above her left breast. Medical examiners estimated that she had been dead for less than an hour when her mutilated body was found.

In Grand Junction, Colorado, Sheryl Bonaventura, who was looking forward to a skiing weekend in Aspen with her boyfriend, disappeared from the Mesa Mall, where she worked. A few hours before, another young woman had been approached in the same mall by a bearded man who handed her a business card imprinted with the name of a Denver modeling agency. He asked her if she would like to pose for a fashion layout, but she wasn't interested. But Sheryl, eighteen and only a few months out of high school, had been talking about a possible modeling career, and had already posed for some professional photos.

Modeling was far from the minds of Sheryl's worried parents, however, when they searched the mall for her and found only her car. They notified Grand Junction Police, who immediately launched an investigation. A message on the National Crime Information Center (NCIC) computer telex had already carried an advisory to law-enforcement agencies to be on the lookout for Wilder. And the trail of missing women and dead bodies he was leaving on his wild cross-country flight indicated that he was heading their way.

When the young woman who'd rejected the advance made by the stranger in the mall contacted police and told them her story, investigators showed her several photographs of middle-aged, balding men with beards. She identified Wilder as the man who approached her.

Using the receipts from his business partner's stolen credit cards, the FBI tracked Wilder to a restaurant in Silverton, Colorado, a small town about a hundred miles south of Grand Junction. A waitress described the customer as a man in his thirties, with thinning blond hair and a beard; he had been with a pretty blonde woman of about twenty years of age. She said the young woman told another waitress that her name was Sheryl Bonaventura, and that her grandfather used to live in Silverton. Speaking in what the waitress described as baby talk, Sheryl added that she and her companion were going to Durango to visit relatives, then to Las Vegas where she and another girl were going to become models.

Shown a collection of photographs, the waitress identified Wilder and Sheryl as the customers. She added that another attractive woman in her teens or early twenties had eaten with the couple and left with them. About thirty-five miles away, in Durango, a few hours later, a man checked into a motel, listing himself and a companion as "Mr. and Mrs. L. K. Kimbrell." A relative of Sheryl's later speculated that based on the way she had reportedly talked in the restaurant, she might have been drugged.

On Sunday, April 1, Michelle Korfman, the vivacious seventeen-year-old daughter of a Las Vegas casino executive, left her family's home to compete in a modeling contest at a mall, and never returned. A good student and budding pianist, Michelle was a leggy five-foot-nine, 130-pound beauty, with blue eyes and long dark brown hair. When she learned that a cover-model competition for the popular teenagers' magazine *Seventeen* would be held in Las Vegas, she had entered as one of the contestants. Judges who looked over hundreds of photographs submitted by young, hopeful, would-be models, had selected Michelle as one of fifteen finalists to compete at the Meadows Mall.

Police found the 1982 Camaro her father had given her parked in a lot behind Caesar's Palace. Her personalized license plate, "TOMISH" (To Michelle), was mounted in a black frame with the slogan "To Daddy's

Girl'' still attached. Detectives also located a woman who reported seeing Michelle leaving the dressing-room area at the department store where the contest was held, with a bearded man. She later picked out a photo of Wilder from a selection of police photos of sex offenders.

Amazingly, authorities actually came up with a photo of Wilder watching the beauty contest as Michelle paraded before the judges, photographers, and guests. The picture was inadvertently snapped when the mother of one of the other girls dropped her camera and the shutter clicked. When the film was developed, the picture showed a closeup of the miniskirted legs of a young model — and watching intently from across the floor in front of her, the balding, middle-aged Wilder.

Local police and FBI agents talked with models, parents, contest authorities, photographers, and everyone else they could find who had been at the competitions. Several of the girls reported they were approached by a man who looked like Wilder, and talked into meeting him at Caesar's Palace for photographic sessions. Although they went to the meeting place, he never showed up.

Investigators also learned that the fugitive had stayed in a modestly priced downtown motel, and another night at a motel on the gambling strip — both times boldly signing the register with his own name. Authorities were still tracking Wilder's movements in the Las Vegas area, when he checked into a motel near the municipal airport in the town of Torrance, California, a few miles south of Los Angeles. He had driven west across the Mojave Desert, and was apparently making no effort to disguise his now nationally known and infamous features. He was still using his business partner's credit card to pay for his lodging, however.

Three days after Michelle Korfman disappeared, sixteen-year-old Tina Marie Risico walked into a delicatessen at the Del Amo Fashion Center after classes to apply for a summer job. The Torrance teenager was slim and attractive, and when a man who had strolled into the deli behind her handed her a business card and offered her $100 to model for photos, she agreed. He had an expensive-looking camera slung around his neck and told the pert blue-eyed blonde that she was perfect for a billboard ad he was working on. Tina Marie rode in his car with him to a remote beach near Santa Monica and posed prettily on the sand while he snapped what he said was a test roll of pictures.

But when she advised him that it was time for her to return home, his personality underwent a chilling metamorphosis. Snarling, he pulled a gun, quickly trussed her up with a stout cord, and loaded her into the car, stolen in Texas from Terry Walden. He then drove more than two hundred miles south to the small town of El Centro, California, about five miles from the Mexican border. Checking into a motel there, he freed Tina Marie, ordering her to cut her hair so she couldn't be easily recognized, and he shaved off his beard. Then he forced the girl back into the car, and minutes later was backtracking, driving northeast through California into Arizona. He finally checked in for the night at a motel in Prescott, about a hundred miles north of Phoenix, tied his helpless prisoner to a bed, and sexually abused and tortured her for hours.

Back in Torrance, police, who had been notified about the missing girl by her worried mother, talked with a clerk at the delicatessen. He told them about the bearded man with the camera, and identified Wilder, from a selection of pictures shown to him by police, as the man Tina had left with.

Wilder checked into a Taos motel on April 7, with his frightened young prisoner still in tow. But the next morning, it was Wilder who was frightened and upset — he had just been placed on the FBI's Most Wanted List. Two days later he received another nasty jolt. Television programs around the country carried taped segments of the suspected serial killer giving an interview with a video dating service. Executives of the Florida dating service had telephoned the FBI office in Miami and advised them that they had videotapes of the fugitive, filmed in 1981, when he had described his likes and dislikes and told about his desire to meet and date attractive young women. FBI release of copies of the tape to local television stations and networks produced a surge of reports around the country from people who believed they had seen the fugitive.

The next stop on Wilder's zig-zag, cross-country sex-and-murder rampage was Merrillville, Indiana, about ten miles southeast of the Illinois state line and at the southern border of the deteriorating steel town of Gary.

Dawnette Sue Wilt, a fresh-faced, sixteen-year-old beauty, was at the bustling Southlake Mall to fill out an application form for a summer job in a clothing boutique. She was busy working on the form when another teenager approached and explained that she already worked there and thought Dawnette would be perfect for the new job. The girl said her name was Tina Marie Wilder. Moments later Dawnette was being introduced to a balding man who said he was the manager of the shop. The man took a quick glance at the attractive high-school junior, and asked if she would like to model clothes for teenagers at the shop. Most teenaged girls would jump at an opportunity to venture into the thrilling world of fashion modeling, no matter on how small a scale, and Dawnette was no exception. She readily agreed to walk to the parking lot with her new acquaintances to sign some model release forms the man said he had in his car.

As soon as the trio reached the car, the man pulled a gun. Dawnette was forced inside the Mercury Cougar, her arms and legs were tied, and tape was pressed over her mouth and eyes. Wilder raped her in the back seat of the car, as the other girl drove east across Indiana to Wauseon, Ohio, a town on the edge of Toledo. There, Dawnette was bundled into a motel, sexually abused again, and tortured with electric shock. The next night, the trio was in Niagara Falls, N.Y., and Dawnette was once more raped and tortured in a motel.

But the nightmare odyssey was nearing an end, for Wilder and for his two young captives. The morning after checking into the Niagara Falls motel, Wilder decided it was time to get rid of the Indiana teenager he had been abusing for two days and nights. He tied and gagged Dawnette and shoved her into the back seat of the car, then ordered Tina into the front seat beside him. Wilder drove southwest to Barrington, in the rustic Finger Lakes region of the state, where he untied Dawnette, but left the tape over her eyes. He shoved the helpless girl ahead of him into a heavily wooded area, where he retied her arms and ordered her to kneel. Then he plunged a knife into her chest and back.

A short time later Wilder and Tina were in a shopping mall in the outskirts of a Rochester suburb where he was stalking another victim.

Miraculously, Dawnette survived. The plucky girl had played dead until she heard the sound of the car pulling away, then she lurched to her feet. The blood from her wounds had made her hands slippery enough to pull them free of the cord, and she stumbled to the road to summon help. Her frantic parents in Indiana were notified a few hours later that their missing daughter had been found, seriously injured but alive, and was in the Soldiers and Sailors Hospital in Penn Yan.

By that time, Wilder had already kidnapped Beth Ann Dodge, his final victim. The thirty-three-year-old mother and Sunday-school teacher was on her way to meet friends for lunch in her 1982 Pontiac Trans-Am when Wilder spotted her. He had been incredibly lucky driving Terry Walden's Cougar so many miles for such a long period of time, when it was obvious that a description of the vehicle must be on every police and sheriff's department hot sheet in the country. It was time to change cars, and the gold Trans-Am looked like just the ticket.

A few minutes after Beth Ann stepped from her car at the Eastview Mall, Wilder confronted her with a drawn gun and pushed her inside the Cougar. With Tina following in the Trans-Am, he drove his frightened passenger to a country road near a gravel pit, forced the woman outside, shoved her to the ground, and shot her once in the back of the neck with a .357 Magnum. Mrs. Dodge's body was found a few hours later. The abandoned Mercury Cougar police had been seeking for so long was parked nearby.

For the first time since the cross-country murder spree had begun, FBI agents and local law-enforcement agencies were only a few hours behind their quarry. Both victims of his latest brutal assaults had been found only a short time after they were attacked. Police streamed into the area, as the focus of the manhunt turned to upstate New York. Nevertheless, aided by a combination of devil's luck and cunning, Wilder once more slipped through their net. Somehow, despite wide dissemination to police agencies of descriptions of Wilder, his companion, and the car he was driving, the fugitive drove unmolested along the heavily patrolled New York State Freeway and clear across the adjoining state of Massachusetts, to Boston.

In Boston, Wilder inexplicably drove Tina Marie to Logan International Airport, bought her a ticket with three crisp new hundred-dollar bills, handed her a fistful of money, and instructed her to take a flight to Los Angeles and return home. He told her to kiss him on the cheek.

"All you gotta do, kid," he advised, "is write a book."

During a newspaper interview some four months later, Tina Marie recalled: "It was heartbreaking. It was so sentimental."

As obedient as she had been in the past, the teenager boarded Delta Airlines Flight 933, and began the long cross-country trip home. She had just survived a horrific nine-day trip with a human monster who at that moment was the most wanted and dangerous criminal in the nation.

Twelve hours later, when Tina Marie stepped off the Delta jet at Los Angeles International Airport, instead of going immediately to the police or telephoning home, she took a taxicab to an Hermosa Beach lingerie boutique. At the boutique, she casually shopped for some lingerie, mentioned to a couple of clerks that she was the girl who had been kidnapped from Torrance several days earlier, paid $104.50 for her purchases, and left. Sometime later, she ran into a couple of friends, who drove her to the Torrance Police Department. Later Tina Marie was quoted in newspapers as saying she thought she had been spared because Wilder had fallen in love with her. Sexually abused as a little girl and living with her mother in the Northern California backwoods where she often went hungry and missed weeks of schooling, Tina also believed her troubled childhood had toughened her sufficiently to help her survive the grueling ordeal with the sadistic killer.

An FBI spokesman in Buffalo said shortly after Tina Marie's release that agency officials considered her Wilder's victim, rather than his accomplice.

"Victims in fear of their life very closely identify with their captors as their only means of survival," remarked Special Agent Michael Kogut. "Some have described it as the Patty Hearst Syndrome." (Patty Hearst, heiress to part of a huge newspaper fortune, was kidnapped by left-wing radicals calling themselves the Symbionese Liberation Army in 1974, and after extensive abuse and brainwashing became sympathetic to them. The condition is also commonly called the "Stockholm Syndrome" so named after bank employees in Sweden released after being held hostage for a long period during a botched hold-up, were found to be protective toward their captors.)

A psychiatric review of Tina Marie's ordeal also indicated that she was a victim, rather than a willing accomplice. In a prepared statement released to the press by police, after examining the teenager at the UCLA Medical Center, Dr. Roland Summit was quoted as saying that she had been "subjected to an unimaginable terroristic action" by her captor.

"He impressed on her that he didn't hesitate to kill. He showed her a ruthlessness and an ability to victimize," the psychiatrist remarked. Wilder had routinely shoved the barrel of a handgun into Tina Marie's mouth and threatened to pull the trigger, as part of the brainwashing technique.

Dr. Summit said the girl was "subjected to sexual humiliation and brainwashing. The pattern follows explicitly one in which terror and obedience are instilled in the victim," he added in an Associated Press report.

Questioned about the girl's seemingly curious action of shopping for lingerie after returning to California, Torrance Police Sergeant Rollo Green remarked: "Tina did exactly as we would have expected." The investigator, who interviewed her for five hours, added, "It's not unusual at all for sexually abused women to want to get rid of the stench in their clothes. That's all they can think of." The teenager was not permitted to change her clothes during the nine days she was held by Wilder, it was explained in a Cox News Service report.

After leaving Tina Marie at the airport, Wilder attempted to snatch one more love slave. Driving out of Boston the next morning along Route 128 he spotted an attractive nineteen-year-old woman standing near her malfunctioning car, a short distance from suburban Beverly. He pulled to a stop and offered to give her a lift to a nearby service station. She accepted the ride, and when she complained as they drove past the station about a mile along the road, the man she had taken for a Good Samaritan pulled out a handgun and ordered her to shut up. She complied, but moments later as he slowed his car to exit from the highway, she pushed open the door and tumbled out onto the shoulder of the road. Wilder speeded away, as she scrambled to her feet and ran for her life.

At 1:30 that afternoon, a balding man pulled a gold, 1982 Pontiac Trans-Am to a stop in front of the pumps at Vic's Getty Oil Station in the village of Colebrook, New Hampshire, about ten miles from the Canadian border. Chatting casually with attendant Wayne Delong he asked if there was any likelihood he would have difficulty with documents or authorities when he drove across the border. As the men talked, a green station wagon with four policemen inside moved slowly past the station.

The officers were Colebrook Chief of Police Wayne Cross, and New Hampshire state troopers Howard Weber, Leo "Chuck" Jellison, and Wayne Fortier. Although newly assigned to the area, Fortier's training and policeman's sixth sense were working overtime for him, and as they passed the gas station the gold Trans-Am triggered a spark of suspicion in his mind. A description of the stolen car and of the suspected killer had been flashed to police across the country, and just that morning he had watched a television news report of the slaying of Beth Ann Dodge in upstate New York.

Colebrook was normally a quiet town, and it was hundreds of miles from Penn Yan. Nevertheless, the Pontiac was disturbing to Fortier.

"That looks like the car that Wilder guy is supposed to be driving," he observed, as they moved past the station. A couple of minutes later, Jellison and Fortier dropped the other trooper and the chief off at the Colebrook Police Station. Swinging the station wagon around, they drove back to the service station to have a look at the gold Trans-Am and the stranger who was driving it.

The Trans-Am had Massachusetts license plates instead of New York tags. But the color, year, and model of the car matched the vehicle described in FBI bulletins. And the driver, who was still talking with Delong, looked suspiciously like the FBI descriptions of the serial-killer suspect, except for the fact he was beardless. However, a light area on his chin and cheeks indicated he could have recently shaved off a beard.

Jellison, who like his companion, was wearing plain clothes, pulled his station wagon between the pumps and the Pontiac and slid out of the car. The officer is a big man, carrying some 250 pounds on his husky six-foot, four-inch frame. He cut an imposing figure as he approached the driver of the Trans-Am, who had broken off the conversation and was returning to his car.

"Excuse me," Jellison said. "I'd like a word with you."

Taking one startled look at the huge man who had just approached him, Wilder dashed for the car.

The door on the passenger's side was locked, and the fugitive raced around to the driver's side, ripped open the door, and scrambled across the seat, snatching a .357 Magnum from the glove compartment.

Jellison was right behind him, and he threw himself on top of Wilder, gripping the killer in a massive bear hug. Silently telling himself to, "Keep his elbows in. Keep his elbows in," the brawny state trooper used his weight and position to try to prevent Wilder from firing the gun. But just seconds after the two men tumbled into the car, a bullet ripped into Jellison's chest. An instant later another shot fired, and the gunman — still gripped tightly by the injured trooper — jerked violently. Then his body suddenly went limp.

It was Friday the thirteenth, and Wilder was dead, sprawled face down across the blood-soaked bucket seat, his legs dangling lifelessly out the open car door. Both shots had struck him in the chest. The first passed completely through his body, striking his heart and continuing on to slam into the big policeman. The second shot also hit Wilder's heart, causing the organ to virtually explode.

Jellison pulled off his bloody shirt and stumbled back to the station wagon to radio for an ambulance. At the nearby Upper Connecticut Valley Hospital it was discovered that the slug that crashed into his chest had bruised a lung and lodged on top of his liver. A doctor remarked that the state trooper had missed death by an inch.

The carnage was now over for Wilder, but the hurt was not over for the families of his victims. For the families of young women presumed dead at Wilder's hands but still missing, the grief was perhaps most difficult to bear.

Sheryl Bonaventura's nude corpse was recovered from the banks of the Kanab River, a few miles across the Utah state line from Page, Arizona, on May 3, 1984, nearly three weeks after the death of her killer. She had been stabbed in the heart, shot, and her left breast had been mutilated.

Michelle Korfman's badly decomposed corpse wasn't discovered until almost a month after Wilder's death. A couple on a bicycle ride in the Angeles National Forest near Los Angeles came upon the body on May 11. It remained unidentified at the Los Angeles County Morgue until June 15, when dental charts provided by the Korfman family at last revealed the fate of their daughter. Michelle had been asphyxiated. William E. Gold, a spokesman for the Los Angeles County Coroner's Office, disclosed that pathologists found grains of soil in her larynx and trachea.

"It's probable the deceased was forced face down into the dirt at some point at or near her death," Gold said.

At this writing, Rosario Gonzalez and Beth Kenyon have not yet been found, and there is no indication that the agony their families have been enduring is nearing a conclusion.

Authorities have speculated that their bodies were disposed of, in or near water. Wilder seemed to have a fixation with water. His home in Boynton Beach was bounded on two sides with water, and the remains of most of the young women he murdered were recovered in or near water. He even took time out to view Niagara Falls with Tina Marie while he was on the run as the most wanted man in America.

Months after Wilder's violent death, authorities were continuing to investigate the possibility that still other murdered and missing girls and young women may have been his victims before or during the terrible forty-seven days that began with the disappearance of Rosario Gonzalez. After his death, color photos of four beautiful women, none of them known victims, were found in his car along with forty-nine hundred-dollar bills, a knife, scissors, silver duct tape, glue, and other items.

Assistant FBI Director O. B. "Buck" Revell was quoted as speculating that Wilder may have killed several other women. "There may be some who lived alone who haven't even been reported missing yet," he remarked.

The disappearance of fifteen-year-old Colleen Osborn from Daytona Beach on March 15, less than three weeks after Rosario vanished, was still baffling police more than two years later. Wilder has been considered as a suspect since detectives learned he was registered in a motel near the Daytona International Speedway on the day the girl vanished. A man fitting his description was also observed near her house at about the time she was last seen.

And the mother of Tammi Lynn Leppert asked the courts for more than $1 million from Wilder's estate because she believed the seventeen-year-old Merritt Island, Florida, model had been abducted and possibly murdered by the serial killer. Tammi was last seen by her family and friends on July 6, 1983, about eight months before Wilder's cross-country rampage began. The sun-bronzed beauty posed for swimsuit ads, had reigned as Miss Teen Florida, and played bit parts in the movies *Scarface* and *Spring Break*.

Mrs. Curtiss was owner of the Galaxy Model Workshop on Merritt Island, and after looking at photographs of Wilder, said she was positive that he had visited her agency several times in 1983. She said her daughter worked at the agency part time. "He talked to her," she added. "She was his contact."

Another claim for an unspecified amount was filed by an Ochopee, Florida, family whose daughter was murdered in March 1984. Ochopee is on the west coast of Florida, just across the state from Dade, Broward, and Palm Beach counties where Wilder is now known to have stalked his pretty young victims for so long. The family did not assert specifically that Wilder was the killer, but said they wanted to preserve their rights in case it was ever proven that he was responsible.

Police in Australia also requested samples of his blood from the FBI, after reopening a near twenty-year-old investigation into the brutal slaying of two fifteen-year-old girls on Wanda Beach at the edge of Sydney. In 1965, Marianne Schmidt and Christine Sharrock made the fatal mistake of walking into the sand dunes with a handsome young man fitting Wilder's description. They were raped, stabbed, strangled, and buried in shallow graves. Sydney police said Wilder, who was nineteen years old and lived near the beach, was questioned in the mutilation-rape slayings, but released.

In South Florida, the books were closed on some previously unsolved sex crimes as well, including the abduction and abuse of a pair of ten- and twelve-year-old girls in June 1983 from Boynton Beach. They had been forced into Wilder's car, made to perform oral sex, then released. The girls provided accurate descriptions of Wilder and of the car he was driving at that time, police said.

A Palm Beach County judge ruled that there was too little evidence to support the claim of Mrs. Curtiss to any of Wilder's estate, but approved more than $7 million in claims from other victims' survivors. Payment was expected to be eventually worked out on a percentage basis as directed by the court, according to the amount left in the estate.

Despite Wilder's general reputation for great wealth, when his will was probated his representatives valued the estate at a fairly modest $445,100. And the IRS filed a lien against the estate for $345,000, with added penalties and interest, claiming Wilder hadn't paid his taxes for 1980. He willed almost everything he owned to his family, but left his Boynton Beach home and another house to a blue-eyed blonde woman friend who had shared a long and close relationship with him.

Wilder's brother, Stephen, claimed the body which was returned to a Boynton Beach funeral home, where quiet services closely guarded by police were held for a small group of mourners. At the request of law-enforcement authorities, a plaster cast was made of Wilder's jaw and teeth so that police could attempt to match impressions with bite marks on the breasts of victims. The brain was removed during the autopsy in New Hampshire.

Scientists had plans for the brain, which was stored

for study in a formaldehyde-filled plastic jar in a laboratory at Boston's Beth Israel Hospital. Medical researchers may work with the tissue for years, extracting and minutely examining cells and configurations in an attempt to determine exactly what it was — some physiological abnormality, tumor, low-grade and difficult-to-detect inflammation or infection, or simply sexual desire, sadism, and viciousness — that caused Christopher Wilder to kidnap, rape, torture, and kill.

CHAPTER 4

THE FATHER FIGURE

ARTHUR GARY BISHOP

(1979-1983)

Graeme Cunningham was an active, healthy thirteen-year-old enjoying his summer break from school, when he walked out of his house to visit a friend — and vanished.

Although the brown-eyed youngster was headed toward a house only a few blocks away, no one could be located who remembered seeing him after he exited from his front door. There had been no reports of anyone suspicious lurking in the quiet middle-class Salt Lake City neighborhood, no sign of any struggle or physical violence, and no screams.

Graeme, it seemed, had simply ceased to exist. The teenager's disappearance was especially frightening for two reasons: The first was that he had been excitedly looking forward to a camping expedition to be taken in just two days with his buddy and an older companion in his early thirties who had become a father figure to Graeme's schoolmate. It was inconceivable that Graeme would run away or voluntarily stay away from home and miss the exciting excursion.

The second thing that created special cause for concern was the close proximity of Graeme's home to that of a bright-eyed six-year-old boy who had mysteriously vanished from his house only a few weeks earlier.

Concerned law-enforcement authorities realized that Graeme's disappearance seemed to fit an ominous pattern that had developed in Salt Lake City where young boys and girls were being snatched off the streets every few months. Some of the youngsters had been found murdered; others had never been found.

In Utah, with its heavy Mormon population which favors large families and which has the highest birthrate of any state in the country, the missing and murdered children had created so much attention and concern that a strict new child-kidnapping law had taken effect just a few weeks before Graeme's disappearance. Considered to be one of the toughest laws of its kind in the nation, the new statute mandated minimum terms of five, ten, and fifteen years for first-degree kidnapping or child rape, depending on the circumstances. Two or more convictions could mean a life sentence without parole.

The baffling pattern of child disappearances began to develop on October 14, 1979, after four-year-old Alonzo Daniels went outside his apartment building to play. The little boy's mother watched for a few minutes while he played with a make-believe airplane, then returned to her work. When she checked on her son a few minutes later, he had vanished. She never saw him alive again.

The worried mother called relatives who helped her search throughout the large apartment complex, but they failed to turn up any sign of him. When the police were called they were equally unsuccessful, even though they made door-to-door searches of all the buildings surrounding the courtyard where the youngster was last seen playing.

Salt Lake County Search and Rescue teams joined local law-enforcement officers, and the search was expanded into the residential neighborhoods surrounding the complex. Hundreds of men, women, and teenagers, including students and faculty members from the University of Utah and members of a Teamsters-union local, volunteered to assist in the growing effort.

Despite hundreds of interviews conducted by police, no one was found who could remember seeing the handsome little olive-skinned, curly-haired boy in the cream-colored t-shirt with the flavors "vanilla," "chocolate," and "lime" written on it, after his mother sent him outside to play. Police couldn't locate a single witness who had seen Alonzo wander away from the courtyard or leave with an adult or another child.

Almost thirteen months later, eleven-year-old Kim Petersen dropped out of sight.

The day before Kim vanished he had confided to his parents that a man he had met at a roller-skating rink wanted to buy his skates. The boy was excited about the proposed transaction because he wanted the money to invest in a new, more expensive pair of skates.

On November 9, 1980, the last day Kim was seen by family members, he rushed into his house and announced that he had just run into the man who wanted his skates on a nearby street corner. Kim speculated he might get as much as $35 in the deal. Then he rushed out of the house with his skates. He never returned.

Investigators turned up some people who recalled seeing Kim talking at the skating rink the day before his disappearance with a chubby-faced man wearing glasses and clad in blue jeans with an army-type parka or jacket. Most of the witnesses said the stranger appeared to be about between thirty and thirty-five years old, although one suggested that he might be as young as twenty-five.

The witnesses agreed to be hypnotized, then helped a police artist make a composite sketch of the mystery man, whom they recalled as being about six feet tall, with dark, short-cut hair and bushy eyebrows. They estimated he weighed two hundred pounds. One of the witnesses said he had seen the man in a silver-gray Camaro with out-of-state plates, which might have been issued in Nevada.

In the middle of the afternoon on October 20, 1981, four-year-old Danny Davis dropped from sight. The youngster had been shopping with his grandfather in a busy supermarket in South Salt Lake County when he vanished.

Store employees and customers joined the frantic grandparent in an immediate search for the missing tow-headed youngster without success. Then police were notified.

Several customers were located who remembered seeing Danny, and two cashiers recalled noticing a little boy resembling him who was fiddling with a gumball machine until a smiling young man showed up and helped him. Detectives showed the cashiers a photograph of Danny, but they weren't positive he was the child they had seen. Both later agreed to be hypnotized in an effort to help provide better descriptions of the boy and the man.

Once again, Salt Lake City citizens responded to the emergency and participated in a sweeping search of the metropolitan area, nearby mountains, desert, and rivers, desperately seeking the missing child. Temperatures dropped into the thirties the first night Danny was gone, giving impetus to the frantic search. The child had been wearing only a pink t-shirt, blue trousers, and thongs when he disappeared. If he was still outside he could die of exposure.

Fliers were distributed, carrying Danny's picture and a detailed description of the boy and of the clothes he was wearing. Police divers searched the Big Cotton-wood Creek in the rugged Wasatch Mountains, and sheriff's deputies combed ponds, ditches, and alleys. The heavily publicized investigation and search was the most intensive ever conducted by the Salt Lake County Sheriff's Department up to that time. A $20,000 reward was posted for Danny's return.

This time the National Crime Information Center, the FBI, and Child Find were all contacted for assistance. Photos and a description of Danny were distributed to law-enforcement agencies throughout the country.

Curiously, police realized, all three disappearances had occurred within two weeks of Hallowe'en. But October 31, 1982, came and went without any new reports of suspected child-kidnappings. It was June 22, 1983, before the next boy vanished from Salt Lake City.

It was Troy Ward's sixth birthday, and a family friend had promised to pick up the excited, freckle-faced boy at 4:00 P.M. and drive him home after play at Liberty Park. When the driver arrived at the corner a few minutes early, Troy wasn't there.

Police were called and officers began to comb a three-square-block area surrounding the park for the child. All they were able to turn up was one witness who said he had seen a little boy resembling Troy walking away from the corner with a young man a few minutes before 4:00 P.M.

"I thought he was the kid's father," the witness said. "The kid acted like he knew him."

It was turning into another bad summer for police assigned to investigate juvenile cases and major crimes in Salt Lake City and neighboring communities.

The previous August three-year-old Rachel Runyan had been forcibly abducted from a school playground in Sunset, Utah, about thirty miles north of Salt Lake City. A short time later, the little girl was found in the nearby mountains. She had been murdered.

An eleven-year-old girl had been bludgeoned to death and left in an empty shed near her home in another case that was still baffling authorities. And there were several other perplexing murders and assaults on children, in the city itself and in the smaller communities, that had stumped investigators for answers since the wave of child-killings had begun in 1979.

Utah's child-kidnappings and murders were attracting national attention, and pressure on police and other authorities was mounting as the fear and paranoia spread.

Worried parents were streaming into police stations and county sheriffs' offices all over the state, voluntarily submitting their children to fingerprinting. Churches, schools, and local civic organizations were booking police spokesmen for talks on the prevention of kidnapping and child-molesting. Police agencies and school authorities were being deluged with reports of strangers behaving suspiciously around playgrounds and other areas where children congregated.

FBI agents and officers from the Salt Lake City Police Department, Salt Lake County Sheriff's Department, and from the Davis County Sheriff's Department which was investigating the kidnap-slaying of the three-year-old Sunset girl met to compare their information and theories in an effort to figure out a pattern in the devilish wave of child-murders and -abductions. They gathered in the Metropolitan Hall of Justice in Salt Lake City to brainstorm the cases.

There were strong indications that the girls had not been victims of the same individual who was preying on Salt Lake City's young boys. Even when considering only the boys' deaths, however, investigators were faced with puzzling dissimilarities.

Although all the boys were pre-pubescent, their ages represented a fairly wide range, from four to eleven. Kim, Danny, and Troy were white, and Alonzo was black, even though he was so light-complexioned he might have easily been mistaken for a Hispanic child. All the children except for Alonzo had light hair.

The children had disappeared at different times of the

day, and at different times of the week, from widely different areas of the city and county. There was no apparent connection with Hallowe'en.

And now, a teenager, Graeme Cunningham, had disappeared just two days before he was expected to leave on the camping and fishing trip to the Sierras near Lake Tahoe.

When Graeme's thirteen-year-old friend telephoned the house the day before leaving to see if the boy had returned home and would still be going, Graeme was still missing.

The night Graeme's buddy returned from his trip, Salt Lake City Police detective Steven Smith and Sergeant Bruce White stopped by his adult friend's apartment to talk to him about the missing teenager. Even the most insignificant bit of information might fit into the puzzling mosaic that authorities were so painstakingly attempting to piece together in their efforts to find Graeme, and the man could be a potentiall valuable witness.

The camper was Roger W. Downs, an amiable, thirty-two-year-old bachelor whom some neighborhood kids regarded as a father figure. He took them on outdoors trips, and was considered by some admiring neighbors to be a caring, responsible adult who was a good influence on the young boys he took such a paternal interest in.

As the detectives talked with the young, easy-going accountant, however, they rapidly became aware that he wasn't being completely honest. Downs readily complied when they asked him to follow them to police headquarters where questioning could continue more privately. Detective Don Bell, a veteran homicide investigator, met them there and joined in the questioning. The detectives were skilled interrogators and as they picked out one inconsistency after another in his statements, the pressure on the glib young man increased.

That night Downs confessed to the sex murders of five boys.

The next day he led a search team to a remote area in the Cedar Fort section of Utah County and pointed to some soft dirt under a stand of shade trees. Three of the bodies were buried there, he advised them. A squad of lawmen unearthed the remains of Alonzo Daniels, Danny Davis, and Kim Petersen from the shallow graves.

Police were then led to Big Cottonwood Creek, some sixty-five miles south of the grave site. There they recovered the bodies of Troy Ward and Graeme Cunningham from a log jam in the debris-filled water. The other child-murders that law-enforcement authorities were investigating in the Salt Lake City area were apparently unconnected to the Bishop case.

The pudgy child-molester admitted killing the boys because he was embarrassed and afraid that they would tell their parents that he had sexually abused them.

He had not been the innocuous good neighbor he appeared to be. Instead, a check of his background revealed that he was a sinister Jekyll-and-Hyde character whose name wasn't even Downs.

His real name was Arthur G. Bishop, and he had been raised with a younger brother in the small farming community of Hinckley, a town of fewer than seven hundred people in central Utah. At first, Arthur seemed to be the kind of son every parent would wish for. He was an honor student throughout his four years at Delta High School, became an Eagle Scout, and as a devout young Mormon, served in the Philippines for a while as a Latter-Day Saints missionary. After completing his mission obligation, he graduated with honors from the Stevens Henager College, as an accounting major.

The first dark clouds on Bishop's promising future appeared in February 1978 when he was charged with a second-degree felony forgery. He was accused of embezzling $8,714 from the car dealership he had worked for the previous July. Apparently contrite, he pleaded guilty to the charges and was sentenced to five years' probation, with the stipulation that he pay restitution. Instead of complying with the terms of probation, he dropped out of sight, and a warrant was issued for his arrest. Approximately a year later, the Mormon Church issued an excommunication order for its errant son.

Careful reconstruction of Bishop's activities after his first unhappy brush with the law revealed that the onetime immaculate son and good citizen became a seemingly aimless nomad, changing jobs, addresses, and names as easily and handily as most people change clothes. A classic trait of serial killers, these wandering ways make it extremely difficult for lawmen to trace them and piece together their multiple crimes into a recognizable pattern.

In October 1978, Bishop was accepted into the Big Brother–Big Sister of Greater Salt Lake program, but was dropped after about a year when officials learned of his forgery conviction. Spokesmen for the organization later revealed that the organization had received anonymous tips that he had molested two children. Although there was no evidence indicating that he had abused his "little brother" during the time with the program, the information from the tipster was passed on to police.

Using the alias "Roger Downs" in 1979 and living in an apartment across the hall from Alonzo Daniels when the four-year-old disappeared, he was one of the neighbors police had questioned.

He was using the same name in 1980 when Kim Petersen disappeared, and was living in an apartment only a few blocks away. Again, as Roger Downs, he lived only a half-block from the supermarket where Danny Davis was abducted in 1981, and although questioned by police, he was not considered a suspect.

A few months before Danny's kidnap and murder, Bishop, who was now calling himself Lynn E. Jones, was working as a bookkeeper for a Salt Lake City ski retailer. One afternoon he didn't return from lunch, and his boss discovered that $10,000 was missing from a company account. Jones's personnel file was gone as well.

Neighbors of the curious young man had also begun to talk among themselves about the rowdy hippies and motorcycle toughs who sometimes hung around him. One woman was especially worried about a ragged youth who delighted in setting fires, until the pudgy host stopped the dangerous hijinks by punching him. The same woman became so nervous about Downs' bizarre behavior, roughneck friends, and the scary child disappearances that she instructed her children to stay away from the weird neighbor.

Arrest of the confessed murderer of five young boys and recovery of the bodies brought an end to the terror that had gripped the normally peaceful city for more than four years. But the shock, pain, and horror would linger for months, especially during Bishop's lurid three-week trial. Authorities eventually revealed that the boys had been bludgeoned, drowned, suffocated, and shot. And there were ugly whispers, hinting at necrophilia.

Investigation of the most heinous series of crimes in the history of Utah revealed that dozens of other boys may have been sexually abused by the pedophile, but permitted to live. Bishop admitted luring one boy into his home, pushing him into the basement, and, at gunpoint, forcing him to pose for nude pictures. He released the frightened youngster after threatening to kill him if he told anyone about the humiliating ordeal. The boy might have become a sixth murder victim if his sister hadn't seen Bishop pick him up.

Salt Lake City Detective Captain Jon Pollei said that

police were deluged with telephone calls and other tips from citizens accusing Bishop of sexually molesting their children, or the children of relatives and acquaintances. "We've got more information now than we can handle," he complained to news reporters with the *Salt Lake City Tribune*. "What I'd like to know is where were those people two and three years ago when we had nothing."

During a search of Bishop's home, detectives recovered a .38-caliber revolver, a mallet, and a blood-stained hammer. They also confiscated a booklet entitled *100 Ways To Disappear and Live Free* and a huge collection of pornography, including dozens of photographs of naked young boys. Some of the photos were of one of the victims, taken after the boy's abduction, police said. Many of the other pictures showed only the nude torsos of pre-pubescent boys, making identification difficult, or impossible.

Bishop was charged with five counts of capital homicide, five counts of kidnapping, and with sexual abuse of a minor.

During the grueling, emotional trial, Deputy County Attorney Robert Stott portrayed Bishop as a ruthless killer and sexual deviant with "a scheming, calculating, cunning mind," who preyed on children.

Bishop's defense attorneys, led by Jo Carol Nesset-Sale, did not contest his damning confession to police. They concentrated instead on efforts to prove that he suffered from psychological and emotional "deficits" that left him sexually addicted to boys, and argued that he should be convicted of manslaughter instead of more serious charges. He grew up without learning to care for others, they claimed, and killed because he didn't want to be exposed as a child-molester.

"Art became, for some reason, stuck or fixated with a sexual attraction to little boys . . . he never outgrew those erotic feelings," Nesset-Sale declared. "He was a lonely, frightened child."

The seven-woman, five-man jury panel deliberated less than five hours, before returning guilty verdicts on each of the kidnapping and first-degree-murder charges. They also found him guilty of one count of sexual abuse of a minor.

According to Utah law, Bishop was permitted to choose whether to have the judge or the jury hear testimony on aggravating and mitigating circumstances during a formal sentencing hearing before a decision was made about imposing the death penalty or life imprisonment. He chose the jury.

The hearing before Third District Judge Jay Banks provided some of the most emotional and grotesque moments of the entire criminal-court procedure. Prosecutors played the convicted killer's taped confession, and as the jury listened, their faces set in grim masks, he described how he abducted, abused, and slaughtered his helpless victims. At times during the grisly recitation, he giggled, and at other times he lapsed into a high-voiced mimicking of the children's agonized pleas for mercy. He told how he lured some of the boys to his homes with promises of candy or ice cream, others with toys or money. And with no indication of remorse, he recounted how he sexually abused them, or photographed them in the nude, how he killed them, and how he continued to fondle some of them after they were dead.

"I'm glad they caught me, because I'd go do it again," he admitted.

The jurors, who were permitted to hear only portions of the confession during the trial, decided that Bishop should die for his appalling crimes. In accordance with Utah law, the convicted child-slayer was given a choice of death by firing squad or by lethal injection.

Bishop had obviously given the morbid choice considerable thought. Speaking in a steady, clear voice, he advised the judge: "I'd prefer the lethal injection, Your Honor." A few moments earlier his voice had wavered with emotion as he stood before the bench and said he was sorry for the murders and the grief he had caused.

Judge Bell sentenced him to death by lethal injection, on each of the five first-degree–murder counts. The serial killer is now on death row awaiting conclusion of the lengthy appeals process.

In a bizarre sidelight to the tragedy, a few weeks before Bishop's apprehension, his twenty-three–year-old brother, Douglas, was arrested on sodomy charges, accused of sexually abusing young boys in Utah County. Douglas was also convicted and sentenced to prison.

Although there was no connection between the two cases, except for the family relationship of the brothers, shortly after conclusion of the sensational murder trials, prison officials at Point of the Mountain, Utah, revealed that there were rumors of a $5,000 bounty placed on the head of Arthur Bishop. The mysterious backers of the reputed reward then reportedly raised the total to $10,000 for the deaths of both brothers.

Captain Craig Rasmussen, chief of prison investigations and security, said of the offer: "These kinds of rumors occur with a high degree of regularity, but we are taking this Bishop case seriously because of the catastrophic results should he actually be attacked after we had been given public warning."

At this writing, more than two years later, apparently no one has tried to collect either of the reputed bounty offers.

CHAPTER 5

THE GOOD OL' BOY MURDERS

DAVID ALAN GORE AND FRED WATERFIELD

(1981-1983)

Pedaling his bicycle toward home, a fourteen-year-old boy was jarred from his reverie when a shrill feminine scream cut through the subdued hum of activity in the quiet small-town neighborhood. The youth took one startled glance in the direction of the shriek and almost fell off his bike.

Barely fifty yards away, a naked teenaged girl was running pell-mell along a driveway, screaming for help. Only a few feet behind, a barrel-chested, red-faced man, also nude, was lumbering after her. He was clutching a gun in one hand.

In moments, the beefy pursuer caught up with the slender girl, curled a muscular arm around her writhing body, and began to drag her back along the driveway toward the house. When they reached a palm tree a few feet from the door, he hurled her to the ground, levelled the gun at her head, and fired.

The shaken youngster pedaled away as fast as he could go, until he reached a friend's house. Dropping his bicycle to the ground, he ran the rest of the way home to tell his mother about the shocking scene he had just witnessed.

Naked girls shot by naked men in plain view of passers-by are not typical of hot July afternoons in Vero Beach, Florida, and the concerned woman loaded her shaken son into the family car and drove to the house where he said the shooting had occurred. Then she drove back to her home and telephoned police.

The anxious mother's call wasn't the only one Vero Beach police logged concerning the bizarre chase and shooting. A few minutes after her call, they received another message on the 911 emergency number from a man inside the house where the shooting had taken place. He reported that he had just witnessed a naked male with a gun chasing a nude woman through the orange groves several blocks away.

Police quickly determined that the second caller was probably David Alan Gore, a burly, hard-drinking one-time auxiliary policeman and ex-convict, known for crimes against women. The house was owned by his relatives.

Based on Gore's reputation for violence, sexual assault, and general orneriness, officers concluded that he likely had been more than a witness to the remarkable chase and shooting, and began to try to talk him into leaving the house peacefully. A cousin of Gore's was located, and joined in the effort.

Meanwhile, no one knew where the girl was, or whether she was dead, or badly wounded and in need of immediate medical assistance. Then an Indian River County Sheriff's investigator began poking around the white Monarch sitting in the carport. He peeped through the car windows, but there was no one inside, and felt the car hood. It was still warm, indicating it had been driven recently. Checking out the back of the car, he knelt down to peer suspiciously at a spot of red liquid in one of the tire tracks. It appeared to be blood. As he was inspecting the liquid, another drop dripped from the trunk of the car.

The officer called to another investigator, and a few moments later they had pried the trunk open. Inside, they found the body of a slim young girl who appeared to be in her mid-teens. She was naked, except for a blood-soaked rag carelessly wrapped around her head. She was dead, from a massive head wound. Her wrists and ankles were discolored, and in some places the flesh had been slashed to the bone, indicating that she had been tightly bound shortly before her death.

The leader of the hastily assembled police team sent for tear gas, and ordered all officers except those armed with shotguns to move away from the house.

That was enough for Gore. He permitted relatives to talk him into giving himself up and surrendered, ending the tense standoff.

Inside the modest home, police found another naked teenager. A whimpering fourteen-year-old girl was handcuffed to the rafters in the steamy attic. She identified herself as a local girl, and said her dead friend was Lynn Carol Elliott, a seventeen-year-old senior at Vero Beach High School.

After the shaken teenager was given a blanket to wrap around herself, she stammered out a hair-raising story of rape and murder. She and her friend had been hitchhiking to the beach when Gore and another man stopped in a truck and motioned the girls inside, she said. The teenagers had taken a few sips from a can of beer Gore gave them when the truck struck a bump in the road and the glove compartment flew open. A handgun was inside, and Gore pulled it out and pointed it at them.

"Wouldn't it be fun to take these two girls home and have some fun with them?" the girl said he asked the driver.

When Lynn started to cry, Gore pointed the gun at her and growled, "Shut up or I'll kill you."

The girls were driven to the house and forced inside at

gunpoint, the fourteen-year-old told investigators. Inside, she said, they were taken to separate bedrooms and tied up. Then Gore began a bizarre rape marathon, going from one girl to the other, and back again. All the time the helpless girls were enduring the sexual assaults, a police-radio scanner in the house was broadcasting emergency calls and other information.

Finally, Gore pulled the younger girl from the bed and half-carried and half-pushed her to another room, where he slashed off her remaining clothes with a knife, and shoved her, still tied and manacled, into a closet. A few minutes later she heard gunshots from outside the house.

Sometime after that, Gore returned and took her to the attic, huddling there with her for about an hour before surrendering, she said.

Gore was as talkative as his young victim. After the obligatory reading of his constitutional right to remain silent, he agreed to make a taped statement. Speaking clearly and easily, he admitted to picking up the girls and to the rapes and the murder, and implicated his cousin, Fred Waterfield.

He said he and his cousin had picked up the two young hitchhikers and driven them to the house. On the way there, however, a car driven by one of Waterfield's relatives passed by.

"I'm sure they seen what we got in the front seat. If these girls end up missing, we're in trouble," Gore quoted Waterfield as warning. Nevertheless, they continued on to the house with the frightened teenagers.

Somehow, after she had been left alone for a few moments, the older girl succeeded in undoing the nylon cord she was tied with and ran from the house, screaming for help, Gore related. So he grabbed his gun and dashed after her, he told the stern-faced investigators.

"She was hollering and screaming and everything, and I fired a warning shot over her head. She sort of turned around to look back and she fell down," he related. "Elliott was still hollering and screaming, so I just shot her to make her shut up."

Gore said that when he saw the boy on the bicycle, he realized that the police would be showing up soon, so he stuffed the teenager's body into the trunk of the car, drove it into the carport, and returned to the house. Waterfield, shaken by the unexpected turn of events, walked out, leaving him alone in the house with the younger girl, Gore continued.

As he began throwing on his clothes, he turned the police scanner on again, and his fears were confirmed, Gore told the investigators. The first police cars were already on their way to the house, and he knew that he needed time to get out, so he dialed the 911 number and reported a chase and shooting out among some orange groves several blocks away. With luck, he reasoned, the call would lure police away long enough for him to make a getaway.

The police weren't fooled, and in minutes the first patrol car pulled to a stop in the driveway. That was when Gore scooped up the trembling fourteen-year-old and carried her to the attic. He crouched there, warning the girl against screaming for help. "If I go down, you're going too," he threatened. The girl, totally subdued, did as she was told, cowering beside her captor while listening helplessly to voices over police loudspeakers that implored: "David, come out!"

As he gave himself up, a sheriff's investigator was already at Waterfield's car-repair shop talking with Gore's cousin. Waterfield was also taken into custody peacefully, but unlike Gore, he maintained a stony silence.

But law-enforcement authorities began to take a long, close look at the brutal cousins, and at recent cases of rape, of thwarted abductions, and of mysterious disappearances of attractive women.

They uncovered a nightmare. And Gore, who claimed to have experienced several miraculous religious experiences in jail that changed his life and attitudes, helped investigators sort it all out.

Aided by new confessions, including a statement made following Gore's first supernatural encounter only eight days after he was jailed, police solved five other murders and a host of lesser crimes.

Gore led authorities to the remains of a mother and daughter from Taiwan, and of a California woman, all reported missing from Indian River County nearly two years earlier. The skull of a teenaged runaway from North Florida was also recovered, but the remains of her female companion were never found, although Gore apparently made a sincere effort to pinpoint their location.

In many ways, the six-foot tall, 275-pound Gore, age thirty-one, was a classic Southern "Good Ol' Boy." He grew up around the citrus groves, cattle ranches, and boating and fishing docks along South Florida's Atlantic Coast. And he developed a reputation as an outdoorsman who knew every grove, stream, and stand of woods in Indian River County, from where the famous Indian River fruit is grown, packed, and shipped around the world. Like most of his peers, he also developed a fondness for girls — and guns. In fact, he liked handling weapons so well that he learned gunsmithing. And while he was attending Vero Beach High School, he belonged to the campus ROTC. But he treated his guns better than most of the women who were unfortunate enough to cross his path. He was fired from one of his jobs as a gas-station attendant after the owner found a hole bored in the wall between the men's and women's restrooms, but playing the peeping Tom would be the least of Gore's offenses against females.

Waterfield, who was a year younger than Gore, was also a local boy. A popular student at Vero Beach High

School where he played on the varsity football team, he was ruggedly handsome, and as mean as his cousin.

According to Gore's confessions, by 1976 the two cousins were teaming up to stalk attractive young females. He related that their first attempt at kidnapping occurred when they were cruising along a state highway near Yeehaw Junction in Indian River County and saw a pretty young woman driving by herself. Freddy shot out her tires and she jumped from her car screaming. When Waterfield threatened to shoot her, she ran onto the highway and flagged down a truck, and Gore and his cousin escaped as the driver stopped to pick her up.

The next time they tried to catch a girl, they had driven a friend to Miami International Airport when they decided to troll for a victim along the beach area. They finally began following a pretty girl with long brown hair who was driving a late-model car, waiting for her to stop and get out so they could jump from their vehicle and grab her, Gore claimed. They gave up and drove home when she turned into a busy area of the city, making their plan too dangerous.

According to Gore their first successful rape occurred a few days later, after Waterfield telephoned him and said his car was in one of the orange groves. When Gore got there, Freddy had a woman, and they took turns raping her at gunpoint. Although the victim reported the rape, she later dropped the charges because she didn't want to testify in open court.

By early 1981, their savage game had moved into high gear. Gore had gotten himself an appointment as an auxiliary deputy with the Indian River County Sheriff's Department. He was assigned to nighttime patrol in residential neighborhoods where it was hoped increased police visibility would reduce home burglaries. During the day he worked with his father as a caretaker at one of the citrus groves. Waterfield had moved north to Orlando where he ran an automotive shop, but he returned frequently to his hometown.

On one of those trips home, Gore later told investigators, Waterfield offered him $1,000 for every pretty girl he could deliver. Gore had already figured out that his position with the sheriff's department would make kidnapping much easier than it had been before.

The first girl he thought pretty enough to earn the $1,000 bounty was seventeen-year-old Ying Hua Ling. The unsuspecting teenager was the daughter of a couple from Taiwan who had recently moved to South Florida where the husband worked as a part-time agriculture inspector for the state and tended a small grove near his home. Gore stalked the girl for two days.

One afternoon he waited about a half-mile down a dirt road from her school-bus stop. As the high-school girl was walking down the road to her home, he flashed his auxiliary deputy sheriff's badge and authoritatively informed her that he wanted to talk to her about official business. Following his orders she obediently climbed into his pickup truck, and he drove her to her house.

When they walked inside Gore was surprised to be confronted by the girl's mother, Hsiang Huaun Ling, who was vacuuming the living-room rug. He pulled his gun and handcuffed the two frightened women together, then led them back outside again to his truck and drove to a nearby citrus grove where a relative worked as a caretaker. He patiently waited for the unsuspecting relative to leave the office for the day, then went inside and telephoned Waterfield in Orlando.

Because Vero Beach is more than an hour's drive from Orlando and Gore had time to kill, he raped each of the women.

According to Gore, Waterfield was furious that he had brought along the older woman. Cursing and ignoring her pitiful pleas for mercy for herself and her daughter, he hogtied her, so that if she struggled she would strangle herself. The mother moaned, coughed, and turned blue in the face as Waterfield brutally raped her daughter a few feet away, Gore told investigators.

Gore killed the two women and after Waterfield had paid him $400 of the promised $1,000 bounty, he left him with the bodies. Then, Gore drove back to the Ling house, where he planned to steal the victims' purses. He left, however, after spotting a relative of the Lings.

In his confession Gore claimed that Waterfield telephoned him the next night and said it was time to get rid of the bodies. Gore drove to a citrus grove about a mile from the Ling house, where he was met by his cousin in a truck carrying two metal drums. Gore dug two holes with a backhoe he had brought along and then he and Waterfield stuffed the bodies of the mother and daughter inside the drums and buried them.

It was five months before Gore spotted the next woman he considered pretty enough to earn the $1,000 bounty. Waterfield had allegedly said that this time he wanted a blonde — and thirty-five-year-old Judith Kay Daley, a receptionist for a doctor in Belmont, California, appeared to be the perfect victim.

A stunningly attractive woman, Mrs. Daley was vacationing in Florida with her two daughters and visiting with relatives in the Vero Beach area. After dropping her teenagers off at busy Jaycee Beach, she moved on toward the quieter beach at Round Island Park, where Gore saw her pull into the parking lot and get out of her car. Watching admiringly as the woman walked toward the beach to sunbathe, he muttered to himself: "Well, now, maybe this is one Freddy can use. . . ."

Gore walked to the woman's car, opened the hood, and removed a coil wire, so the car wouldn't start. Then he found a spot safely distant from his prey and used binoculars to watch her sunbathe.

Almost two hours later, when Mrs. Daley returned to her car and discovered that it wouldn't start, Gore, who was waiting nearby, pretended to be helpful. She agreed when he offered to drive her to a pay telephone where she could call a relative for assistance. As soon as she slid into the passenger seat beside him, he pulled a gun and handcuffed her. Then he drove to the pay phone and made two calls, he related. One was to a relative of his prisoner, "passing a message" to pick up her children at Jaycee Beach. The second call was to Waterfield.

"I got a package for you," he announced.

Gore sexually abused his helpless victim while he was waiting for his cousin. Then he tied her up, stuffed her into the trunk tool box of the truck, and drove around until Waterfield arrived.

Gore said Waterfield was in a hurry and explained that he had to return quickly to Orlando. He raped Mrs. Daley, then left, Gore told investigators.

Gore killed Mrs. Daley, then drove around with her body until he dumped it into a reptile-infested canal bordering a swamp. "I fed her to the alligators," he confessed.

About a week after Mrs. Daley's abduction and rape-murder, authorities were given their first clue that something was terribly wrong with the strutting young auxiliary deputy. The concerned father of a pretty nineteen-year-old girl complained to the sheriff's department that a deputy had stopped his daughter while she was driving along a state highway and tried to lure her to a secluded spot along the Indian River with the excuse that he was investigating a burglary. The girl was too cautious to fall for the ruse, and after she identified Gore as the deputy, he was dropped from the auxiliary force.

The moody bully's luck turned even worse a few days

later when a bank teller spotted him crouching in the back seat of a car parked in front of a Vero Beach medical clinic. She flagged down a sheriff's department patrol car, and deputies found him inside the parked vehicle with a .357 Magnun, handcuffs, and a police scanner.

Gore, whose wife of seven years had divorced him and moved out of state with their son, told a jury that he had heard she was in town and would be at the clinic. He had claimed that he merely wanted to see if she was really taking his son to the doctor, but after he was tied to the shocking series of Indian River abductions and sex murders, he later admitted that it had been a "cock-and-bull story I made up" in an effort to win leniency from the jury.

But there had already been too many complaints about his dangerous behavior. One woman had reported that he secretly slashed a tire on her car, played Good Samaritan by offering to fix it, then talked her into following him to an isolated location in the county. Fortunately, she became alarmed at the last minute and drove away.

Another time Gore started a conversation with a good-looking woman and changed her flat tire before he discovered that she was a police officer in a nearby community. He quickly abandoned his scheme to kidnap her.

After the caper in front of the clinic, Gore was arrested on a charge of armed trespassing of an automobile and was sentenced to a five-year prison term. Even though he refused the prison psychiatric counseling the judge had recommended, he was paroled only eighteen months later in March 1983. A few weeks after his release, equipped with a pistol, handcuffs, rope, and a cooler filled with beer, he and Waterfield resumed their unholy search in Indian River County for new victims to rape and murder. By this time, Waterfield had closed his Orlando auto-repair shop and opened a new one in Vero Beach called "Freddy's Four-By-Four."

On May 20, less than nine weeks after Gore's release from prison, he and his cousin did some drinking and doping and decided to drive to Daytona Beach to look for women, according to one of the confessions. They found a hooker there, paid her forty dollars to have sex with both of them, then dropped her off and drove back to Orlando. Still unsatisfied, they then prowled Orange Blossom Trail, an area in the southwest part of the city known for the prostitutes and homosexuals who gather there. They picked up another hooker, but she leaped from the van and escaped after Gore pulled a gun.

Frustrated and in a nasty mood, they began the drive back to Vero Beach. Gore had dozed off when he was awakened with a jolt as his cousin jammed on the brakes and pulled off Interstate 95 near Melbourne.

"There are two hitchhikers back there. Get the gun ready, we'll get these," Waterfield excitedly told his companion. In moments, Waterfield had backed the van, stopped, and two teenaged girls got inside and sat down on a beer cooler in the back. They were Barbara Byer and her girlfriend, Angelica Lavallee, both four-teen years old, and both runaways.

It wasn't the first time Barbara had run away. Or the second. In fact, the troubled teenager had been in counseling at the Orange County Mental Health Center for her chronic runaway problems and refusal to live according to family rules. The last time the junior-high-school student's father had brought her back home, she told him she wouldn't stay and just walked away. Barbara and Angelica were best friends, and are thought to have been heading for Fort Lauderdale to visit a former schoolmate when they had the bad luck to hitch a ride with the murderous cousins.

According to the confession, the girls had barely sat

down before Gore pulled out his pistol and ordered them to lie down on the floor of the van. They were too frightened to talk as he clambered into the back and began roughly pulling off their clothes. When they were nude, he tied them up. Before he could rape either of them, Waterfield pulled to the side of the road and ordered him to trade places, Gore said.

Warning the girls to keep their mouths closed and to cooperate, Waterfield raped one, then the other, in turn, continuing for about a half-hour until Gore drove into Vero Beach. At Waterfield's direction, Gore said, he dropped his cousin off at the auto-repair shop.

Gore said he drove the girls to a secluded citrus grove, untied Angelica, handed her clothes to her, and ordered her to start walking because he was letting her go. He followed her a few steps into the grove and shot her in the back of the head. Then he returned and told Barbara that he had let her girlfriend go and later would do the same for her if she behaved. Reasoning that Waterfield might want to rape her again, he drove her back to the shop.

But Waterfield was angry because he had returned with one of the girls, and ordered him to get rid of her as well, Gore told investigators. So he drove her back to the grove, and calmly fired two shots into the back of her head. Then he returned to his house and took a two-hour nap.

Later that day the ruthless cousins returned to the grove to get rid of the bodies. They dug two holes, and Gore cut up Barbara's body with a hunting knife, severing her head, arms, and legs. Then they buried the pieces and covered them up.

The grisly dismemberment and burial had taken so much time and so tired them, that they decided against burying Angelica. They dumped her body into the same canal where Mrs. Daley's remains had been disposed of, Gore related.

For more than two months after the girls' disappearance, their distraught parents did not know what had happened to their daughters until Gore made his startling confession to the murders. While carrying out the kidnappings, rapes, and murders, he told a prosecutor, he was the enforcer, the man with the gun. "Freddy played the nice guy."

The game-playing ended with the kidnap, rape, and murder of Lynn Elliott and the sexual assault and terrorizing of her friend. Seemingly contrite and filled with the ecstasy of his proclaimed religious conversion, Gore signed an agreement with the state attorney, promising to testify against anyone prosecuted for the kidnap, sexual battery, or murder of the Lings, Mrs. Daley, Barbara Byer, and Angelica Lavallee. In exchange he asked for a promise that the death penalty would not be sought against him in those cases.

Gore confessed to those murders and was given consecutive life sentences in prison. There was no agreement, however, not to seek the death penalty against him on the first-degree–murder charges in the slaying of Lynn Elliott, and he was scheduled for trial across the state in St. Petersburg. Because of the sensational pretrial publicity the case had been venued to the city on Tampa Bay and State Attorney Bob Stone demanded the death penalty.

Gore's attorneys claimed witnesses had confused him with Waterfield, his look-alike cousin, who was the real master villain. But a crime-laboratory expert testified for the prosecution that analysis of seminal fluid, blood, and saliva indicated that someone of Gore's blood type, not Waterfield's, had sexually assaulted Miss Elliott.

A tape recording of the confession made by Gore at the Indian River Sheriff's Office shortly after his arrest was also played at the trial. It was especially horrifying because of his matter-of-fact recitation of the perverse ordeal the girls had been submitted to.

But the state's key witness was the girl who had survived the kidnapping and vicious sexual assaults a year earlier. The teenager, now fifteen, spoke evenly and calmly throughout most of her time on the stand, except when she was asked to identify one of the men who had kidnapped and abused her. Then her voice broke and her eyes brimmed with tears.

"Right there. That's him right there," she said, pointing at the defendant. Gore sat motionlessly at the defense table, with his head down.

After an exhausting trial, a jury of six men and six women returned a verdict of guilty of first-degree murder, guilty of two counts of kidnapping, and guilty of three counts of sexual battery. Circuit Judge L. B. "Buck" Vocelle sentenced Gore to die in the electric chair for the murder. He also ordered life sentences for the kidnapping and sexual-battery convictions.

"If there's any case that merits a death penalty, this case does, and the court does impose a death penalty upon David Alan Gore," the judge sternly intoned.

Still stoutly claiming innocence, Waterfield went on trial in the Charlotte County seat of Punta Gorda, for the murder of Lynn Elliott and the kidnapping of her and her companion. State Attorney Robert Stone contended that even though Waterfield was not the killer, he had masterminded the depraved scheme that had led to the teenager's death, and that he had played the "good guy" of a "good guy, bad guy" team.

Defense Attorney Michael Bloom argued that his client was afraid of his gun-wielding cousin, and failed to summon police because he was too shaken up to think straight after leaving the house before Lynn escaped and was shot — not after the shooting, as Gore had contended. Waterfield's attorney branded Gore as a "pathological liar" and a "convicted, maniacal, psychopathical killer."

In earlier grand-jury testimony that was read aloud during the trial, Waterfield had claimed that he had tried to talk his brutal cousin out of hurting the teenagers, until Gore threatened to kill him too.

But the young girl who survived the ordeal testified that Waterfield didn't do a thing to try and protect her or her friend.

The jury found Waterfield guilty of manslaughter, but acquitted him of kidnapping the two girls. "There just wasn't enough evidence Waterfield was active in the kidnapping. That was the main thing," Jury Foreman Nester Deobil was quoted as saying.

He told newsmen from *The Post* in West Palm Beach that Waterfield's failure to summon police to help the girls he knew were at Gore's house led the jury to return the manslaughter conviction. Waterfield was sentenced to the maximum fifteen-year prison term.

Although neither cousin testified at the Punta Gorda trial, Gore kept his word and took the stand against his cousin in the twin cases based on the kidnap, rape, and murder of the two fourteen-year-old runaways from Orlando. He was the star witness.

Bolstered by loyal family support, Waterfield stubbornly continued to insist that he was innocent, and blamed his burly cousin for the ghastly wave of kidnappings, rapes, and murders. He insisted that he wasn't even with Gore on the fateful drive when Barbara and Angelica were picked up, and claimed that he was as much a victim of his cousin's evil as the girls were.

A jury in the Lake County seat of Tavares where the trial was venued decided differently. The panel convicted Waterfield of two counts each of kidnapping and first-degree murder. He was sentenced to two consecutive life terms in prison for the murders and two life terms for the kidnappings to run concurrently with the others. The judge stipulated that Waterfield was not to be considered eligible for parole for at least fifty years.

The state attorney did not seek the death penalty because Gore, who had confessed to personally carrying out the cold-blooded executions, had already been sentenced to the lesser penalty of life imprisonment for the twin murders. "I cannot in good faith seek the death sentence," he said.

With Waterfield safely behind bars for a long term, charges against him in the kidnappings, sexual assaults, and murder of Mrs. Daley and the Lings were dismissed.

A short time after his cousin's trial for the kidnap-murder of the Orlando runaways, Gore was married in a civil ceremony at the Indian River County Jail. Claiming to be a changed man, he had courted the bride from his cell by an exchange of letters through the Christian Penpal Association. His feet were shackled during the brief ceremony, and for security reasons the bride was not permitted to carry a bouquet or purse. Only Gore's public defender, the attorney's secretary, and two jailers witnessed the marriage rite.

CHAPTER 6

THE MAN WHO HATED WOMEN

CORAL EUGENE WATTS

(197?-1982)

Coral Eugene Watts hated women. So convinced was he of their corruption and unredeemable evil that he murdered at least thirteen — perhaps as many as thirty or forty — during a fanatical ten-year outburst of violence.

He didn't bother to rape or rob his randomly selected victims before he killed them — by stabbing, strangling, hanging, or drowning — and he usually burned something that had belonged to his prey, in a weird ritualistic act that he was convinced would finally rid the world of what he believed were their evil spirits.

Houston police first heard of Watts in 1981 when they were contacted by homicide investigators in Ann Arbor, Michigan, and warned that he was on his way to the Texas metropolis to look for work. They were informed that he had a reputation among several Michigan police agencies for unprovoked attacks on women, had served time in jail, been confined to a mental hospital — and was a suspect in several savage murders of females.

A file photo taken from a colored snapshot of Leonard Lake, federal fugitive and self-styled survivalist who committed suicide in police custody. *AP/WIDE WORLD PHOTOS*

Charles Ng, wanted in connection with the discovery of 19 bodies at a California cabin, is presently in a Canadian prison and the subject of an extradition wrangle between Canada and U.S. *AP/WIDE WORLD PHOTOS*

Alton Coleman and Debra Brown in custody after their Midwestern sex-and-murder rampage. *AP/WIDE WORLD PHOTOS*

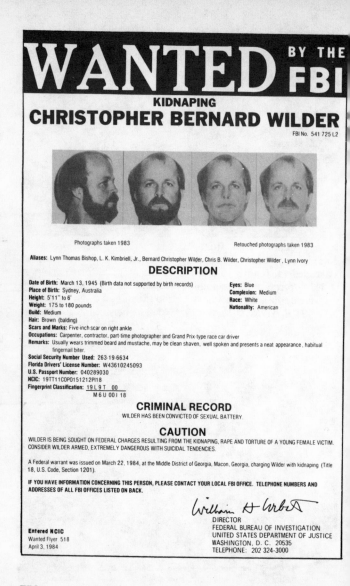

FBI poster showing the change in serial killer Christopher Wilder's appearance after he shaved off his beard to avoid capture.

Rosario T. Gonzalez

Elizabeth Ann Kenyon

Two of Wilder's victims who are still missing.

Arthur Bishop enters 3rd District Court during his trial in Salt Lake City for the abduction and slaying of 5 boys. *AP/WIDE WORLD PHOTOS*

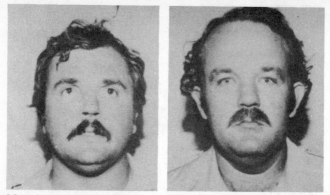

Mug shots of cousins Fred Waterfield (left) and David Alan Gore (right) who were convicted of kidnapping and murdering Florida women. *Photo courtesy of Indian River Sheriff's department*

Left: Confessed mass-murderer Coral Eugene Watts leaving the Harris County district attorney's office after questioning. *AP/WIDE WORLD PHOTOS*

Right: Labelled a "thrill killer" by the press, Richard Biegenwald who is now serving a life sentence for the murder of two young women, killed his victims simply "because he wanted to see someone die." *AP/WIDE WORLD PHOTOS*

Robert Hansen, who admitted to the murders of 17 Anchorage, Alaska women, poses in an undated photo with a mountain goat he killed with a bow and arrow. *AP/WIDE WORLD PHOTOS*

Christine Falling, the baby-sitter who is serving a life sentence for the murder of 3 of her charges. *AP/WIDE WORLD PHOTOS*

Douglas Daniel Clark turns toward defense attorney Penny White in a Los Angeles courtroom where the jury decided Clark should die in the gas chamber for the "Sunset Slayer" sex killings of 6 women. *AP/WIDE WORLD PHOTOS*

Although considered by police to be the slayer of Atlanta's children, controversy still rages about conviction of Wayne B. Williams (above) for the murder of 2 Atlanta adults. Williams is currently serving two consecutive life sentences in a Georgia prison. *AP/WIDE WORLD PHOTOS*

Clifford Robert Olson, the serial killer whose confession to the murders of Vancouver children in return for payments to his family from the RCMP led to the most damned and widely-publicized investigative decision in the RCMP's proud history. *AP/WIDE WORLD PHOTOS*

Carol Bundy wipes a tear from her eye as she listens to her attorney in Superior Court in Los Angeles where she was sentenced to 52 years to life in prison for her part in the "Sunset Slayer" murders. *AP/WIDE WORLD PHOTOS*

Gerald Gallego lights up as he hears the jury find him quilty of murdering 2 college sweethearts in order to fulfill his fantasies of finding sexual slaves. *AP/WIDE WORLD PHOTOS*

Charlene Gallego (right) sits beside defense attorney Fran Laethem before pleading guilty to aiding her husband in the lurid murders he committed. *AP/WIDE WORLD PHOTOS*

Kenneth A. Bianchi (left) sobs in the courtroom after pleading guilty to the slayings of 2 Western Washington coeds. Bianchi and his cousin, Angelo Buono, were charged with a total of 25 counts in 10 of the "Hillside Strangler" murder cases in Los Angeles. *AP/WIDE WORLD PHOTOS*

Richard Cottingham, a 20th century "Ripper" whose lust to kill prostitutes led to his conviction and present life imprisonment. *By permission of The Bergen Evening Record Corporation, Hackensack, N.J.*

Angelo Buono, Jr., with hands manacled, is escorted by unidentified officer at Los Angeles court. He is currently serving a life prison term for his part in the "Hillside Strangler" slayings. *AP/WIDE WORLD PHOTOS*

Almost all of his adult life Watts had been in and out of trouble for his violent acts and assaults on women. One of ten children, he was born in Fort Hood, Texas, in 1953, but attended public schools in West Virginia, and in Inkster, Michigan, a footstep away from Detroit. He had a few brushes with the law as a teenager, but first came to the serious attention of homicide investigators in 1974 in Kalamazoo, Michigan.

Despite his diminished intellectual capacity (his I.Q. was recorded as being 75) and a predictably uninspired record as a student, Watts had been deemed college material and successfully enrolled as a freshman at Western Michigan University. He was attending classes on the Kalamazoo campus when the body of Gloria Steele, a nineteen-year-old coed, was found on October 30. She had been literally chopped to pieces, her remains showing thirty-three knife wounds, but the girl had not been raped or robbed.

Investigators quickly zeroed in on Watts as a prime suspect in the apparently unprovoked slaying. Just five days before the murder, a muscular but lean young black man had burst through the door of a campus apartment and attacked a terrified twenty-two–year–old student, choking her into unconsciousness. She identified the intruder as Watts.

Another woman had also identified Watts as the man who beat and choked her after she answered a knock at her door, but the charge against him was dropped after he pleaded guilty to the assault on the twenty-two–year–old student.

The cleverness by which Watts outmaneuvered homicide investigators working on Gloria Steele's murder belied his low I.Q. He had himself committed to a state mental hospital, and backed by an attorney, rebuffed police efforts to question him about the crime.

On December 19, 1975, however, Watts appeared in court and was sentenced to a year in the Kalamazoo

County jail for his attack on the coed he had choked into unconsciousness. By that time the trail in the homicide case involving Gloria Steele had grown cold.

After he'd completed his jail term, Watts moved to Ann Arbor, then to Detroit. Concerned about his record of violence police could do little more than try to keep track of his whereabouts and exchange information. Watts fathered a child and also married briefly, but by May 1980 he was divorced and single again. Years later he remarked to a psychologist that his wife of two months had learned about his troubles with the law and became frightened of him.

It seemed she had good reason to worry, because her husband had become a suspect in more murders of women. One of the most highly publicized was the vicious 1979 Hallowe'en-night slaying of thirty-five-year-old Mrs. Jeanne Clyne in the exclusive Detroit suburb of Grosse Pointe Farms. Mrs. Clyne, a former reporter for *The Detroit News*, was stabbed to death as she was walking home from a doctor's appointment. A neighbor discovered her body when he stepped outside his home to look for his children who were out trick-or-treating.

Although investigators learned that Watts was living with a relative in Grosse Pointe Farms at the time, and that he resembled a man who had been seen jogging in the area when the woman was killed, there was no solid evidence to link him to the crime.

A few weeks later, when he was in Ann Arbor, Watts became a suspect in a particularly alarming series of murders attributed to an elusive killer who had become known as the "Sunday Morning Slasher." In 1980, just a few months apart, two University of Michigan coeds and an older Ann Arbor woman were stabbed to death with a sharp instrument. Eighteen-year-old Shirley Small died in April; twenty-year-old Glenda Richmond died in July, and twenty-nine-year-old Rebecca Huff was killed in September. Each of the women was attacked on a Sunday morning, between 3:00 and 5:00 A.M. None of the victims was raped or robbed, and there was no indication that any of them had previously known their killer. Several other distressingly similar murders of women had also occurred during the same general time period in the southeastern Michigan area and across the U.S. border, in Windsor, Ontario.

In July 1980, Ann Arbor police spearheaded formation of a task force of police agencies from southeast Michigan and Ontario to collect, exchange, and correlate information about the shocking series of murders.

Once when he was being tailed, Watts was picked up on a traffic charge, after officers became concerned that he was stalking a victim. But during the brief time he was in custody, he exercised his constitutional right to refuse to answer questions.

In mid-November 1980, Ann Arbor police obtained a court order permitting them to secretly attach a homing device on his car. Officers used the surveillance method for the forty-five days allowed by the court order, and then renewed it for another forty-five days.

Police followed the suspect with a helicopter, and in a series of vehicles, following in one car for a while and then, in classic movie fashion, switching to new teams of officers in different cars in order to allay suspicion. Detroit police and Michigan state police also participated in the surveillance effort, but Watts seemed to have a sixth sense that let him know when he was being followed. He was never observed committing an illegal act, or acting in any manner that would seem to pose a danger to others.

In March 1981, Watts was laid off by the Detroit trucking company where he worked as a mechanic, and police learned that he was planning to move to Houston.

But despite their concern when they learned that the

leading suspect in Michigan's grisly "Sunday Morning Slasher" murders was resettling in their city, there was little that Houston police could do to protect their citizens except initiate weekend surveillance of the newcomer.

Watts went to work as a mechanic for a trucking company in Houston, and local police picked up the surveillance. They continued to keep track of him after he was laid off and took a new job with a company that serviced oil-well drilling equipment. And they stuck to him after he was fired from that job and signed on as a mechanic with the Houston municipal transit company. But the job of tailing him was difficult.

Just as in Michigan, Watts seemed to know when the police were hugging his trail. In order to avoid violating his civil rights, officers were restricted to surveillance by car. As far as they knew, he hadn't committed any crimes in Houston, and he was well aware of constitutional protections of his rights. Perhaps surprisingly for someone with his purported antipathy for women, he dated regularly. He even began sporadic attendance at a local church. Sometimes Watts lived with friends, and at other times he lived in his car. Consequently there were days and nights when no one knew where he was going or where he had been.

The surveillance was eventually relaxed. But by that time, unusually large numbers of young women had already died violently on weekends in Houston and in nearby Texas cities. Many of the murders were eerily similar to Michigan's still unsolved "Sunday Morning Slasher" slayings. Several of the victims were killed on Sundays, either by stabbing, strangling, hanging, or drowning. Not only had the victims apparently not known their assailants, but the usual motives of rape or robbery were absent.

Psychological profiles developed by the FBI and local police agencies indicated the obvious, that the slayer had an obsessive desire to murder females. And like other serial slayers, it was also obvious that he would continue to kill until he died, was imprisoned for another crime, put away in a mental institution, or brought to justice for the slayings.

Mrs. Edith Anna Ledet, a thirty-four-year-old medical student in her fourth year at the University of Texas medical school in the nearby city of Galveston, was stabbed to death as she jogged shortly before dawn on March 27, 1981. A newspaper carrier found the body of the woman, who was the daughter of a Dallas judge, on the east edge of the campus a few blocks from her apartment.

Near midnight on Saturday, September 12, twenty-five-year-old Elizabeth Montgomery screamed and stumbled toward her apartment, where she died in the arms of her boyfriend. A man had plunged a knife into her chest as she was walking her dog.

About two hours later on Sunday morning, September 13, Susan Marie Wolfe, a twenty-one-year-old supermarket employee, was about to enter her apartment when a man slipped up behind her and fatally stabbed her six times in the chest and once in her arm.

The new year was only four days old when twenty-seven-year-old Phyllis Ellen Tamm was found hanging from a tree near Rice University at about dawn on a crisp January morning. She had been hanged with an article of her own clothing.

An attractive Rice University architecture student, Margaret Everson Fossi, was the next to be found murdered. A relative had become concerned when she failed to return home early Sunday morning. Checking her car for clues the police pried open the trunk. The body of the twenty-five-year-old married woman was stuffed inside. Her larynx had been crushed, as if it had been struck sharply with a heavy blow, and she had died of asphyxia.

The body of Elena Semander, a twenty-year-old University of Houston physical-education student, was found dumped into a trash bin behind an apartment on Sunday, February 7. The woman, who had last been seen by friends as she left a nightclub at about 2:00 A.M., had been strangled with her blouse and was wearing only underpants. The rest of her clothing was recovered from a dumpster a couple of blocks away, and her purse, containing her credit cards and cash, was found in her car.

In March, Frank LaQua, a cook at a truck stop in the town of Brookshire, about forty miles north of Houston, filed a report with local police notifying them that his fourteen-year-old daughter, Emily Elizabeth, had apparently run away. The girl had been in town only two days after she and a girlfriend left Seattle where they had been living with Emily's mother, and hitchhiked to Texas. Emily, who had a history of running away, had decided she wanted to stay with her father.

On April 15, thirty-four-year-old married postal employee Carrie Mae Jefferson failed to return home after her night shift.

The same day, twenty-five-year-old Suzanne Searles left a party in Bear Creek Park. Alerted by co-workers after she failed to show up for her job as a production artist with a typography company the following Monday, investigators checked her car which was parked at her apartment and found her broken glasses and the contents of her purse scattered throughout the vehicle.

Twenty-six-year-old Yolanda Sanchez Degracia was discovered at about 6:00 A.M. on April 16, murdered near her home. She had been stabbed six times.

Mrs. Harriet Semander, whose pretty daughter Elena was one of the victims, began to suspect that the unusually large number of young women being murdered or attacked in Houston might be linked to the same killer. She asked police to issue a public warning. They refused.

"I was told that would start a panic, people would be frightened," she was later quoted in a *Houston Chronicle* newspaper article. "Meanwhile, another girl was killed."

Mrs. Semander went to the news media with her suspicions, and was interviewed by a local television reporter. At last, the public had been informed that there was a good chance that a serial killer was stalking and murdering women in their city.

The families of three slain or missing women contacted Mrs. Semander and they began comparing newspaper stories and looking for a tie-in to link the slayings. The parents finally managed to arrange a meeting with Chief of Police Lee P. Brown to pursue their theory that the same individual was responsible for several of the murders. Mrs. Semander told the press that the chief didn't agree. The *modus operandi* in the killings was not the same, he told the parents, and blamed the media for blowing things out of proportion.

It was not as though the Houston police were unfamiliar with serial killers! In 1973 Houstonians had been shocked when the shooting death of a former candy-maker, Dean Corll, exposed a ghastly three-year series of savage homosexual murders that claimed the lives of at least twenty-seven boys. Corll enlisted the help of two teenagers in some of the slayings, and after overpowering his victims, tied them to a plywood torture board where he abused them — sometimes for days — before strangling them to death. Parents of some of the missing boys, who went to police, later complained that authorities refused to consider the possibility of kidnap or murder and insisted that the missing youths were merely runaways. The slayings didn't end until seventeen-year-old Elmer Wayne

Henley, one of Corll's young accomplices, shot him to death during a quarrel.

And in 1975, Houston police arrested an escapee from a mental hospital in Michigan on charges of rape and sexual abuse. The suspect surprised authorities, while in custody, by confessing to the murder of a Houston woman and three others, in Ann Arbor, Michigan, in Toledo, Ohio, and in Seattle, Washington. He finally agreed to plead guilty to the murder in Seattle, in exchange for a guarantee he wouldn't be prosecuted for the other slayings.

Although police hadn't agreed to issue a public warning, they were determined to stop the senseless slaughter and find the madman who was killing Houston's young women. A team of skilled homicide investigators were assigned to the slayings. Factors that were making the manhunt especially difficult, however, were the apparent lack of a motive and what seemed to be the almost entirely random selection of victims.

Usually when young women are murdered and there is no evidence of rape or robbery, police first check out their husbands, boyfriends, neighbors, co-workers, or other people who knew them. When robbery and rape are committed, even by strangers, there are usually clues left behind. It may be the killer's sperm, a strand of hair, clothing, fiber, a dropped cigarette butt, any of a myriad of telltale signs to point a determined investigator to the killer's trail.

But except for a bloody, hooded sweatshirt found near the corpse of Mrs. Ledet, which had been sent to FBI laboratories for study, police had few clues to help them track down whoever it was who was killing the Texas women.

When police finally got the break they had been hoping for, it had nothing to do with the painstaking investigation and the thousands of manhours they had invested in finding the killer.

It was about seven o'clock on Sunday morning, May 23, when Patrolmen L. W. Domain and D. R. Schmidt responded in their squad car to what is one of the most common, yet potentially explosive, of all police calls. The dispatcher sent them to the apartment of two young women, Lori Lister and Melinda Aquilar, to handle what was believed to be a domestic disturbance.

But alarmed neighbors had not telephoned for help because of a mere squabble between two roommates. As the squad car pulled to a stop in front of the building, the officers heard what sounded like a heavy foot slamming into a door. Seconds later, an athletic-looking black man darted from the apartment, leaped a half dozen steps in a single bound, and fled through the courtyard. Although he was fast, he made the mistake of turning into an opening between the apartments that led him into a dead end. The two policemen and a neighbor who had joined in the chase had him handcuffed in moments.

While Domain stayed with the prisoner, Schmidt hurried back to the apartment where he found neighbors desperately working to revive a young woman who had been dumped into a bathtub. The woman had been badly beaten as well as choked, but she was revived and paramedics soon arrived and began treating her and her roommate — who had leaped headfirst over a porch railing to get help even though her hands were tied behind her.

As police began sorting things out, they learned that the woman pulled from the half-filled tub was twenty-one-year-old Lori Lister. Her roommate who had leaped over the porch railing was Melinda Aguilar.

According to their stories, their ordeal had started a short time earlier when a strange man suddenly attacked Miss Lister in the parking lot of the apartment complex, and choked her into unconsciousness. Then he used her key to unlock the apartment, and walked inside. Miss

Aguilar had been sleeping on the front-room couch, and before she could scramble away, the wiry intruder jerked the petite, five-foot-tall woman to her feet and began to choke her. Moments later he was dragging her into the bedroom, where he forced her hands behind her back and bound them with a wire coat hanger and a belt.

Apparently satisfied that she was helpless and would cause no immediate trouble, the intruder walked back downstairs and dragged Miss Lister back into the apartment where he resumed beating her. Finally, he pulled her into the bathroom, dumped her into the tub and filled it with water.

Fearful that she was about to be murdered, Miss Aguilar struggled to her feet and plunged over a four-foot-high porch railing. Her head struck an outcropping of the porch, flipping her over so that she landed on her knees on the grass. Then she was on her feet, running and screaming for help. "Someone," she shrieked, "is trying to kill me!"

The prisoner refused to talk to police, but he was quickly identified as twenty-eight–year–old Coral Eugene Watts.

The Sunday morning that Watts was arrested, the body of another attractive young woman was found in the bathtub of the Houston home she shared with her mother. An autopsy disclosed that Michelle Marie Maday had been strangled on the day of her twentieth birthday.

In custody at last, Watts was lodged in the Harris County Jail under $50,000 bail and charged with two counts of attempted murder, aggravated assault, and burglary of a habitation.

A few weeks later, at the request of his court-appointed attorneys, he was admitted to Rusk State Hospital in Austin for treatment. After conducting a battery of psychological tests, Dr. J. A. Hunter, a psychiatrist at the hospital, reported that Watts hated women and had been sane on May 23 when he allegedly assaulted the two roommates in their apartment.

Dr. Jerome Sherman, a Houston psychiatrist, who examined Watts for the defense, reported that the suspect was a paranoid schizophrenic.

"Mr. Watts appears to perceive the world around him as pure fantasies which revolve to a large extent around the struggle against the 'evil' he sees everywhere," the doctor said.

He added that females, whom Watts perceived to be deceitful, unfaithful, and parasitic, were the object of much of the suspect's hostility. At one time during their interview, the psychiatrist said, Watts cried while talking about the death of an uncle he believed to have been killed by a female member of the family.

There was an obvious similarity in Watts's assault on the Lister and Aguilar women and the unsolved murders of some of the other women in Houston who had been slain during the previous fifteen months. But suspecting him of the murders and proving that he was responsible were two different matters. Authorities needed solid evidence, or a confession. They had neither.

On August 9, 1982, jury selection was about to begin for Watts's trial, when his attorneys advised the judge and the assistant district attorney assigned to the case that their client wanted to plea bargain.

They said he would plead guilty to the burglary of the apartment, accept a fifty-year prison sentence, and cooperate with authorities by detailing his part in the murders of Houston women he was suspected of killing.

In return, he demanded a guarantee that he would not be prosecuted in the slayings.

Harris County District Attorney John B. Holmes was faced with a difficult decision. He had already met with relatives of several of the victims and he was fully aware of the grief and loss they had suffered. But he was also aware of the special grief of those families who did not know if their missing female relatives were alive or dead. The deal that was being offered might well solve some of the dismal mysteries and lead to the recovery of bodies for proper burial.

However, if Watts was indeed responsible for one or more of the unprovoked brutal murders he was suspected of, the death penalty would not be undeserved.

But there was no guarantee under Texas law that Watts could even be convicted of murder, and no certainty that even if found guilty he would ever face a death sentence. The state's capital-punishment law is one of the factors Holmes had to consider when weighing the chances of winning a death sentence or life term for the suspected killer. In Texas, capital murder, which provides for a life sentence or execution by lethal injection, applies only in situations in which the slayings occur during the course of another felony. There was no evidence that the women he was suspected of murdering had been the victims of other felonies such as rape, robbery, or kidnapping. Consequently, a capital murder conviction could be extremely difficult to obtain.

The apparent motiveless nature of the crimes, which did not involve sex or personal gain, might also go a long way in helping bolster possible acquittal by reason of insanity.

Holmes opted to deal, but not for a fifty-year sentence. He insisted on a sixty-year prison term.

Although tacking on the extra ten years might not appear to make much of a difference, there was a solid reason for Holmes's insistence on a sixty-year sentence. Because, in Texas, all convicts are eligible for parole after serving one-third of their terms, sixty years is the equivalent of a life sentence. Prisoners sentenced to life are eligible for parole consideration after twenty years.

Holmes explained to the press that although sixty years might appear to be too light a sentence for a suspected multiple murderer, it was the best that authorities could do. "We didn't have a stitch of evidence to go on in the killings," the DA said. "We figured that at least this way we'd get the bodies and the life sentence."

Through his attorneys, Watts agreed to the sixty-year stipulation, and he was returned to the Houston municipal jail for what developed into a grueling three-week interrogation. Watts kept his word, and delivered impassive admissions to the murders of Susan Marie Wolfe, Carrie Mae Jefferson, Elizabeth Montgomery, Margaret Everson Fossi, Elena Semander, Suzanne Searles, Yolanda Garcia, Phyllis Ellen Tamm, Michelle Marie Maday, and Edith Ledet. Those admissions were not unexpected. But the prisoner had some bombshell revelations to drop, as well.

He admitted to his interrogators that he had slashed the throat of a nineteen-year-old outside her apartment in the port city of Galveston on January 30, 1982. A few weeks earlier, an ex-convict had been found guilty of attempted murder in the non-fatal assault on the young cocktail waitress, and had been sentenced to life in prison under Texas's habitual-criminal law. Follow-up investigation stemming from Watts's confession confirmed that the ex-convict was innocent, and he was released.

Watts's unemotional recitation also cleared up a near year-old Austin case, previously considered by authorities to be an accidental death.

When the body of Linda Katherine Tilley, a twenty-two–year–old University of Texas coed, was found floating in a swimming pool on September 5, 1981, authorities theorized she had tripped over a hose and fallen into the pool. Watts's startling confession indicated differently. "It would have been one of those perfect crimes," Travis County Medical Examiner Roberto Bayardo later told reporters. "There was no evidence."

But Watts told Austin police that he had begun following a lone woman in a car in Houston on the night of September 4, and trailed her nearly 160 miles west, to Austin.

Near an Austin apartment complex the woman Watts was following turned, and he assumed that she had pulled into a parking place. Minutes later he pounced on Miss Tilley as she was walking from her car in the parking area to her apartment. Watts said that during the struggle they tumbled into the pool and he held her face down in the water until she drowned.

After Watts's surprising confession investigators checked out the young coed's movements on the night she was killed and learned that she had not been anywhere near Houston. When the woman he'd been trailing turned off the road Watts had momentarily lost sight of his original quarry. By a cruel twist of fate, he apparently mistook the university student who had been driving home from a date for the girl he had been stalking.

The Houston woman wasn't the only intended victim who escaped the murderous mechanic. He told police that a few minutes after he killed Edith Anna Ledet in Galveston, he jumped on the back of another woman, intending to add her to his murder list. But his hands were still slippery with blood from the earlier killing, and the lucky woman twisted free and fled. He admitted to another non-fatal attack in the tiny town of Seabrook, on Galveston Bay, as well.

The prisoner explained that most of his victims were selected by chance or whim. He said he merely drove around until he spotted a lone young woman he felt was the one he wanted. Then he would follow her until there were no witnesses around and he believed conditions were safest. Finally, he would sneak up behind his unsuspecting victim, kill her, and flee. His technique was simple, and devilishly successful.

Texas State District Judge Douglas Shaver later

observed of the suspect: "He would just periodically see a woman and decided that because he believes women are evil, that that particular woman was evil and needed to be killed — and he'd kill them."

A few months before Watts's capture, he altered his pattern and began carrying a shovel in his car so that he could bury some of the women.

Watts shared an intriguing quality with many other serial killers. He had a phenomenal memory for details dealing with his selection of victims, his attacks, and disposal of the bodies. He remembered the clothing his victims wore, the make and color of their cars, and provided other information that helped investigators confirm his involvement in specific attacks.

He led Cecil Wingo, chief investigator for the Harris County Medical Examiner's office, and a group of six detectives to a weed-choked vacant lot in West Houston where they uncovered the badly decomposed remains of a woman from a shallow grave. She was dressed only in a brassiere and socks. Dental charts were used to identify her as Suzanne Searles.

A few days after the first body was recovered, at the direction of a team of officers, trustees from the Houston Municipal Jail dug up another body near a Houston bayou. The victim was wearing only panties, a brassiere, and a blouse. Dental charts identified the remains as those of Carrie Mae Jefferson.

Acting on information provided by Watts, police in Brookshire also recovered the body of a young girl from a culvert. It was the suspected runaway, Emily Elizabeth LaQua, and an autopsy disclosed that she had been strangled.

By that time, officials from police departments and district-attorneys' offices in several other states, including Michigan, Ohio, Indiana, Louisiana, and Florida, were telephoning with suspicions about his possible involvement in unsolved murders in their jurisdictions, or were flying to Houston to talk with the suspect.

After receiving a promise of immunity, Watts admitted to the murder of Mrs. Clyne in Grosse Pointe Farms. Michigan investigators quoted him as saying that he stabbed the woman eleven times in the chest with a sharpened screwdriver, then drove away to buy some potato chips before going home.

Dominick Carnovale, assistant prosecutor in Wayne County, Michigan, said that details given by Watts about the Grosse Pointe Farms slaying could only have been provided by someone involved. However, in a 1982 Associated Press article Carnovale added that although prosecutors suspected Watts in other Detroit slayings, authorities had indicated they would not offer immunity in order to clear up these crimes.

A few minutes before noon on September 3, 1982, journalists, relatives and acquaintances of the dead women and a few friends of the defendant gathered in Judge Shaver's Houston courtroom to witness Watts's sentencing on the burglary charge. Frustration at the confessed serial killer's avoidance of more serious charges, and more serious penalties, was obvious on the faces of many of the spectators, and security was heavy. Prosecutors and some other court officers were wearing bulletproof vests. Spectators were screened with metal detectors to make sure they were not carrying weapons, before being allowed to enter, and about a half-hour before the proceedings began, a German shepherd dog, trained to sniff out bombs, had roamed the courtroom.

Harris County Medical Examiner, Dr. Joseph Jachimczyk, testified during the proceeding that, based on his experience, the bathtub water that Watts used in his effort to drown the trussed-up victim was a deadly weapon. Judge Shaver concurred, consequently ruling that Watts was convicted of a violent crime, which meant he would not be eligible for parole before serving twenty years, or one-third of the sixty-year sentence. Without the introduction of a deadly weapon, Watts could conceivably have been eligible for parole in about eleven years. Watts listened impassively, with his hands shoved casually into the pockets of his gray slacks, as the agreed-upon sixty-year prison sentence was imposed. Judge Shaver was not as devoid of emotion when he addressed the prisoner who had so senselessly ended an untold number of young lives in violence and spread such grief. Staring hard at Watts, the jurist declared that if the defendant ever misbehaved in prison: "I hope they put you so deep in the penitentiary that they'll have to pipe sunlight in to you."

CHAPTER 7

THE THRILL KILLER

RICHARD BIEGENWALD

(1958-1983)

Before they finally decided he had earned another chance, the New Jersey State Parole Board had rejected convicted murderer Richard Biegenwald's plea for early release three times.

In 1975, when the spare, scarfaced convict walked out of the New Jersey State Prison at Rahway, he had served seventeen years of a life sentence for a holdup slaying committed when Biegenwald was eighteen. The victim of the youthful indiscretion was Stephen F. Sladowski, a grocer who was also an assistant municipal prosecutor in Bayonne.

But the cold-blooded murder of the Bayonne father of four was not the first time Biegenwald had gotten into serious trouble. In fact, he had been in trouble most of his life, and by the time he walked out of the Rahway penitentiary he had spent more than a quarter of a century in jails, prisons, juvenile and psychiatric institutions in three different states.

According to various court and family-service–agency

records, Biegenwald's father, an alcoholic who had no interest in his wife and child, often beat his young son. Richard was barely five years old when he set fire to his house on Staten Island, and was committed to the Psychiatric Center in Rockland County, New York. He was only eight years old when he began drinking and gambling, and as a nine-year-old, he had received a series of electroshock-therapy treatments in the psychiatric unit of New York's Bellevue Hospital. A couple of years later, he was placed in the State Training School for Boys in Warwick, New York, where he was blamed for burglaries and for inciting other children to escape.

During visits home he stole money from his mother, and at the age of eleven, Richard set himself on fire. He survived the attempt at self-immolation little the worse for wear, and was released from state custody long enough to graduate from the eighth grade at a Staten Island school when he was sixteen. Although his high-school career lasted only a few weeks, his criminal career would last a lifetime.

The recent high-school dropout made his way to Tennessee, stole a car in Nashville, was apprehended, and did time in a federal prison. After his release a few months later, he returned to Staten Island, stole another vehicle, and shot Sladowski to death during a robbery. Biegenwald and an accomplice in the stickup were arrested in Maryland two days later, after firing a shotgun at a state trooper who flagged them down for speeding. Biegenwald was sentenced to life in prison.

But those bad old days appeared to be behind him when he was released seventeen years later. He had worked as a dental technician, printer, and machine mechanic, and wasn't without legitimate job skills to help him survive outside prison walls. He found jobs painting houses, and soon, moved on to auto-body shops where he painted cars. He reported faithfully to his parole board, seemed to have settled down, and for the first time in his life showed serious signs of becoming a hardworking, honest, contributing member of society.

He even developed a surprising romantic relationship with a teenaged blonde beauty he met while visiting his widowed mother, Mrs. Sally Biegenwald, who lived in a modest but neatly kept blue bungalow in the quiet Charleston section of Staten Island.

The teenager was Dianne Merseles, a pretty sixteen-year-old neighbor of Biegenwald's mother. Dianne was an outstanding student, and had been raised by a warm, loving family in a pleasant home. She seemed a strange match for the skinny, pock-faced loser with the red hair and wispy beard who had spent more years in prisons and other institutions than she had lived. Despite Biegenwald's grubby appearance and unsavory past, however, it wasn't long before Dianne announced to her baffled family and friends that she was in love with her neighbor's son, and intended to marry him.

By that time Biegenwald was in trouble again. Since the middle of 1977 he had not checked in with his parole officers. Police, who were looking for him to question him as a suspect in a rape, finally tracked him down in Brooklyn in June 1980, and he was arrested and locked up in the Brooklyn House of Detention. He and Dianne were married there.

Although the rape charges were dropped after the victim was unable to pick him out of a lineup, he was returned to the New Jersey State Prison at Rahway as a parole violator. Six months later he was released and he and his bride moved into their first home together at Point Pleasant Beach, where Biegenwald found a job as a maintenance man for a real-estate company.

He was in Point Pleasant when an old cellmate from his first hitch at Rahway looked him up. Dherran Fitzgerald, five years older than Biegenwald, was an athletic, two-hundred-pound skydiver and career criminal. His big-talking ways and brash derring-do had kept him in trouble most of his adult life, and he had served nearly twenty years in prison for kidnapping, robbery, and various other serious offenses.

Fitzgerald had not been idle since his separation from his former cellmate. He had been paroled, rearrested when he was caught sitting in a stolen car with a gun and a ski mask outside a New Jersey shopping center, imprisoned, and paroled again. According to later statements made to police, he had then immediately sought out another former-convict friend from Pennsylvania, William J. Ward, who was on the run after escaping from the New Jersey State Prison at Leesburg three years earlier. The two men hooked up in a scheme to run guns from Florida to New Jersey.

It wasn't long before Fitzgerald was in trouble again, and police began looking for him as a suspected shoplifter. When the Biegenwalds began taking care of a rambling old woodframe house in Asbury Park, N.J., that had been converted to apartments, and moved into one of the flats, Fitzgerald set up housekeeping in another of the apartments. An attractive twenty-one–year–old woman who worked with Dianne at a diner also moved in, renting a basement room that Biegenwald had constructed.

The little group of tenants remained together for several months, until Dianne's friend found a new job selling jewelry. She moved out, and another young woman took her place and moved in.

On January 4, 1983, two frightened boys discovered the body of a teenaged girl dumped behind a fast-food restaurant in Ocean Township, a few miles north of Asbury Park. She had been shot four times in the head. According to newspaper accounts, she was fully dressed and there were no indications of sexual assault.

Grieving relatives identified the once-beautiful victim as Anna Olesiewicz, an eighteen-year-old girl from

Camden, New Jersey, who was last seen by friends near the Asbury Park boardwalk during the busy Labor Day weekend of 1982.

When the jewelry salesgirl read about the shocking discovery of the body dumped in Ocean Township she went to the police. On January 22, a squad of armed policemen surrounded the old house in Asbury Park and arrested Biegenwald, Fitzgerald, Dianne, and their new female tenant. She, however, was released a short time later without charges.

But police had hit the jackpot as far as the two ex-convicts were concerned. Investigators were quoted in press reports as revealing that a search of the house turned up floor plans to several area banks and businesses, four pipe-bombs, several automatic pistols, a machine gun, a drill press and grinder, a bottle of knockout drops, a cocaine-freebasing device, marijuana, an "Anarchist Cookbook," and a deadly poisonous live puff adder. More importantly, both the jewelry salesgirl who had moved out of the house and Fitzgerald were talking. They related chilling stories of obsessive evil, and random, senseless cruelty.

Fitzgerald told detectives that Biegenwald once asked him to look at something in the garage next to the Point Pleasant Beach house. Inside the garage, Biegenwald lifted a piece of canvas and revealed the body of a dead girl, her face still hidden by a bag. Fitzgerald said Biegenwald advised him that the girl had to be killed for "business reasons."

Fitzgerald said he agreed to help his friend transport the corpse to Staten Island and bury it. While digging into the hard clay in the flower beds behind Biegenwald's mother's house, with only the moon for light, Fitzgerald told police that his shovel uncovered the remains of another young woman. Biegenwald reputedly explained that she had also died as the result of a business deal gone bad.

The loquacious ex-convict led investigators to the double grave where they unearthed the decomposing bodies of two teenaged females. One of the girls had been shot twice in the head, dismembered, and buried in green plastic trash bags. She was identified as seventeen-year-old Maria Ciallella, an Ocean County, New Jersey, girl who had been last seen alive shortly after midnight on Hallowe'en, 1981.

A police patrolman had passed and recognized the friendly high-school student as she was walking down a lonely road toward her house in Brick Township. He planned to give her a ride home after responding to the radio call he was on, but when he returned a few minutes later, she was gone.

Miss Ciallella's remains were buried under the body of another victim, eventually identified as seventeen-year-old Deborah Osborne. A petite girl who worked as a motel chambermaid, Deborah was last seen by friends on April 8, 1982, when she left a bar-lounge in Point Pleasant. Pathologists reported that she had been stabbed in the chest and abdomen.

Fitzgerald also told investigators that he had acted as a lookout a few months earlier while the pot-bellied Biegenwald dug a shallow grave in an isolated area a few miles north of Asbury Park, and buried another teenager. Following his directions, police had dug up the body of seventeen-year-old Betsy Bacon who was wearing only panties when her body was unearthed. Two bullets had been fired into the head of the Sea Girt, New Jersey, teenager, who had walked out of her house shortly before midnight on November 20, 1982, to buy a pack of cigarettes at a nearby store.

The revelations of the former tenant of the Asbury Park house were equally graphic and shocking. She eventually confessed to investigators that she had become Biegenwald's protégée, and he sometimes drove her to the boardwalk to hunt for easy murder victims, especially teenaged girls. Although he was hairy, dirty, and uneducated, the morose ex-convict had a strange Manson-like ability to charm and manipulate attractive young women. His intended protégée insisted to police, however, that she always found some way to avoid assisting in or witnessing a murder when she was with the curiously magnetic killer. She said that one evening Biegenwald awakened her at about midnight, and she looked out a window toward the driveway where she saw someone sitting in his car. Unable to rouse her to full wakefulness, Biegenwald left the house alone, and the young salesgirl went back to sleep.

According to the young woman's account, the next morning she noticed sand and what appeared to be mud in the car. (Investigators later indicated that the mud was apparently a mixture of blood and sand.) The woman related that she asked Biegenwald if he had picked up a victim and he replied that he had. Then he led her to the garage, lifted an old mattress, and displayed the body of a dead girl. The salesgirl said he made her touch one of the victim's legs she would know what a corpse felt like. About a month later he presented her with a sapphire ring he had taken from the dead body.

Police and prosecutors later disclosed that the dead girl was Anna Olesiewicz, and that Biegenwald had lured her away from the boardwalk by promising her some marijuana.

From the examination of the remains and witnesses' statements, there was no indication that any of the young victims had been sexually abused. Fitzgerald told authorities that Biegenwald explained he was bitter over his long years of incarceration, and that committing the murders calmed him and released his tensions.

Monmouth County Prosecutor Alexander D. Lehrer presented the evidence pertaining to the senseless slayings of the innocent teenagers to a grand jury in

Freehold, then filed first-degree murder charges. He said Biegenwald had killed simply "because he wanted to see somebody die."

The press responded to the information by labelling Biegenwald a "thrill killer."

But the suspect was soon linked to two other murders, neither involving a young female, and apparently neither committed solely for the perverted joy of killing.

New charges were filed against Biegenwald for the fatal shooting of the escaped convict William J. Ward. When his remains were recovered from a hastily dug grave behind a cemetery just outside Neptune City, a few miles from Asbury Park, it was discovered that his head had been shattered by five bullets.

Fitzgerald told interrogators that he got into a fistfight with Ward while they were in Biegenwald's apartment in Asbury Park. The men fought their way out onto a patio and were struggling over a gun, when Biegenwald suddenly stormed from the house and shot Ward several times in the head, at point-blank range.

Two women living in the building later admitted to police that they had seen Fitzgerald and Biegenwald with the bloodied victim a few minutes after the shooting. One woman said that when she looked out a door she saw Ward sprawled on the patio, his head bloodied. Fitzgerald was standing by his side, and Biegenwald was near his feet holding a gun, she said. Frightened, she slammed her door closed.

The other witness said she looked outside and saw Biegenwald and Fitzgerald supporting a man between them whose head was covered with blood. She related that the pair told her not to bother calling for help, because they were taking the injured man to a hospital. Several other people learned about the incident within the week, but no one notified police. They explained that they had remained quiet because they were afraid of Biegenwald.

Acting on a tip from an informant, police unearthed the body of another ex-convict who had served time in a New Jersey prison for check forgery, and was last seen alive by associates in June 1978. Since parole from prison in 1968, John A. Petrone had become known as a police informant. Investigators claimed they had information that made Biegenwald a suspect in the shooting death of the fifty-seven–year–old auto salesman. Petrone's body, minus the jawbone, was found buried under a mound of earth, some old tires, and an abandoned car frame in a remote wildlife preserve.

Detectives also checked into the possibility that Biegenwald may have been linked to the slaying of seventeen-year-old Virginia Clayton, whose fully clothed body was discovered only four miles from the site of Petrone's makeshift grave in the same wildlife preserve. The teenager was last seen alive by family members on September 8, 1982, after leaving her house in Freehold Township to hitchhike to a babysitting assignment. Her body, stabbed several times, was found three days later.

Biegenwald was not charged with either the Petrone slaying or that of the babysitter. But he was indicted by a grand jury and charged with five counts of first-degree murder in the slayings of the other four girls and of Ward. Each case was to be tried separately.

His old prison buddy, Fitzgerald, entered into a plea-bargain agreement with authorities who consented not to prosecute him on murder charges, in exchange for his continued cooperation in the investigation and for his testimony against Biegenwald in the upcoming trials. Fitzgerald pleaded guilty to charges of illegal possession of weapons and of hindering the arrest of Biegenwald, by helping him bury Anna's body, and was sentenced to five years in prison on each count.

Biegenwald's young wife, Dianne, was charged with hindering her husband's arrest. She pleaded guilty in

October 1983 and was placed on probation. While her husband was behind bars awaiting trial, she gave birth to a daughter. Biegenwald first saw his child when his wife brought her along on a visit at Trenton State Prison.

No charges were filed against Dianne's former co-worker at the diner who told police of Biegenwald's thwarted scheme to groom her for a life of crime.

The first murder charges against Biegenwald to come to trial were those filed in the slaying of Miss Olesiewicz, and his attorneys sought to convince the jury that the forty-nine–year–old Fitzgerald was the real killer. Fitzgerald was the state's star witness at the six-day trial in Freehold, and was brought to the courtroom under heavy guard from the Trenton State Prison. On the stand, the fast-talking braggart was accused by Biegenwald's defense attorneys of being a necrophile, a "sickie" who sexually violated the bodies of dying young women as he killed them. Three convicts who had known him and Biegenwald in prison testified that Fitzgerald had talked to them of perverse fantasies about murdering females during sexual activity.

Terry O. James, a convicted armed robber who worked in the kitchen at Trenton State Prison with Fitzgerald, said the muscular braggart showed him a newspaper article about the murder of Miss Olesiewicz. Fitzgerald boasted that she was "one of the girls he killed," James testified. James added that Fitzgerald "figured they wanted Biegenwald so bad that he could do whatever he wanted and get through. He figured they'd put it all on Richie." The conversation reputedly occurred several months after police swooped down and arrested the occupants of the house in Asbury Park.

Marcus Albuquerque, another convicted armed robber, testified that Fitzgerald once told him that there was "something special about killing women while having sex with them."

Charles Layton, imprisoned at Trenton for aggravated assault and witness tampering and who had known Fitzgerald since 1969, described him as a sick person who was thrilled by watching people die and liked to "have sex with them while they are dying."

Fitzgerald denied their stories, but conceded during the lurid six-day proceeding in Freehold that he had once boasted to police he was a mercenary who killed people as part of his job. He insisted during testimony that he had been lying, however, and claimed he had never killed anyone.

Fitzgerald admitted that two days after her murder he had helped Biegenwald stuff Miss Olesiewicz's body into the trunk of a car and move it from the garage to a wooded area behind the fast-food restaurant where it was eventually found. He also claimed that Biegenwald shot the teenager to death as part of a "training exercise" for his protégée. The young jewelry salesgirl confirmed that Biegenwald had wanted her to kill Anna. "This was supposed to be my victim," she testified.

The jury chose to believe the prosecution witnesses, and returned a verdict of guilty to first-degree murder. Acting on the jury's recommendation, Superior Court Judge Patrick McGann, Jr., sentenced the pale, impassive forty-three-year-old defendant to be executed. The sentence marked him as the second man scheduled to die by lethal injection since the state's new death-penalty law had been enacted the previous year.

Two months later, Biegenwald was found guilty of murdering Ward. Judge McGann ruled that the prosecution could not mention Biegenwald's previous murder conviction for the slaying of Miss Olesiewicz because it was still under appeal, and the jury recommended a life sentence. Again Biegenwald showed no emotion as he was sentenced to life in prison.

Biegenwald later was given life sentences for the slayings of both Maria Ciallella and of Deborah Osborne.

He has not been tried in the murder of Betsy Bacon. In early 1986, Assistant Monmouth County Prosecutor James Fagen told the author that the case will be brought to trial only if Biegenwald escapes execution in the Olesiewicz slaying. If that occurs and Biegenwald is tried for the Bacon murder, Fagen said, the death penalty will be sought.

CHAPTER 8

THE MAN WHO HUNTED GIRLS

ROBERT HANSEN

(1973-1983)

Robert Hansen could never get dates with the prettiest girls in high school.

In fact, the skinny stutterer with the pimply face was virtually shut out of the dating game during his teenage years. Rejection bothered him constantly, eating away at him until he developed a deep-seated hatred for females, particularly the long-legged young beauties with enticing figures whom he had so desperately desired.

So when he grew up he left his home in Pocahontas, Iowa, and traveled to Alaska, where he murdered at least seventeen young women — most by flying them into the wilderness, stripping them naked, and hunting them down like animals, with a knife or big-game rifle.

According to Victor Krumm, a state of Alaska district attorney, after the kill-crazy vendetta was at last brought to an end, Hansen told investigators that he had suffered a "feeling of rejection by women" since his youth. "He nevertheless liked and respected women who he felt, in his mind, were good,'' the district attorney added.

Hansen felt no remorse about killing the young women he selected as victims. Most of them were prostitutes or barroom dancers drawn by the fast money to be made in the land of glaciers, snow, and virgin forests.

Some of the girls who populated Anchorage's riproaring red-light district found their way north by themselves, or came with husbands, boyfriends, and pimps who were willing to live off their earnings. Some were veteran hookers, and others were topless dancers recruited by a Seattle talent agency for the nudie bars and clubs catering to the sexual desires of loggers, hunters, trappers, and fishermen. By the time these women had reached Anchorage they were tough and streetwise.

A few of the girls, however, were relative newcomers to the vice business, still too trusting and naive to recognize the danger signals sent out by the occasional bar customer or trick who wanted more sinister satisfaction than mere companionship or a quick, furtive act of sex.

But to Hansen, the girls from the red-light strip were all the same. "He considered them inferior, so it was all right to kill them to appease his resentment toward women," explained Krumm.

While the ghastly ten-year wave of rape and murder was raging police had found it hard to believe that the respected local family man could have had anything to do with the shocking crimes. It was difficult to think of the timid businessman as a cold-blooded killer of helpless women, even after the story told by an hysterical teenager Officer Gregg Baker spotted tearing headlong down Anchorage's Fifth Avenue with a handcuff trailing from one wrist.

At first the terrified girl could only gasp: "He was going to kill me! He was going to kill me!"

Finally, after she was taken to police headquarters and the tears had stopped, the seventeen-year-old told investigators that she was a prostitute and had gone to a nice house in the suburbs with a trick who had offered her $200 to perform oral sex.

Once they arrived at the house he took her to the basement and talked her into stripping so he could fondle her breasts. As soon as she was nude, he locked a handcuff on one wrist, slammed her against a post, encircled her arms around it, and snapped on the other cuff. Now that she was helpless, her captor immediately began calling her filthy names, stuttering as his excitement mounted, while he tortured and sexually abused her.

After two horror-filled hours, she was released and ordered to get dressed. The scrawny, pockmarked man then snapped the cuffs on one of her wrists and one of his own and told her that he was going to fly her to a cabin he owned in the woods. He often took captive girls there and kept them for a week or more until he tired of tormenting them, he told her. Then he killed them!

Forcing the sobbing girl into his car, he drove to nearby Merrill Field, where he kept a private airplane. Desperately, the girl looked around for someone to help her but the airfield was dark and deserted.

The streetwise teenager knew that if she climbed into the airplane it would be only a matter of hours, or days, until she was dead. She already knew too much about her captor, and about other girls who had flown into the woods with him and never returned. She also knew where he lived. She was certain that he could not allow her to return to Anchorage alive.

When he uncuffed her wrist and ordered her to climb inside the aircraft cabin, she made her break for freedom. Jerking away, she ran, as the man charged after her, cursing.

But few forty-four-year-old men can catch up to a

healthy seventeen-year-old, especially one who is running for her life. The uneven footrace was no contest, and when the girl reached the first streetlights on the edge of the city, her winded pursuer gave up and melted back into the shadows. Moments later she was spotted by Officer Baker.

After initial questioning at police headquarters, the teenager climbed into a squad car with a pair of detectives and directed them to the suburban house where she said she had been tortured.

"Are you sure this is the place?" one of the policemen asked when she pointed out the comfortable, well-kept home, recognized by the officers as the house owned by Robert Hansen. She was sure.

Both men knew that Hansen had red hair, a pockmarked face, and stuttered — just as the girl had described. But Hansen was a respected businessman who had lived in the city for seventeen years, was married, had a teenaged daughter about the same age as the young hooker, and operated a popular bakery where he sold pastries to the morning-coffee crowd. He was also known locally as an avid big-game hunter. He flew his own airplane into the wilderness for his hunting jaunts, and had been nationally recognized for bagging trophy-sized Dall mountain sheep with a bow and arrow.

The policemen drove the girl to Merrill Field, where she pointed out a Piper Super Cub. Outfitted with over-sized tires for landing and taking off in snow, it was the big-game hunter's private airplane.

Back at police headquarters the girl dictated a formal statement, tracing her nightmarish ordeal in detail. Hansen was picked up at his home and voluntarily returned to headquarters with the officers. Stuttering badly, he insisted that he was anxious to clear up what was obviously a terrible mistake — or a blatant attempt by the teenaged prostitute to shake him down.

Confidently, the skinny businessman declared that he

couldn't possibly have picked up and tortured the girl. Because his wife and daughter were vacationing in Europe, he had spent the evening having dinner with a business friend, he explained. In fact, as they were dining, he said, another acquaintance had dropped by. The second friend had dropped him off at his house only a few minutes before the police arrived. Police telephoned the businessmen, and both confirmed Hansen's alibi.

Still, the girl stubbornly insisted that Hansen was the trick who had lured her to his home, tortured her, then driven her in handcuffs to Merrill Field before her escape. She positively identified him, and when she was asked to go over her story again it was the same in every detail. The policemen were seasoned investigators who had heard lies before, and had broken witnesses who were lying, but the girl stuck to her story. And it had the disturbing ring of truth.

Nevertheless, they did not have the type of case that most prosecutors would consider taking to court. Police had little more than the word of a badly frightened teenaged hooker. Balanced against her accusations were the statements of three prominent Anchorage businessmen. The officers filed their paperwork on the case, and turned their attention to other business.

A few months later, hunters stumbled onto a suspicious mound of dirt as they were tracking game along the Knik River, about twenty-eight miles from Anchorage. A few inches below the surface they discovered the stiffened nude body of a young woman. Her clothes had been tossed into the shallow grave beside her, along with two brass shell casings fired from a .223-caliber Ruger Mini-14 rifle.

Searching through missing-persons files, Alaska state troopers soon identified the corpse as that of Sherry Morrow, a twenty-three–year–old topless dancer whose boyfriend had reported her missing about a year earlier, in November 1981.

The gruesome discovery was especially disturbing because just about the time that the Morrow woman disappeared, a party of hunters had found the remains of another murder victim in a shallow grave along the banks of the same river. Although decomposition was far more advanced and there was little except a skeleton remaining of the earlier victim, she had been identified as Paula Golding.

A few months before her death, it would have been difficult to imagine Paula Golding sharing the same dismal fate as the topless dancers who were mysteriously disappearing from Anchorage's bustling vice strip. She had been a secretary until a botulism scare led to the shutdown of some of the local canneries, and the economic slowdown had spread to other businesses.

Suddenly, the thirty-year-old woman found herself adrift in a depressed job market along with scores of other men and women. Pretty, with a nice figure and soft blonde hair, she found work in a topless bar. She could have done worse. The dancers in some of the bars performed bottomless, and although it was strictly against the law, and violations could cost an owner stiff fines and his liquor license, dancers in some of the bars were said to work also as prostitutes.

Paula worked just eight days before she disappeared. After her remains had been discovered along the frozen riverbank, the club manager told investigators that when she didn't show up for work he assumed she had found another job and quit. Neither the bar owner nor any of the girls who had known Paula during her brief career as one of the city's topless dancers could recall seeing her leaving with anyone when her last workshift had ended at about 2:00 A.M., a year earlier.

Although the evidence found at the two grave sites was sparse, it was revealing. There seemed to be little doubt that the two pitiful women were victims of the same depraved killer. Both Paula and Sherry had been exotic dancers, and their graves were similar and close to each other. There were no bullet holes in their clothing, and they had apparently been naked when they were shot to death. It was very likely that the killer was the same man responsible for the sudden disappearance of a dozen or more other young women who had vanished from the city's sin strip since 1973.

Paula's upper spine had been shattered by a slug from a .223-caliber Ruger Mini-14 rifle. The shell casings found in Sherry's grave were from the same type of high-velocity weapon. Prized by big-game hunters, Ruger Mini-14s are expensive and especially popular with men who shoot wolves from airplanes.

When the local gun shops and stores were canvassed, it was discovered that, despite the high costs, scores of people owned the high-velocity rifles in the area. Further, it was possible that the death weapon had not been purchased at a local gunshop, but had been brought to Alaska from out of state, or ordered by mail.

Investigators seemed to have reached a dead end. However, that changed quickly when detectives going through missing-persons reports came across the slender file on Hansen's embarrassing brush with the teenaged hooker. The baker's wilderness cabin wasn't far from where the graves of the two young women were found.

Clues began to add up. Hansen was a dedicated outdoorsman with his own airplane, who thrilled at the opportunity to stalk and bag elusive prey. And he had already been a longtime resident of Anchorage when the first victim's remains had been found in 1980, in an isolated grave.

Portions of the first corpse found by construction workers in a shallow grave along the Eklutna Road had never been identified because part of the body had been dragged away and eaten by bears. What was left of her body was buried with the name, "Eklutna Annie," after the road where her grave was found.

Bears had also ravaged the second known victim, who had been dumped in a gravel pit near Seward. Investigators came up with a possible name, Joanna Messina, but could not locate her family or a hometown. Police learned that both Joanna and Sherry Morrow had worked Seattle's topless bars before making their way to Anchorage, and five other missing dancers were also known to have Seattle connections.

The girls who danced and hustled on Anchorage's sin strip usually changed names as often as they changed jobs and boyfriends. And they didn't talk much about their background. The lack of information about their true identities and their pasts helped obscure any previous records of brushes with police. The problem was further compounded by the transitory nature of the bar girls, who drifted into town from who knows where to work a few weeks or a few months, then moved on, leaving no one behind to miss them when they were gone.

Investigators did discover that one of the missing women had told friends she was going to meet a man for lunch, then pose for nude photos he planned to take. Another said she was going to meet a runt of a man who had offered her $300 for an hour of her time. Neither of the women had been seen by their friends again.

The police officers realized that mere suspicions about Hansen weren't enough to justify hauling him in to the police headquarters for a new round of questioning. And without more information or evidence, there was no chance that a judge could be talked into issuing a search warrant so Hansen's home could be checked for a Ruger Mini-14 that marked shell casings with the same distinct pattern as those found near the remains of the Golding and Morrow women.

It appeared that the only chance of getting another crack at the spindly baker would be by breaking down his alibi. If one of the witnesses who supported him when the teenaged hooker had made her accusations could be induced to change his story, obtaining a search warrant would be practically assured.

The detectives took their suspicions to Krumm and talked it over. The men came up with a scheme to call a special grand jury to hear evidence in the case of the young prostitute, and to notify the alibi witnesses of plans to subpoena them to testify. It would be made clear to the two businessmen that if they perjured themselves before a grand jury, it could mean prosecution and a possible prison term.

Confronted with the prospect of getting into serious trouble, Hansen's friends quickly changed their stories. They admitted lying about spending the evening with him, and explained that when he told them a story about getting into a jam with a hooker they agreed to help with a cover-up. By the time they had learned what he had done to the girl, they'd been afraid they would get into serious trouble if they changed their statements and told the truth.

Neither of the original statements had been made under oath, so no charges were laid against the businessmen. But Krumm obtained search warrants for Hansen's house, his bakery, his car, and his cabin on the Alaskan tundra.

Investigators found the evidence they were looking for. They confiscated a .223-caliber Ruger Mini-14 rifle, and ballistics experts reported that test firing showed it had identical firing-pin marks to those found on shell casings in the graves of the Golding and Morrow women.

They also turned up an aviation map with twenty different locations marked, many on the rugged Kenai Peninsula, southeast of Anchorage. The detectives immediately recognized four of the marks. They pinpointed the two graves along the Knik River, the grave of Eklutna Annie, and the gravel pit near Seward.

The reason for the sixteen other marks seemed chillingly obvious. There was still an unknown number of pretty young women who had abruptly disappeared from the streets and bars in the city's red-light district during the past ten years. However, a search for their bodies at that time wasn't practical, because the ground was frozen and covered with snow. It would be weeks before the thaw permitted a search to get under way.

Hansen had been booked on charges of rape and attempted kidnapping of the teenaged hooker and was being held in the Anchorage municipal jail. With the consent of both city police and Hansen, officers from the Alaska State Police Criminal Investigations Bureau transported him to their headquarters to be questioned by Sergeants Glen Flothe and Lyle Hugsven, and by District Attorney Krumm and his assistant, Frank Rothschild. The suspect waived his rights to remain silent and to have an attorney present.

The lawmen began by informing him of some of the evidence they had already accumulated, and of their intentions, as soon as the weather permitted, to begin searching for bodies at the sixteen mystery locations pinpointed on the map.

Stuttering, and nervously wiping away the sweat beading on his forehead, Hansen offered to talk if he could make a deal that would prevent his family from suffering through the ordeal of a sordid trial. He offered to plead guilty to the murders of the four women whose bodies had already been found if, in return, he received a promise that he would be sentenced immediately, and would not be prosecuted for any other murders. There was no death penalty in Alaska, but conviction on four first-degree–murder charges would ensure that he remained in prison for the rest of his life.

Krumm told him he had a deal.

That was the beginning of a grisly twelve-hour taped confession, recorded over two exhausting days. The lawmen listened quietly, interrupting only when it was absolutely necessary to pin down important details about identities, dates, and locations, while Hansen unfolded a chilling tale of savagery and sexual depravity. He admitted to slaughtering at least seventeen women, but conceded that there may have been many more victims. He said he kidnapped thirty or forty other women, but released them after hours, sometimes days, of sex and torture.

Those who agreed to satisfy his demands, while convincing him that their submission was due to sincere attraction, were allowed to live. But if a girl suggested or demanded money for sex, he became enraged, and most of those girls were killed.

"If they came across with what I wanted, we'd come back to town," he said. "I'd tell them if they made any trouble for me, I had connections and would have them put in jail for being prostitutes."

"What about those who didn't come across?" he was asked.

"They . . . they're still out there," Hansen stammered.

Hansen never knew the names of most of his victims, but recalled Paula, Sherry, Joanna, and Eklutna Annie because of the newspaper stories about the discovery of their bodies. Most of his victims he recalled only by the color of their hair, the size of their breasts, or by some particularly vicious form of torture he submitted them to before killing them.

He said the woman believed to be Joanna Messina was his first victim. He met her on the dock in Seward and she explained she was camping out with her dog while waiting for a job to open up at a cannery.

Hansen told his interrogators that he thought she liked him, and took her to dinner, then to the gravel pit to have sex. But he lost his temper when she told him she was broke and wanted money, so he shot her in the head with a pistol. Then he returned to her camp and killed the dog.

Eklutna Annie was the next victim. According to his statement, he picked her up on the street and drove her to Eklutna Road for sex. When he refused to give her money, he continued, she drew a knife from her stocking, but he took it away and cut her throat.

Hansen seemed to remember details of Paula Golding's death with particular relish. After he had sated himself with rape and torture, he turned the naked blonde out of the cabin, gave her a head start, then hunted her down with his rifle. She became a terrified substitute for the big-game animals he liked to stalk.

The grim investigators listened silently as he told how the panic-stricken woman raced nude along the sandy bank of the river, unmindful of the frigid air and of the sharp rocks and pebbles slashing her bare feet. Finally, exhausted and unable to run farther, she scurried under a stand of brush and lay there shivering and panting for breath.

Hansen took his time. Calmly and deliberately, he walked along the river bank, following her footprints in the sand. When he spotted her in the brush, he called out, then waited for her to run. Somehow, she found the strength to stagger to her feet in a last desperate effort to live.

The hunter lifted his rifle to his shoulder, peered through the scope until the crosshairs centered between her shoulders, and squeezed the trigger. After that, it was all over but the burial.

"It was like going after a trophy Dall sheep or a grizzly bear," the callous killer recalled.

The hunt was so exhilarating to him, in fact, that he picked up Sherry Morrow, so they could play "the same kind of game." He had planned to kill the teenaged hooker the same way, he admitted. But she got away.

After Hansen completed his statement, he flew with troopers in a helicopter to point out the exact locations of other graves marked on the map.

On February 28, 1984, his guilty plea to four counts of murder was accepted by Judge Ralph Moody. In a statement urging that Hansen receive the maximum sentence, Rothschild pointed out that the defendant was renowned as a local big-game hunter.

"But killing animals was not enough. He chose to put women in the role of animals. He turned them loose, naked in wild country where they could not escape, and then hunted them down with a rifle as if they were animals. It was a game for him, done for the thrill, at the expense of human life," Rothschild declared.

Judge Moody sentenced Hansen to life in prison on one count of murder, to ninety-nine years on each of the other three counts, and forty years each for the kidnapping and rape of the teenager. The most prolific killer in Alaska's history had been sentenced, at the age of forty-five, to a total of 461 years in prison without parole.

After the hearing, Krumm revealed that there may have been many more than seventeen victims, as Hansen admitted only to the murders of women he considered to be prostitutes. But investigators learned that he had advertised in the singles personal column of a newspaper, with an invitation advising he was: "Looking for a woman to join me in finding what's around the next bend, over the next hill."

Said Krumm: "I think he's kept that secret and likely will continue to keep it unless we find the bodies of women who may have accepted the challenge of going around the next bend and over the next hill."

CHAPTER 9

THE BABY-SITTER

CHRISTINE FALLING

(1980-1982)

Christine Falling appeared to be a baby-sitter with a curse on her.

Five babies died mysteriously while they were under the care of the apparently gentle teenager. Three others she was minding were rushed to hospitals after being suddenly stricken with puzzling ailments, but recovered. And an old man died unexpectedly on the very day she began working for him.

For two and a half years death dogged Christine's footsteps.

Although Christine's backwoods Florida relatives and neighbors muttered darkly of a jinx or curse, some baffled authorities speculated that she might be a modern-day Typhoid Mary, an unwitting carrier of a deadly unknown virus.

Other medical and legal officials suggested that the tiny victims may have succumbed to a little-known form of encephalitis, or that Christine was simply an unlucky victim of circumstances who happened to be caring for a succession of babies who were stricken with Sudden Infant Death Syndrome (SIDS). (Also known as "crib death," SIDS is frequently cited when infants die suddenly and there is no known cause of death.)

When it began to be hinted that the sitter might have played a sinister role in the bewildering deaths, other residents of the rustic communities of Lakeland, Perry, and Blountstown rallied to her support. So did some of the bereaved parents. There could have been no sitter who was more loving, protective, and tenderly caring of their babies than Christine, her supporters insisted.

In fact, it seemed that no one could have taken the shocking series of deaths any harder than Christine, herself. It was the worst tragedy yet in a young life that had already been filled with deprivation and pain.

"I don't understand why this is happening to me," she tearfully confessed. "It all seems like a weird coincidence. I never used to be afraid to baby-sit, but now I don't want to take the chance again. I love children."

Obese, dim-witted, and epileptic, Christine, it appeared, was born under an unlucky star. All of her life she had known poverty — not only of material goods but of the spirit, as well.

The world that Christine Laverne Slaughter Falling was born into on March 12, 1963, was as bleak and bare as the sun-parched landscape of North Florida's Panhandle. Her mother, Ann Slaughter, although only sixteen, already had an eighteen-month-old daughter, Carol, and was married to a sixty-five–year–old man, Tom Slaughter.

Many of the homes that Christine's neighbors lived in were tarpaper shacks, miserable lean-tos tossed together out of mismatched pieces of throwaway lumber, or rusting housetrailers that were years past their prime. Surrounded by a jumble of junk cars and pickup trucks, the homes sat in dirt yards from which a few scrub trees typically jutted.

Work was hard to find, and usually low paying. Christine's hometown of Perry was in logging country and men with enough gumption and persistence just might be lucky enough to land a choice job at Buckeye, the local paper plant. The women applied for jobs as clerks at the local K-Mart or at one of the supermarkets. Others had to, or preferred to, make do with welfare.

So far as members of the family know, Christine's young mother bore four children. And although Tom Slaughter gave each of them his name and did his level best to care for them, he claimed only one, a boy who died in infancy, as his own.

Every now and then Christine's mother would just take off and leave the little house in Perry, usually heading for Blountstown about a hundred miles west.

Tom was proud of all the youngsters and tried to take good care of them. Carol and Christine later recalled that one day, while Ann was away on one of her jaunts and Tom was in the woods cutting timber, he was struck by a falling tree as they played nearby. His head was split open and he suffered internal injuries.

Somehow, the wiry old man survived. But he was hospitalized for a long time, and there was no one to care for the babies.

Not long after that, Jesse and Dolly Falling adopted the sisters. Childless and desperately hungry to satisfy her maternal instincts, Dolly quickly agreed when her husband asked if she wanted the girls. She made sure that they studied the Bible, and were no strangers to the inside of a church.

But taking the girls to church regularly provided no guarantee that the little family would be a happy one, or that Christine wouldn't get into occasional devilment.

For example, there was the time when Christine and some of her girlfriends decided to find out for themselves if cats really did have nine lives. On Sunday nights when "Aunt Dolly" took her to church, she and her friends sometimes would slip outside, catch some cats, and toss them as high as they could into the air, or wring their necks.

Christine learned that cats did not have nine lives. Once they were dead, they were dead to stay.

Despite the cruel experiments, Christine insisted that she loved cats. Just like she insisted she loved the babies who died.

And despite the churchgoing and the motherly affection heaped on them by Dolly, there was a darker side to the relationship between the girls and their adoptive parents. There were terrible family fights, and after one particularly bad flareup when the police were called, authorities placed eleven-year-old Carol and nine-year-old Christine in Great Oaks Village, a children's refuge two hundred miles downstate in Orlando.

Christine didn't do well during the one year she was at Great Oaks. Staff members reported that she was a compulsive liar and a thief, and one report noted that she would do anything for attention, even if she knew her behavior would lead to punishment.

Records at the refuge show that when an employee was required to indicate special interests that Christine exhibited, the response was that there had been none. And in reply to a question, "What would you single out for praise in the child's behavior?" the answer was: "Nothing."

After the sisters were returned to the Falling home, another fight led them to pack their belongings in a grocery sack and move into an apartment with a girlfriend. Fourteen-year-old Carol took advantage of a school program that permitted her to attend classes half the day and work the other half. But six weeks after Christine left the Falling home, the twelve-year-old girl headed for Blountstown, where she searched for, and found, her mother.

On September 19, 1977, Christine, who was fourteen,

married a young man in his early twenties. During the turbulent six weeks the marriage lasted, she once heaved a twenty-five–pound stereo at her husband during a violent burst of temper.

About a year after her brief unhappy marriage had ended, she began a series of bizarre visits to the local hospital. In two years she made fifty visits to the emergency room, complaining of a bewildering array of troubles, including snakebite, red spots, bleeding tonsils, dislocated bones, falls, burns from hot grease, and vaginal bleeding — which she soberly advised doctors was "not normal menses." The doctors decided that the bleeding was, indeed, normal. Months after the hospital trips, however, the Calhoun County Sheriff and a deputy puzzled over how a girl who was considered to be semi-literate, with a vocabulary that barely reached the sixth-grade level, had picked up a word like "menses."

Her surprising use of the word, and other terms previously believed to be too sophisticated for her limited vocabulary and understanding, hardly fit in with her replies to questions posed to her during a 1982 literacy test.

At that time, Christine had declared:

This is the 19th century.
Russia bombed Pearl Harbor.
Columbus was on the *Mayflower* and discovered Florida.
Abraham Lincoln was the "founder" of electricity — or perhaps it was George Washington.
Elephants gestate for two years, and their babies weigh twenty tons.

A dull student, Christine wasn't bright enough to land a clerking job in a store, and was so fat — over two hundred pounds after she reached her early teens — that younger children trailed after her, mocking her with cruel chants of: "Christine, Christine, beauty queen!"

When she began baby-sitting, she was almost the same age her mother had been when she had given birth to her first child. She was good at taking care of other people's children. She cuddled them, fed them their bottles, or gave them candy and cookies. She liked the little girls better than the boys, because their clothes were prettier and she enjoyed dressing them up.

However, Christine didn't enjoy her "young 'uns" when they were grumpy, or cried. That made her nervous, and then all she could think of was how to make them quiet down.

The first known victim of Christine's compulsion to kill was two-year-old Cassidy Marie "Muffin" Johnson.

It was sultry and hot even for a Panhandle winter in Blountstown, when Muffin was rushed to the offices of Dr. Robert Frederick Boedy on February 25, 1980. The young family physician made a tentative diagnosis of encephalitis, a brain inflammation. But he wasn't completely satisfied with that. A bump and bruises on Muffin's head made him suspicious that the little girl might have been a victim of child abuse.

Christine explained that she had been sitting with Muffin for about two hours when the baby suddenly lost consciousness. A short while earlier, Muffin had taken a nasty fall from her crib and hit her head, the sitter added.

Dr. Boedy decided that Muffin needed more intensive care in the Tallahassee Memorial Regional Medical Center, and sent along a note suggesting that authorities check out the baby-sitter. However, when Muffin's frantic parents arrived with her at the Tallahassee hospital, the note was apparently missed, or ignored.

The seemingly heart-broken baby-sitter was praised

by emergency workers for wrapping her tiny charge in blankets, holding her close, and breathing into her mouth during the mad dash to the hospital.

Doctors who examined the unconscious tot reported finding inconclusive signs of encephalitis. During the next forty-eight hours, Muffin showed signs of improving and of regaining consciousness, but on the third day she suffered seizures and died.

An autopsy indicated no evidence of encephalitis. A doctor reported examining bruised bone and scalp tissue that indicated a blow to the head, but the injury was not considered to be serious enough to cause a coma. Muffin's grieving parents buried their baby.

The next of Christine's charges to die was four-year-old Jeffrey Michael Davis. It was a year after Muffin's mysterious death, and Christine had been in the city of Lakeland in Central Florida for about two months, when she was asked to baby-sit by Jeffrey's parents who were distant relatives. They had gone out into the wetlands to collect earthworms for local fishermen by fishbaiting. (Fishbaiting involves sticking a pitchfork or other implement into the ground and jerking the handle back and forth, causing the metal tynes to vibrate and drive worms to the surface. A bucket of about five hundred worms could bring anywhere from $17 to $28, depending on the season and the demand.)

Christine told investigators that while she was baby-sitting with Jeffrey in his home and he was taking his morning nap, she realized he wasn't breathing. An autopsy indicated that he had died of myocarditis, or heart inflammation, an ailment which is rarely fatal.

Three days after Jeffrey died, Christine was sitting with his first cousin, two-year-old Joseph "Joe Boy" Spring, while his parents were attending Jeffrey's funeral.

Before they returned home, their baby had also failed to survive a nap. Christine said he awoke with a scream, and was dead before she could get to his crib.

An autopsy indicated that, like Jeffrey, Joe Boy had also died of myocarditis. But this time, doctors isolated a virus known as Coxsackie A-8, which is transmitted from person to person by contact with fecal matter.

Tissue from Jeffrey's body was not suitable for testing, but medical investigators said they suspected he had the same virus. However, tests on Christine and other members of the two bereaved families failed to turn up any sign of Coxsackie A-8. The water supply was also ruled out as a possible source of infection.

The puzzled families buried their babies, and consoled Christine. The fat, stringy-haired sitter needed a lot of consoling. She seemed to be the innocent victim of a bewildering streak of bad luck. Baby-sitting was about her only source of income, and she admittedly just loved "young 'uns." But three times in barely one year, infants under her care had died tragic, unexpected deaths. Still others had taken ill, suddenly passing out or experiencing serious breathing problems before they recovered in hospitals or under local doctors' care.

Christine began to mutter that she felt as if she had a curse upon her. But medical investigators, and journalists who learned of the apparent series of tragic coincidences dogging the baby-sitter, began to talk of the possibility that she might somehow be personally deadly to the infants.

But relatives and neighbors who had known Christine for years and shared her hardscrabble existence, were quick to come to her defense. They talked about how well she had treated the tykes she baby-sat. When the babies were hot and fussy, she gave them cookies, let them sip out of her glasses of iced tea, or washed them and dressed them in fresh, cool clothes. And she always felt just terrible about the little ones who died. She had merely been unlucky, they explained, when talk turned to the unfortunate youngsters.

Newspaper reporters now began to write sympathetic stories about Christine and how her hard luck had caused the sitter's business to fall off. And some doctors, although refusing to reject outright the possibility that Christine might be host to a killer germ, suggested that the baby deaths weren't really all that unusual among Florida's poor. It wasn't surprising, they said, that the infant mortality rate should be higher among the poor than among more affluent families where better nutrition and hygiene often ensured both healthier parents and offspring.

Shaken by the latest tragedies, the dour teenager with the dull gray-blue eyes decided she should stay away from the "young 'uns" for a while. She took a job as a housekeeper for seventy-seven–year–old William Swindle, who lived in a tiny cottage on a truck farm near Perry. The day she went to work for the old man, he was found mysteriously dead on the floor of his kitchen, but there was no autopsy, and no suggestions that he had died of other than natural causes.

On July 14, 1981, Christine was back in the baby-sitting business in Perry. Doctors had given her a clean bill of health, and she had changed her mind about staying away from "young 'uns."

"The way I look at it, there's some reason God is letting me go through this," she philosophically explained. "If God hadn't wanted me to go through this, He wouldn't have let it happen."

The next baby to die while in Christine's care was the baby daughter of her stepsister, Geneva Daniels. Eight-month-old Jennifer Yvonne Daniels was bright and cheerful when she was carried into the Taylor County Health Department office, to get an oral dose of polio vaccine and shots for whooping cough, diphtheria, and tetanus. But she began to cry when she was given an injection and she was still crying when Christine carried her outside.

Mrs. Daniels drove to a nearby supermarket and went inside to buy some diapers, leaving Christine in the car, holding the infant. When the young mother returned to the car her baby was dead, but Christine waited until they were driving away to warn her that something was wrong. She said that Jennifer had suddenly stopped crying, and when she looked down the baby wasn't breathing.

The frantic mother and the sitter rushed the baby to Doctors' Memorial Hospital, where the emergency room staff desperately tried to revive the limp infant, but their efforts were in vain.

An autopsy failed to reveal any obvious cause of death, and the case was officially logged as another instance of sudden infant death syndrome. At Jennifer's funeral, Christine fainted when the organist played "Precious Memories," and later, the troubled teenager suggested that the infant had died of "a 'yemonia sickness."

The last child to die under the baby-sitter's care was ten-week-old Travis DeWayne Coleman.

Christine had moved back to Blountstown and was living in a trailer with her boyfriend, Robert Johnson, on July 2, 1982, when the child's mother, seventeen-year-old Lisa Coleman, dropped Travis off to spend the day and night. Hospitalized for five days at Tallahassee Memorial, Travis had apparently won a nasty bout with pneumonia. Now, after the strain and worry of the baby's illness, the young mother wanted some time off.

When Christine awoke the next morning, Travis was dead. The last time she had seen him alive was at about 4:00 A.M., when she fed him his formula, changed his diaper, and put him back to sleep, she told authorities.

Again an autopsy was performed. Initial laboratory tests on tissue samples from the little boy indicated that he had died of a lack of oxygen. Panama City Medical Examiner Dr. Joseph Sapala told news reporters that lack of oxygen could be attributed to SIDS. It could also be attributed to suffocation, said Dr. Sapala who had recently been hired to investigate deaths resulting from homicide, suicide, accidents, or mysterious causes in a North Florida district covering six Panhandle counties.

However, there still remained those, including medical professionals, who found it difficult to believe that the dumpy, vacant-eyed sitter had anything to do with causing the deaths of her charges.

Dr. Flora Wellings, who had run tests on Christine for the Florida Epidemiology Research Center and studied tissues of babies who died earlier under the lethal sitter's care, was quoted in the *Tallahassee Democrat* as saying "I think this is a girl who is a victim of circumstances. I have no scientific reason to think otherwise."

Nevertheless, the fifth infant death to occur under the care of the same baby-sitter in approximately thirty months was curious enough to spark a new round of suspicions, questions, and publicity. Dr. Sapala tested the baby's blood for traces of Dilantin and phenobarbital, drugs commonly used to treat epilepsy, in case some of Christine's medicine could somehow have been swallowed by Travis. There was no trace of either drug in the blood, and blood and stool samples taken from Christine and tested in a Tampa laboratory failed to turn up any evidence of a killer virus she might have unwittingly passed on to the youngster.

Christine continued to insist that she was the innocent victim of a series of horrid coincidences. But a psychiatrist had described her as suicidal, and a few days after Travis's death, she voluntarily entered the psychiatric unit of a Tallahassee hospital.

While Christine was hospitalized, Dr. Sapala was called to testify before a grand jury. During the autopsy on

Travis, he had found severe internal ruptures and other signs indicating the little boy had been smothered. The grand jury returned three indictments against Christine for first-degree murder.

She had already admitted to a family member that she had been killing children. And in a taped confession at the hospital, she told authorities: "I love young 'uns. I don't know why I done what I done. . . . The way I done it, I seen it done on TV shows. I had my own way, though. Simple and easy. No one would hear them scream."

Christine called her terrible murder technique "smotheration."

"I did it like, you know, simple, but it weren't simple. I pulled a blanket over the face. Pulled it back. Then again I did the blanket pulling over the face . . . jus' the right amount for the little 'un. A voice would say to me, 'Kill the baby,' over and over . . . very slow, and then I would come to and realize what happened."

Christine never confessed to the murders of Joe Boy and Jeffrey to police or to prosecuting attorneys either before or after her arrest. And she hasn't owned up to any responsibility for the death of William Swindell.

But faced with the possibility of the death penalty after she was charged with the murders of Muffin, Jennifer, and Travis, she plea bargained. She pleaded guilty to three counts of first-degree murder, and was sentenced to life in confinement with no possibility of parole for at least twenty-five years. She is serving her sentence near Fort Lauderdale in the Broward Correctional Institution, a maximum-security prison for five hundred of the most dangerous women in Florida.

CHAPTER 10

THE ATLANTA CHILD MURDERS

WAYNE B. WILLIAMS

(1980-1981)

Someone was killing Atlanta's black children. And for a time it appeared that one of the greatest manhunts in the history of the United States could not stop the slaughter.

Despite the most determined efforts of the Atlanta Police Department, the FBI, the Georgia Bureau of Investigation, five county sheriff's departments, five nationally known detectives on loan from other big-city police agencies, two computer experts, the National Center for Disease Control, and numerous volunteer psychics, the frightful butchery continued unabated for twenty-two months during 1980 and 1981.

Some of the victims' relatives, politicians, and civil-rights leaders charged that Atlanta's black children were being murdered as part of a white racist plot.

Still other charges relating the dreadful slayings to crazed cultists who pedaled drugs and pornography, worshipped Satan, and practiced ritualistic murder, were dismissed out of hand. Roy Innis, then National Staff Director of the Congress on Racial Equality

(CORE), was perhaps the most prominent figure to blame most of the child-killings, as well as many others, on the devil cult.

The number of victims officially attributed to Atlanta's shocking serial killings eventually reached thirty. But some investigators are convinced there were many more, and there are persistent claims that the murders are still occurring.

The youngest confirmed victim was seven, the oldest twenty-eight. Both males and females were included in the official count of the dead, although most were boys or young men. Victims were shot, stabbed, strangled, asphyxiated, and bludgeoned. Several of the children and adults knew one another.

The horror sneaked up on Atlanta during the humid, hot days of mid-summer, 1979. It was July 28 when a woman searching for redeemable cans and bottles in the southwest area of the city spotted the body of a teenaged boy. His leg was tightly secured by a tangle of kudzu vines spread over a steep ravine alongside Niskey Lake Road, and he had been shot. Police investigators called to the scene, soon discovered a second dead body, barely a hundred yards from the first. The second body was also that of a teenaged boy, who like the first, was dressed entirely in black.

One of the victims was quickly identified as fourteen-year-old Edward Hope Smith. Medical examiners made the identification by matching the victim's teeth with his dental records. The teenager had lived within easy walking distance from where his body was found.

Identification of the second victim was more difficult, but after his mother, Lois Evans, filed a missing persons report with the Atlanta Police Department authorities eventually announced that the second fourteen-year-old was Alfred Evans. The cause of death was unknown. Investigators finally concluded that both deaths were drug related, and there were no arrests.

Fourteen-year-old Milton Harvey was the next to disappear. About six weeks after the Smith and Evans murders, young Harvey's prized bicycle was found abandoned along a dusty road. The boy, who had skipped school that day because he was ashamed of his tattered shoes, was never seen alive again.

Then nine-year-old Yusef Bell vanished. On October 22, he had gone to a nearby store to buy a can of snuff for a neighbor woman. About three weeks after Yusef dropped out of sight, the decomposed body of Milton Harvey was found sprawled among the rotting food and decayed jumble of a dump in the Atlanta suburb of East Point. Yusef's remains were found next, stuffed into the maintenance trap among the shattered glass, broken boards, and plaster of an abandoned school, by a man who said he had forced his way inside to find a place to urinate. A family friend spared Yusef's mother, Camille Bell, the agony of identifying the body.

The holidays had passed and the blustery winds of March were already sweeping the dirt and paper refuse along Atlanta's grimy streets when the body of a young girl was discovered in a weed-filled lot. Her hands had been tied behind her back to a tree, she had been strangled with an electrical cord, and raped. Someone else's panties were stuffed down her throat. The victim was identified as Angel Lanier, a twelve-year-old girl whose mother had just brought her to Atlanta from Chicago the previous January.

A week later, ten-year-old Jeffrey Mathis dropped out of sight, after leaving his home to buy a pack of cigarettes for his mother.

By this time, journalists were beginning to realize that something terrible and frightening was happening to Atlanta's black children. They had been talking to Camille Bell, Yusef's mother, who was kicking up a fuss and wanted authorities to arrest and punish the person who was responsible for the death of her son.

Suddenly it seemed that almost overnight local and national news stories were carrying the message: Atlanta's black children were being systematically murdered.

A deadly and baffling pattern seemed to have developed. The victims were all young, black, and poor. Most were boys, and several of the bodies were found carefully laid out in positions that appeared to have been deliberately chosen by the killer, with arms folded over the chest, or reaching straight out from the shoulders. Most of the victims had been smothered or strangled.

Social activist and comedian Dick Gregory got into the act early, talking darkly about a Frankenstein-like conspiracy supposedly involving the Atlanta-based U.S. Center for Disease Control (CDC). He claimed an ingredient from the blood of black children was needed for the manufacture of interferon, a substance reputedly to be used in the treatment of cancer and herpes. Sickle cells found in the blood of blacks provided the best source of the coveted ingredient, the comedian declared.

As suspicion became alarm, and alarm became hysteria, other wild stories began circulating. A few of the youngsters had been bathed or cleaned up after they vanished from the streets. Yusef was one of them. His feet were clean when his body was found, although when last seen he had been walking the streets barefoot. It was said that the children were being kidnapped by a madman or blood cultist who washed and cleaned them before slaughtering them in some depraved sacrificial rite.

Other people talked of an evil host of depraved child-killers, and of copycat murderers — crazies inspired by the earlier slayings to commit their own outrages on children. A few citizens loudly complained that the men who controlled Atlanta's power structure didn't care about the poor, black ghetto children who were dying, and claimed that if the victims had been white the murders would have been solved long before.

Then fourteen-year-old Eric Middlebrooks was lured from his home by a telephone call a few hours before his body was found, stabbed and bludgeoned to death. Eleven-year-old Christopher Phillipe Richardson was the next to disappear, apparently as he was on his way to a swimming pool. His skeletal remains, lying only a few feet from those of another victim, were not found for eight months.

LaTonya Wilson, the only other female officially attributed to the serial killings, was apparently snatched from her bed the night before her seventh birthday by someone who removed a window pane in the housing project where she lived with her family. Acting on the possibility that the little girl might have been kidnapped and transported across state lines, the FBI quietly entered the case.

Atlanta police initially reported that ten-year-old Aaron Wyche died when he tumbled from a bridge. The cause of death was listed as accidental and as asphyxia because it was presumed he had fallen and landed in a position that twisted his neck and cut off his air. Family members insisted that he was afraid of heights and would not have been playing on the bridge. His name was added to the list of murder victims several months after his body was found.

Anthony Carter was seen playing with a neighborhood buddy at 1:30 A.M., before dropping from sight. The nine-year-old's body, stabbed front and back, was found the next evening.

The baffling killings were tearing Atlanta apart. Racial tensions flared as agitators blamed the killings on a mysterious white man, or white men, who had embarked on a mini-holocaust dedicated to wiping out the city's black youngsters. Some reports circulating through the poor neighborhoods insistently blamed a mythical Ku Klux Klan genocide squad believed to be targeting the young victims for murder before they could grow up and father children. An unfortunate explosion at an Atlanta day-care center in which a black teacher and four of her black preschoolers were killed, further enflamed passions. There were rumors that a bomb had been set off by white racists, even though a faulty gas furnace was quickly pinpointed as the cause of the blast. Nevertheless, harried police investigated a well-known Ku Klux Klansman, carefully tracing his movements and those of some of his associates. There were no indictments, no charges, and no arrests.

Based on the now widespread publicity and knowledge of the murders, it seemed highly unlikely to trained observers that a white man could be moving freely enough through the city's hostile black neighborhoods to enable him to continue kidnapping and murdering the children.

Atlanta's first black mayor, Maynard H. Jackson, and his Public Safety Commissioner, Lee Brown, a veteran black lawman who held a Ph.D. in criminology, were appalled at the waste of young lives. And the killings were a public-relations disaster for the already troubled city that only five years before had drawn hundreds of thousands to its glittering underground shopping centers and after-dark playgrounds. The onetime southern Renaissance city had changed considerably by 1979, not necessarily for the best. That year, national crime statistics compiled by the FBI identified Atlanta as the murder capital of the United States, with more killings per capita than any other city in the country.

Atlanta is a city of some 450,000, but its greater metropolitan area is home to more than four times that many people. And many of the homes the population lives in, especially in the poor, black neighborhoods on the troubled city's seamy underside where the murders were occurring, were occupied by women who were raising their children alone and without the benefit of adult male protection.

The police department, in recent years, had been rocked by a series of bitter internal quarrels and scandals, which at one time had two men simultaneously claiming to be chief. No-holds-barred racial political infighting had chased scores of experienced white officers into early retirement or other jobs and produced an embarrassing cheating scam designed to assure promotion of blacks over whites through fixed examinations. The examination scandal helped pave the way for the exit of Lee Brown's predecessor. It was a period, then, when Atlanta hardly needed more troubles or additional negative publicity.

Beleaguered authorities announced a strict 7:00 P.M. to 6:00 A.M. curfew for all children under sixteen. Mayor Jackson also announced a $100,000 reward for information leading to the arrest and conviction of the person, or persons, responsible for the murders.

Bolstered by a substantial pledge from heavyweight boxing champion Muhammad Ali and by corporate and private gifts, the reward was soon expanded to $500,000.

Costs of running the investigation, and of educating the city's children to beware of strangers, were also mounting. At one point it was estimated that the investigation was costing the city $250,000 per month.

Hollywood celebrities Sammy Davis, Jr., and Frank Sinatra headed a star-studded benefit concert at Atlanta's Civic Center that raised about $250,000 for the increasingly expensive investigation and helped to keep the effort to end the murders in the national spotlight. Pennies from school children, dollars from housewives, jealously hoarded $5 and $10 checks from prison inmates, and a $10,000 gift from actor Burt Reynolds added to the war chest. Even former Ku Klux Klan leader David Duke offered to donate a $1,400 fee for a speech at the

University of Montana to be applied to the costs of the probe. Duke explained that he was motivated to offer help because he was afraid the murders would cause "additional violence against white people, not only in Atlanta, but around the country." Mayor Jackson announced that Chicago Mayor Jane Byrne had mailed a check for $10,000 raised from concerned citizens in the Windy City. In Philadelphia, the city council adopted a resolution calling on all Americans to wear green ribbons as an expression of sympathy and concern. The National Council of Christians and Jews picked up the idea, and promoted it around the country.

Atlanta police revealed a list of names of victims believed to have died at the hands of the same serial killer or killers. The reward, they said, applied only if the person or persons responsible for murders appearing on the list was caught. The action immediately set off another round of bitter controversy, as critics loudly complained that: (1) The list did not include names of all of the victims; or (2) The list included children who could not possibly have been victims of the same killer.

The longer the list grew, the more controversial it became. Some of the victims' mothers met with the city council's Public Safety Commission committee, and soon after that, Brown announced that a special Task Force on Missing and Murdered Children had been established to assist in the investigation. The new agency eventually grew to include forty investigators from eight different police jurisdictions. Among others, the Atlanta-based national CDC at which Gregory had pointed an accusatory finger, assigned a team of epidemiologists, working with county health experts, to the job of pinpointing common denominators among the victims and compiling psychological profiles of children who could be potential targets of the killer. Mothers joined with a local minister and formed the Committee to Stop Children's Murders. The investigation had become an organizational nightmare. And still the murders continued!

Earl Lee Terrell went swimming at a public pool with a group of friends. But he was thrown out by a lifeguard after he began scampering behind some of the little girls at the poolside, and mischievously jerking down the bottoms of their suits. The frisky eleven-year-old, whose friends called him "Peanut," never returned home. But the night he vanished, a mysterious telephone call was made to his relatives by a man who said he was holding Earl in Alabama and that the family could have him back by paying $200. The stranger hung up after promising to call back with more information, but he never did.

Earl's disappearance did not immediately lead investigators to the missing youngster, but to a child-pornography ring instead. Three men, including one who lived within sight of the pool where Earl had gotten into trouble with the lifeguard, were subsequently convicted and imprisoned for their involvement in the sleazy operation. The pornographers where white, and police announced that all the boys appearing in the approximately two thousand photographs that were confiscated were also white. There was no connection between the pornography ring and the murders, authorities stressed.

But a teenager was later quoted in police reports as claiming that Earl, and another eventual murder victim, several times committed homosexual acts with one of the pornographers. And there was considerable muttering on the street that some of the other murdered boys were victimized by white adult homosexuals and pornographers.

The Atlanta child murders were now international news. New deaths were being reported on television and in newspapers as far away as Japan and Europe. Political pressures were mounting, and Mayor Jackson publicly demanded that the FBI enter the case. The agency had, of course, already done so after LaTonya's abduction.

As police launched a Kids Don't Go With Strangers campaign, new contributions to the reward fund continued to come in from business and civic groups. Prayer vigils were held in Atlanta, and in both black and white communities around the nation, seeking an end to the horror. Atlanta had become a city under siege!

More than 3,000 concerned citizens, adults and children, men and women, blacks and whites, volunteered to comb the city's garbage-littered vacant lots, ramshackle housing projects, kudzu-choked ravines, and dilapidated vacant buildings on weekends to seek out the children who were still missing and suspected victims of the killer. One of the first big sweeps yielded the pitiful skeleton of little LaTonya Wilson, abandoned in a vacant lot. It was four months after she had vanished from her bed.

Then Dorothy Allison was recruited to assist in the search for bodies of the missing children. A Nutley, New Jersey, housewife, Mrs. Allison is one of the nation's best-known police psychics, and the city agreed to pay for her travel and other expenses while she was working on the case.

At a news conference, Mrs. Allison announced that none of her "little angels" would be killed while she was in the city. "I can guarantee that he won't murder while I'm here," she promised. "I will control him." She also revealed that she had already determined that the killer was a black man from the Atlanta area. She left five days later, reporting that she had provided police with two names to check out. There were no new reports of murdered or missing children thought to be victims of the killer while Mrs. Allison was in the city, and police continued their investigation along more conventional methods.

Clifford Jones, a gregarious thirteen-year-old who had left Cleveland with his mother to begin a summer visit with his grandmother in Atlanta, was snatched off the street and strangled a few days after his arrival.

Ten-year-old Darron Glass, who had run away from several foster homes, was reported missing and added to the list. Twelve-year-old Charles Stephens and nine-year-old Aaron Jackson were the next to die.

In November 1980, the same month that voters elected President Jimmy Carter's former U.S. ambassador to the United Nations, Andrew Young, as Atlanta's new mayor, sixteen-year-old Patrick Rogers was killed. An ambitious youth, Patrick was one of fourteen children and sold newspapers to earn spending money. Shortly after Patrick's slaying, police released a composite drawing of a white man with long, stringy blond hair who was reportedly seen near the spot where the teenager's body was found.

The first names added to the list in the new year of 1981 were those of fourteen-year-old Lubie Geter, an adventurous youngster whom other teenagers were to tell police was linked to Earl Terrell and the pornography ring, and Terry Pue, age fifteen. FBI laboratory technicians obtained fingerprints from Terry's body, using a substance called Kromekote, which lifts the uniquely swirled images from patterns of skin oils picked up on a specially treated paper.

Eleven-year-old Patrick Baltazar and thirteen-year-old Curtis Walker died in February.

By March, a crazy, or a killer, was claiming to be the child slayer, sending in taunting letters written to the *Atlanta Constitution* and the *Atlanta Journal*. Someone was making similar claims in anonymous telephone calls to the minister of a church near the spot where one of the bodies of the victims was found. The letters, sprinkled with police jargon, led to widespread speculation that the killer was a policeman, or posed as a policeman to gain the children's trust.

The terror was building. Mothers sent their children outside with whistles around their necks in case they needed help. Atlanta youngsters were skipping school more often than ever before. They wet the bed, awoke shrieking with terrible nightmares about the shadowy killer they called "The Man," and huddled miserably near trusted adults with equally frightened brothers and sisters. Whites hesitated to venture into black neighborhoods, apprehensive that they would be accused of being the killer. Red-jacketed vigilantes from the Atlanta Youth Against Crime began helping police patrol the streets and shopping malls. In New York, a contingent of Guardian Angels boarded a train and traveled to Atlanta to help out. Fear was pervasive throughout the city.

The same month Ronald Reagan succeeded Georgia's own Jimmy Carter as U.S. president, fifteen-year-old "Jo-Jo" Bell and thirteen-year-old Timothy Hill died. A few days after Reagan was sworn into office, the U.S. Justice Department was ordered to take an active role in bringing the Atlanta child murders to an end. Federal funds amounting to $1.5 million were earmarked to help pay the staggering costs of the burgeoning manhunt.

Thousands of bits of information about the missing and murdered children were fed into computers at the Behavioral Science Unit of the FBI Academy in Quantico, Virginia. Information correlated and compared by the sophisticated electronic brains included descriptions of personal property of some of the victims, such as music magazines, and the fact that fragments of sheet music had been found near some of the bodies. The result was an amazing psychological profile of the killer who was so systematically slaughtering Atlanta's youngsters. The FBI advised investigators to look for a middle-aged male, probably black, who was hungry for prestige and imagined himself to be a talented musician.

Two more names were added to the list of victims but this time they were not children. Eddie "Bubba" Duncan and Larry Rogers were each twenty-one, and both were mentally retarded. Duncan's body, and that of the long missing Timothy Hill, were pulled from the chilly Chattahoochee River only twenty-four hours apart on the last two days of March.

Tempers among police agencies flared when FBI Director William Webster reported in a newspaper interview that three or four of the slayings were "substantially solved." Criticism increased and threatened to flare into a full-fledged quarrel between agencies, when Mike Twibell, the agent in charge of the FBI office in Macon, Georgia, assured a civic club a few hours later that his boss had made the statement "with the full facts behind him." Four of the twenty-three youths on the list were killed by their parents because they were nuisances, he indicated.

"There's no great crime wave sweeping Atlanta," Twibell declared. "About the same number were missing in Cthe same period ofc '78," he said. "The only difference is now the bodies are being recovered."

(No parents were ever charged in the deaths of children or young men whose slayings were investigated by the task force.)

In April 1981, when the horror had been continuing for twenty-one months, Roy Innis swept into town. Surrounded by an entourage of grim-faced lieutenants, the outspoken civil-rights leader announced at a press conference in front of City Hall that he had a photo of the killer. Innis eventually identified a young woman as his source of inside information.

The woman, who was living in Florida, then claimed

that cultists were committing the crimes as part of a grotesque scheme involving drugs, pornography, and ritualistic murder. She said her former boyfriend, a black man, had boasted to her of being involved in six of the slayings. He had kidnapped the children and turned them over to whites, who actually carried out the killings, she related.

The woman quoted her onetime boyfriend as confiding to her that he worked with a long-haired blond man. Her former sweetheart had recently threatened to murder two retarded youths, she said. She added that she had a brother who was mentally retarded and that when she learned that Duncan and Rogers had been killed, she knew she had to come forward and tell her story.

The dramatic yarn was intriguing, but the task force had already begun focusing attention on a young man who bore an amazing resemblance to the profile produced by the FBI. He was Wayne B. Williams, a bright, young media whiz and police groupie who lived with his retired schoolteacher parents, Homer and Faye Williams, in a comfortable and well-kept middle-class home in northwest Atlanta.

On the surface, Williams hardly seemed the type of man to be picked out as a suspect in the dreadful serial slayings of a score of children and young men. He was still in high school when he constructed his own low-powered radio station and operated it from the basement of his parents' home. His radio-station activities helped distinguish him as one of Atlanta's brightest young men, and won him praise in a national magazine story for his electronic genius. He had even hosted a former Atlanta mayor, a mayor-to-be, and Benjamin Hooks, who later became director of the National Association for the Advancement of Colored People, on the radio shows broadcast from the tidy home on Penelope Road.

By the time he was twenty-two, he had developed into

an articulate and industrious entrepreneur who had already built an enviable reputation as an electronics wizard, freelance news photographer, media consultant, and music producer. He was ambitious and enterprising, had a fast, inquiring mind, and despite some claims that he was spoiled, overbearing, and arrogant, he appeared to be the type of young man capable of doing almost anything he wished.

Although he had dropped out of Georgia State University after about a year, no one who knew him thought that it was because he couldn't keep up academically. L. W. Butts, his former principal at Fredrick Douglass High School, surmised in a 1981 UPI release that Williams may have left college because "it wasn't enough of a challenge."

Williams was familiar to many Atlanta police officers and journalists long before his name came up in the investigation of the child-murders. He roamed the city at night, monitoring law-enforcement activities with a police scanner to pick up emergency calls. He often beat local news-hawks to the scene of fires, accidents, and crimes, where he took photos which he later sold.

On one occasion he was arrested on a charge of impersonating a law officer after using flashing red lights while following up on a promising police call. The charge was eventually reduced to unauthorized use of emergency lights, and disposed of in traffic court. For a while, he owned a used police car.

When the task force began taking a closer look at the round-faced, bespectacled black youth, however, they developed considerable interest in his efforts to manage and produce professional recording artists. Copies of Williams' flyers citing his efforts to produce and promote musicians were found on or among the possessions of four of the murder victims. Williams had formed a black singing group called Gemini, named after his personal sign of the horoscope, which he claimed would someday be as popular as the Jackson Five. Some Atlantans believed that the killer was a kind of Pied Piper who had found a way to lure the city's children off the streets. It was suggested that perhaps Williams had enticed the children by trading on their dreams of becoming wealthy and famous musicians.

Michael Cameron McIntosh and Jimmy Ray Payne were added to the victims list in April. McIntosh, a twenty-three–year–old man described as "mentally slow," was suffocated before his nude body was dumped in the muddy waters of the Chattahoochee. Although older than the earlier victims, McIntosh was small, five feet, five inches tall and about one hundred pounds, approximately the same size as several of the teenagers believed to have fallen prey to "The Man." Despite his small stature, however, McIntosh had an impressive police record that included charges of armed robbery.

The bloated body of twenty-one–year–old Payne was also pulled from the Chattahoochee just a week after McIntosh's remains were recovered.

Again in April, the corpse of twenty-eight–year–old John Porter was discovered lying on a sidewalk in front of a vacant lot in Atlanta. He had been stabbed six times. An ex-convict, Porter was known to have held long disjointed conversations with himself, and had been kicked out of one of his homes for sexually molesting a pre-school boy. His slaying was not added to the list until weeks after his death.

In mid-May, the body of seventeen-year-old William Barrett was found lying along a roadway. He was fully clothed, had been strangled with what authorities described as "something soft, like a scarf or a towel," then stabbed in the stomach. Examination of the body determined that the stab wounds were not deep enough to have been life-threatening, and, indeed, appeared to have been made after death. Although Barrett did not exactly fit the victim profile, he was added to the task force's list because of similarities, such as gender, race, and cause of death, to the other cases. He was the sixteenth known victim to have died of some form of asphyxiation.

Finally, in the early, pre-dawn hours of May 22, 1981, investigators got the big break they had been hoping for. Three Atlanta policemen and an FBI agent were on stakeout duty in the northwest outskirts of the city at the South Cobb Drive Bridge over the Chattahoochee River when a rookie officer heard a loud splash that sounded as if something had been dropped into the water. He and another rookie, hidden in underbrush on the other side of the river, looked up and saw the lights of a car stopped on the bridge above them. One of the policemen radioed another member of the stakeout team in a chase car.

As the pursuit policeman prepared to stop the driver of the mystery car, a green station wagon, it pulled across the bridge and into a parking lot in front of a liquor store. The driver turned the vehicle around, began moving slowly back across the bridge in the opposite direction, and then speeded up. The Atlanta policeman who was shadowing the suspicious driver was joined by the FBI agent in a second car. The mini-caravan continued for nearly two miles before police flashed their emergency lights and stopped the station wagon.

Leaping from his vehicle, one of the officers ran to the green car, shouting: "Don't move! FBI! Put your hands on top of the car."

The driver slid cautiously out of his car seat. He was a light-skinned, slightly pudgy black man who appeared to be in his early twenties, was wearing glasses and had an Afro hairstyle. Following directions, he stood with his legs spread a few feet from his car, then obediently leaned over and braced himself with his hands on the roof as the lawmen flashed a light on cards in his billfold which identified him as Wayne B. Williams.

Approximately two hours later, after the arrival of other FBI agents, and a search of his car, Williams was allowed to leave. It was almost 5:00 A.M. Barely four hours later, under the direction of the FBI, dragging operations were under way along the Chattahoochee, downriver from the bridge. Officers were searching for a body.

At about the same time, two FBI agents were knocking at the door of the neat, red-brick bungalow occupied by Williams, his parents, and a German shepherd dog. The agents questioned him for about two hours. Williams later told reporters that they left after telling him they planned to return to take "samples" of possible evidence from his home. He said they rejected his offer to take the samples at that time. The task force had not yet been notified of the developments in the case.

The next day a special team of FBI surveillance experts arrived in Atlanta and began a twenty-four–hour watch on Williams. Two and a half days after the police rookie heard the mysterious splash, the swollen corpse of Nathaniel Cater bobbed to the surface of the river, a few hundred yards downstream from the bridge.

Investigators said that the location and condition of the body perfectly matched the timing of the splash, although forensic experts said the twenty-four–year-old hard-drinking laborer could have died before his corpse was dumped into the river. Surveillance of Williams was stepped up, with several cars dogging his tracks at the same time whenever he left his house. Small airplanes and helicopters were also used for backup.

On June 3, after nearly two weeks of playing cat and mouse, FBI agents took Williams into custody as he was about to make a call from a telephone booth. He was driven to FBI headquarters, his car was impounded, and a search warrant was executed on the vehicle and on his home. Williams was questioned and underwent three lie detector tests, reportedly giving several deceptive answers, before he was again released twelve hours later.

At 7:00 A.M. the same morning Williams gave an impromptu press conference in front of his house, distributed copies of his résumé, and claimed that at 2:45 A.M., on May 22, he was driving in the area of the bridge because he was looking for a woman vocalist he expected to interview in about four hours prior to a singing audition that afternoon. He explained that he wanted to locate her address before returning home. Williams vociferously denied any involvement in the murders, and angrily accused law-enforcement authorities and the press of slandering him.

Investigators later revealed that they had obtained green, yellow, and purple fibers as well as dog hairs among carpet samples, sweepings, blankets, and clothing taken from Williams' home that were similar to fibers and animal hair found on several of the victims' bodies.

At times Williams appeared to hate the constant presence of the surveillance team, while at others, he seemed to bask in the attention. Once he reportedly led an aircraft tracking him from overhead almost to the airspace over busy Hartsfield International Airport in Atlanta before it turned back. As the close surveillance continued, federal, state, city, and county officials met at the Georgia state governor's mansion to compare notes on the complex case.

Two days later, Williams was arrested and charged with Cater's murder, after playfully eluding his FBI and police tail during a high-speed romp through the darkened city. He led them to the street in front of Public Safety Commissioner Brown's house, reportedly waited for them to catch up, then honked his horn, laughed, and again speeded away. He led his pursuers past the house of Mayor Jackson before he was finally stopped and taken into custody.

First-degree–murder charges in the Payne slaying were filed against Williams a few days later. Authorities said that analysis and comparison of microscopic fibers and dog hairs taken from Williams' house and car finally enabled them to file the charges.

A suspect in the Atlanta child slayings that had held the city in a grip of terror for two years was finally in custody and facing trial — for the alleged murder of two adults.

At the trial, Williams was painted by the prosecution as a bright young man who hated his own race so intently that he had openly suggested killing youthful black males in order to eliminate future generations, and as a homosexual, or bisexual, who paid boys to have sex with him. One witness testified that Williams used derogatory nicknames to describe other blacks. Another claimed that he saw Williams and Nathaniel Cater holding hands only a few hours before the incident occurred on the South Cobb Drive Bridge. And fifteen-year-old Darrell Davis testified that Williams gave him $2 in 1980 after fondling him sexually. (Davis died in a shooting in 1984.)

Prosecutors contended that Williams also murdered for the challenge and that he revelled in his ability to outwit the massive task force put together to track down the serial killer.

One of the most devastating developments for the defendant, however, was a ruling by Judge Clarence Cooper permitting the prosecution to offer testimony about the deaths of ten other young people on the task force's list of victims, in order to establish that the slayings were part of a pattern.

Williams testified in his own defense, and hotly

denied the motives presented by the prosecution by insisting that he was not homosexual, and did not detest poor, young blacks. "I haven't killed nobody," he declared. "I haven't thought about it. I don't plan on doing it to nobody." Davis, he charged, was "a bare faced liar."

A girlfriend testified that she had engaged in sexual relations with him, a revelation apparently designed by the defense to prove that he was not homosexual. Her testimony, however, still left open the question of his bisexuality.

Williams' fiercely loyal sixty-four-year-old mother, who had retired in 1980 after nearly forty years as a schoolteacher, told the court and the jury that Wayne had been a model son. He was innocent, she said.

"Wayne's character has been drug through the mud, his daddy's character has been drug through the mud, and I been drug," she complained. "In fact, they have ruined the Williams family and they continue to lie and lie. But they have not produced evidence my son is a killer."

During the closing arguments of the exhausting nine-week trial, however, the State described Williams as a "mad-dog killer." Prosecutor Gordon Miller stressed the importance of the fiber matchup from the bodies of the victims and items found in the defendant's home. The combination defied odds of one in 150 million, he claimed, and was "so significant as to amount to a signature, just as if the defendant had signed his name on the death warrants" of the victims.

Defense Attorney Al Binder insisted that his client was innocent and "the most misunderstood man I ever met." He ridiculed the idea that Williams could hurl a 140-pound body such as Cater's over a bridge railing without a long struggle.

"Look at him," Binder demanded. "This pudgy, fat

little boy. Do you think there's any muscle here?'' the lawyer scoffed, punching Williams' arm. "And they say he's sinister.''

The jury was apparently unimpressed. The panel of eight blacks and four whites found Williams guilty of both counts of murder, and Judge Cooper ordered two consecutive life sentences.

Three days after the jury verdict, police announced that although he was not charged, Williams was responsible for twenty-two more of the serial slayings. It would have been a waste of time and taxpayers' money, as well as an unnecessary security risk to try a man already serving twin life sentences, authorities claimed.

Yet, despite the convictions and official police insistence that Williams was the main killer of Atlanta's children and young blacks during the terrible twenty-two months, not everyone, including some of the victims' relatives, is convinced he is guilty.

Some mothers still believe there was a police cover-up and their children died either at the hands of a ring of vicious homosexuals who may have used the children in pornographic and "snuff" movies, or of a dope ring that employed the youngsters as couriers before eliminating them.

As late as November 1985, a high-powered team of attorneys filed for a new trial, charging that Williams was the victim of a "massive miscarriage of justice." Lawyers cited hundreds of newly uncovered police documents, and named the Ku Klux Klansman investigated years earlier, and members of his family, as possibly being connected to at least one of the murders.

Civil-rights lawyer William Kunstler, who was once Martin Luther King's private counsel, claimed fears of racial violence may have caused black city officials to conceal Klan information and to unfairly target Williams as a scapegoat. Kunstler was joined in the bid to reopen the case by the mothers of nine of the victims, by Harvard Law School Professor Alan Dershowitz, and by black author James Baldwin.

Abby Mann, who produced a television docudrama *The Atlanta Child Murders*, provided additional high-profile support when he appeared with Kunstler and others at a press conference promoting the bid to reopen the case. And Chet Dettlinger, a criminal-justice analyst and former assistant to the Atlanta Chief of Police, co-authored with Jeff Prugh *The List*, a comprehensive study of the murders which criticized handling of the case and strongly recommends another, closer, look.

In early 1987, Fulton County District Attorney Lewis Slater rejected angry demands by parents and other relatives of thirteen of the victims to reopen the case. "We tried Mr. Williams in 1982 on the two strongest cases we had," he said.

Meanwhile, as others continue to grapple with the complex riddle created by the horror visited on Atlanta's children, the man who was convicted — of the murders of two adults — and was publicly blamed by authorities for twenty-two other slayings in the series, is serving his life sentences at the Georgia State Correctional Department's Classification and Diagnostic Center in Jackson.

CHAPTER 11

THE VANCOUVER BUTCHER

CLIFFORD ROBERT OLSON

(1980-1981)

Twelve-year-old Christine Weller had been missing five weeks when her pitifully mutilated body was found on Christmas Day.

The fresh-faced pre-teen from the quiet suburb of Surrey, just south of Vancouver in Canada's ruggedly beautiful province of British Columbia, had been viciously stabbed and slashed to death.

Law-enforcement authorities were unaware of it at the time, but Christine's death was the first in a series of savage sexual assaults and brutal murders that would claim the lives of at least ten more girls and boys from the Vancouver area and lead to one of the most damned and widely publicized investigative decisions in the proud history of the Royal Canadian Mounted Police.

But the bitter wrangle was still months in the future as police from Surrey and nearby Richmond, where the girl's body was found, began the painstakingly detailed homicide investigation.

The probe of Christine's murder was still under way

more than four months later, on April 16, 1981, when another Surrey girl, thirteen-year-old Colleen Daignault, walked out of a friend's house to go home. She was never seen alive again by her friends or family.

Less than a week later, Darren Johnsrud, a sixteen-year-old boy from Saskatoon in the province of Saskatchewan who was visiting relatives in the Vancouver area, vanished from a bustling shopping center. His body was found on May 2, dumped in a wooded area. His skull had been fractured.

On May 19, sixteen-year-old Sandra Lynn Wolfsteiner of suburban Langley hitchhiked a ride in a gray car. She was never seen alive again.

Thirteen-year-old Ada Court, who lived in the town of Coquitlam, had just finished baby-sitting at the house of her brother and sister-in-law on June 21 and was walking home when she dropped out of sight.

If police from the various communities in and around Vancouver were starting to put together the disturbing spate of child-disappearances and the as yet unsolved murder of Christine Weller as part of a deadly pattern, Simon Partington would have been blissfully unaware of their suspicions. The carefree, shaggy-haired nine-year-old had his mind on other things as he hopped on the bicycle his parents had given him on the same day that Christine's body was discovered, and pedaled away from his house in Vancouver to return a book he had borrowed from a neighborhood chum. Later that afternoon, after he had failed to return home, Simon's worried mother telephoned police.

A woman who was questioned by police recalled seeing a youngster who looked like Simon talking with a husky, heavyset man, apparently in his early thirties. A report from another witness placed the boy at a Surrey shopping center where he was seen pushing his bicycle and walking alongside a rugged man about thirty to thirty-five years old who was wearing blue jeans and a t-shirt. Police also learned that several children had found Simon's prized bicycle, abandoned.

The witnesses' descriptions of the man seen with Simon were so rich in detail that a Vancouver Police Department artist made a composite drawing of the stranger. And fliers were widely distributed in the Vancouver area, carrying a description of the missing boy. Within the next few weeks, police logged more than three hundred telephone calls from concerned citizens who thought they had seen Simon, the stranger, or the two together. Despite the calls, as well as the inclusion of experienced RCMP investigators into the rapidly expanding search, authorities were unable to turn up the boy, his suspected abductor, or a body.

In early July, fourteen-year-old Judy Kozma was waiting at a bus stop near her home in suburban New Westminster when a van with a man and a teenaged boy inside stopped and the driver offered her a ride. Although cautious about accepting rides from strangers, Judy had met the driver before at a fast-food restaurant where she worked as a cashier. When he offered her a job washing windows for $10 an hour, the industrious girl was so excited about the prospect of such a well-paying part-time job she climbed inside the van. A few minutes later, at the driver's insistence, the teenaged boy was dropped off.

Judy never returned that night to the home she and her family had just moved into a few days earlier. But four nights later, on July 13, the building manager was awakened by a telephone call. The woman couldn't make out a message, only a tiny voice that appeared to be whimpering or moaning on the other end of the line. It sounded like young Judy Kozma, whose family was so new in the building they didn't yet have a telephone. The building manager telephoned police.

On July 25, the mutilated nude body of a dark-haired girl was discovered in Weaver Lake near the town of

Agassiz in the Frazer Valley. She had been stabbed nineteen times, and the remains were so badly decomposed that it was four days before the girl was identified as the missing Judy Kozma.

Two days before Judy's body was found, Raymond King vanished. The fifteen-year-old boy was last seen at his home in New Westminster after telling his father that he was going to the Manpower Youth Employment Office to look for a summer job. His rapidly decomposing remains, also stripped of clothing, were found about two weeks later, dumped along the shoreline of Lake Weaver, not far from where Judy's body was abandoned.

The day after Raymond's corpse was recovered, distraught parents of some of the missing children got together to produce 10,000 posters. "Our Children Are Missing — Yours Could Be Next," they cautioned.

Seeking the missing children, their remains, clothing, or other clues, a team of more than twenty policemen and tracking dogs combed a sealed-off area around rugged Lake Weaver. A police diver scoured the lake bottom, but when the massive search was finally called off, the effort had failed to yield a single clue.

RCMP officers and local police departments from Vancouver and the Lower Mainland communities of Agassiz, Burnaby, Coquitlam, Langley, Maple Ridge, Mission, and New Westminster gathered in the city to compare notes and map out a new strategy. They hoped a more coordinated effort would stop the killings and bring the sinister butcher of Greater Vancouver's children to justice.

The RCMP also asked law-enforcement agencies in the United States and Great Britain for tips on any available new police technologies in use in their countries which might be helpful in the investigation. They were told there was nothing that could be done that they weren't already doing.

A reward fund totalling $16,000 was collected and

helped generate hundreds of tips and leads from the public, which were being followed up. A family friend of one of the suspected victims also appeared on the Canadian television network's popular "Canada AM" program, calling for federal funds to help in the increasingly desperate search for the dreaded child-killer.

During a press conference, an RCMP spokesman confirmed that the three bodies recovered since the first of the year had each been stripped of clothing. Decomposition of the bodies of the two girls was so far advanced that it had not been possible to determine if they had been sexually molested. Forensic experts were still checking the boy for evidence of sexual abuse.

But a hiker had found ripped pieces of female clothing in a wooded area of Whistler Mountain, north of Vancouver. And a brassiere was recovered in nearby Maple Ridge. "The slacks had at least one cut from the crotch to the cuff," RCMP Superintendent Bruce Northrop revealed to the press. He added that the shirt was also shredded. Search teams, including dogs, returned to the Whistler Mountain area. Police helicopters were also pressed into the search, combing both the Whistler and the Agassiz valleys.

Known sex offenders throughout the Lower Mainland had been tracked down and interviewed and Superintendent Northrop said the probe was the largest he had witnessed in nearly thirty years with the RCMP.

Deputy Chief of Police Ed Cadenhead, of New Westminster, told newsmen that it was believed one person was responsible for the chilling string of disappearances and child-murders.

"In this case we think we're dealing with a guy who doesn't care about the age or the sex of the victims," he remarked. "We've got guys incarcerated who are like that. They're just weird."

Nevertheless, it had not yet been proven that a single individual was responsible for all the slayings and disappearances. Each case was, therefore, handled as a separate investigation, and evidence was shared with a special team of analysts who were making comparisons and seeking similarities that might link up the murders.

Information gathered in the wide-ranging effort to solve the grim mystery was being fed into a police computer. Included in the data was a roster of everyone in British Columbia, both children and adults, who had been reported missing and still hadn't turned up since the first of the year.

It wasn't announced to the press, but the investigative team was already focusing much of its attention on a burly, bearded ex-convict who in the twenty-five years since his seventeenth birthday had piled up an impressive rap sheet with ninety-four convictions ranging from fraud to armed robbery and vicious sexual offenses.

Born as a New Year's baby in 1940, Clifford Robert Olson grew up in the picturesque Vancouver suburb of Richmond, where four decades later the tragically mutilated body of Christine Weller was found. For most of his life Olson had been in trouble. Years after he had left the schoolyards for the exercise yards of provincial prisons and the cramped idleness of local lockups, Olson's former teachers remembered him as a liar, con artist, and thief. His onetime schoolmates and fellow cons remembered him as a mean-tempered bully, strong and scrappy enough that for a while he was believed to have serious potential as a professional boxer. Professional fighting, however, requires discipline and the ability to work smoothly with managers and trainers, characteristics Olson lacked.

He didn't get along any better in prison than he did on the outside. Behind the bars, he had an unenviable and dangerous reputation as a homosexual rapist and informer whose thin lips curled in a perpetual sneer. While in protective custody at the British Columbia

Penitentiary he helped fellow inmate Gary Marcoux write vivid descriptions of the rape, murder, and mutilation of a nine-year-old girl. Then he testified in the sensational trial, at which the incriminating letters were used to convict Marcoux of the lurid sex-slaying.

As a free man, Olson continued his informant activities, sandwiching his surreptitious meetings with police officers between fitful work as a carpenter and other more unsavory activities.

Olson was living with his wife, Joan, and infant son, Clifford, in an apartment in Coquitlam when he became an official suspect at a meeting of detectives and officials from several agencies on July 15. He had married the forty-year-old mother of his son four days before the Wolfsteiner girl was killed.

Investigators had begun taking a close look at the unsavory career criminal after the owner of a Coquitlam restaurant and popular teenage hangout notified local police that an athletic-looking man with a ragged, dark beard had asked her to round up a couple of girls for a job cleaning windows in his apartment. He promised to pay $10 an hour. The stranger had previously claimed that he also had work for boys, but every time she sent a youth over to the apartment, the job offer was suddenly withdrawn. Suspicious of the dubious employer, and protective of the youngsters who frequented her business, the woman refused to pass on the plea for window-washing help to any of the teenaged girls she knew.

The stranger returned one day, however, and asked two girls who were already in the restaurant if they wanted to work for $10 an hour. Excited about the appealing job offer, they left with him. But later they confided to the restaurant owner that they had stopped off for a beer with their affable companion, then left him after he tried to get too cozy. The stranger was Clifford Olson.

Officers shadowing Olson quickly learned that he had highly suspicious habits. He drove for hours, restlessly patroling streets and highways and stopping frequently to try to pick up girls. At other times he led them to other policemen, whom he conferred with briefly, once passing on information about drug dealing before taking off again.

A couple of days after the surveillance began, Olson gathered up his wife and son, and drove them south across the U.S. border through Washington and Oregon to Knotts Berry Farm near Los Angeles. He was back home a few days later and, while the chain of surveillance was broken, killed Raymond King. Then he killed Sigrun Arnd, Terri Lynn Carson, and Louise Chartrand.

It was near the end of July when the parents of Sigrun, an adventuresome eighteen-year-old West German tourist who was hitchhiking to Vancouver to visit friends, heard from her for the last time. Weeks later, dental charts mailed from West Germany confirmed that she had become a victim of the depraved serial killer. She was murdered on July 25, the same day Judy Kozma's remains were found.

Then Terri Lynn Carson left her home in the same Surrey apartment building where Christine Weller had lived. She had talked with a neighbor about applying for a job in a pet store in a Surrey shopping center. Instead the fifteen-year-old became another of Olson's victims.

On the day that Terri was last seen by her family, police had resumed their surveillance of Olson, but it was too late for the unfortunate teenager. She had been picked up, murdered, and her body dumped a short distance from where the bodies of Raymond King and Judy Kozma had been found.

But the surveillance was in time to rescue two other girls from Olson, who along with a couple of other men, had picked up the teenagers and was plying them with alcohol. It was shortly after midnight when cautious officers moved in to break up the party and arrest Olson. He was out of jail again by 3:00 A.M., and drove away into the early-morning darkness, temporarily free of his police tail. Police later claimed that there had been no point in following him at that time, because the street-wise suspect would have known they were watching.

On July 30, seventeen-year-old Louise Chartrand dropped from sight after setting out from her home in Maple Ridge to hitchhike to work. The shredded pieces of clothing found in the Whistler Mountain area belonged to her, but no other trace of her was turned up.

Olson appeared in court on July 31, then left for Calgary, in the neighboring province of Alberta.

When he came back to the Vancouver area, a week later, a crack, full-time RCMP surveillance team picked up his trail. There would be no more breaks in the surveillance, but for nearly a week, the peripatetic wanderer did nothing that would help tie him to the child-disappearances and -murders. Police were so anxious not to alert Olson to their shadowy presence that they silently permitted him to break into a house near Victoria, without making any effort to stop the crime in progress or to make an arrest.

They finally moved in and made an arrest, sooner than they had wanted to, after Olson picked up two girls who were hitchhiking on Vancouver Island. The arresting officers considered the girls to have been in grave danger, and authorities were forced to temporarily settle for charging the murder suspect with impaired driving.

But the discovery in Olson's rented van of an address book containing the name of Judy Kozma provided an important piece of circumstantial evidence, and Olson was charged with first-degree murder in her slaying. The address book also contained the names and telephone numbers of several of Judy's friends, and some of the teenagers had reported being frightened by mysterious calls from a sinister stranger who threatened them with death and sexual abuse.

Authorities were concerned about the lack of witnesses, however, and about the scarcity of other evidence. With only the material then in hand, some were convinced that the chances of obtaining a conviction at a trial would be touch and go.

Six days after he was jailed, Olson began talking about making a deal. He wanted a guarantee that if he was convicted of murdering the missing children, he would be permitted to serve his sentence in a psychiatric hospital instead of a penitentiary. He was well aware that even men who have committed some of the most vicious crimes imaginable hold a special loathing for child-molesters and child-killers. Murdering or injuring a child-molester or child-killer can be considered an important symbol of prison status, and for their own protection sex criminals who prey on children are usually isolated from other inmates.

During Ontario's bloody Kingston Penitentiary riot in 1971, a gang of inmates raged into a protective cell-block for sexual offenders and dragged thirteen screaming convicts outside. The sex criminals were tied to chairs, then savagely beaten with iron bars and clubs, and slashed and stabbed with knives. Two child-molesters died from the dreadful assault, and others were scarred for life.

When an attorney advised Olson that police were not empowered to make a deal involving sentencing, Olson then switched his demands from protection to money. The suspect suggested he would help investigators find the bodies of the missing children — in return for payments to his family for every body found. It was a proposal that the Mounties considered more favorably.

An RCMP report that was later revealed in *Maclean's* magazine pointed out: "The prime consideration in recommending the $100,000 plan was to locate the bodies which would be solid evidence necessary to prove that Olson was indeed responsible."

The proposal included payment for details about the slaying of four youngsters whose bodies had already been recovered, and $10,000 each for the remains of six youngsters who were still missing. Although personally repulsed at the idea of paying a bounty to the family of a child-murderer in order to recover the bodies of his victims, Allan Williams, British Columbia's Attorney General, nevertheless researched the law and determined that the agreement would be legal and would not endanger prosecution. Then, reluctantly, he approved the proposal.

Williams was later quoted in the *Maclean's* article as saying he wanted to "put to rest the uncertainty and grief that parents of the children were experiencing and to give the victims a Christian burial."

The federal government agreed to provide some $75,000 of the total amount promised, based on a federal-provincial cost-sharing plan for the RCMP.

At the cagey criminal's insistence, the money was placed into a trust account for his wife, Joan, and their infant son, with $10,000 to be released each time a body was recovered. He was taking no chances that the RCMP negotiators, or other officials, would go back on their word after he had led search teams to the remains of his victims and withdraw the ransom. Once the details surrounding the method of payment had been ironed out, the killer began keeping his part of the bargain.

As Olson led search teams to the shallow graves in isolated peat and cranberry bogs, thick forests, abandoned gravel pits, and logged-over timber land, he recounted the slayings in vivid detail. He appeared to relish the opportunity to relive, in the presence of grim-faced witnesses, the last moments of his terrified victims as he exercised the awesome power of life and death over them. While he tramped through a forest of tree stumps near Surrey, leading a small posse of lawmen in a search for the remains of Colleen Daignault, he boasted about how he slashed the frightened teenager's clothing off with a knife, then raped her. He explained that he was drunk when he carried out the savage sexual assault, and afterwards smashed her skull with one bone-crushing blow from a hammer.

At other times he bragged about picking up girls and plying them with rye whiskey and sodas. From talking with girls whose lives he had spared after raping them, and from pathology reports that disclosed traces of chloral hydrate in the bodies of girls who were not spared, investigators already knew that he sometimes laced the drinks with knockout drops, potent enough to fell a strong man.

Olson was charged with ten counts of first-degree murder and his trial began on January 11, 1982, in Vancouver, before Justice Harry McKay. According to a later report in *Maclean's* magazine, Olson's attorney, Robert Shantz, planned to cite his client's involvement in the notorious Marcoux case as part of the defense. It was believed that the lawyer would contend that Olson had become so obsessed with the method of the child's sex-and-mutilation slaying that his own behavior had been affected. At the request of Shantz, five psychiatrists examined Olson, and they determined that he was a psychopath.

But on the third day of the trial, Olson surprised courtroom observers who had been predicting an insanity defense and were looking forward to weeks of fascinating legal drama, by abruptly changing his plea from innocent to guilty to eleven counts of murder. The guilty plea included one more murder count than he had been charged with, the slaying of Sandra Wolfsteiner. Her murder had not been included in the original charges because of the inability to positively identify her remains from the small number of bones recovered.

The man who had so callously snuffed out the lives of eleven children and young women, piously claimed that he wanted to spare further anguish, not only to his own family but to the heartbroken families of his victims. Justice McKay sentenced him to eleven concurrent life terms in prison, which according to Canadian law, would enable him to become eligible for parole in twenty-five years. Canada abolished the death penalty in 1976, five years before Olson's murderous outburst began. The Justice sternly observed that it would be "foolhardy" to ever again permit Olson to become a free man, and added that no punishment "a civilized country could give you" would be adequate.

On the same day, the RCMP's unprecedented $100,000 deal with Olson was publicly revealed for the first time. The revelation created a furor in the nation's press, and cries of outrage some 2,500 miles away in Ottawa where Parliament was in session. Highly placed government authorities were criticized for permitting the RCMP to participate in the deal, and politicians, legal experts, and private citizens complained that a ghastly precedent had been established. They claimed a clear message had been sent to criminals that murder could be profitable. There were calls for a federal inquiry, and even Shantz, Olson's own attorney, publicly labeled the deal as morally and legally wrong, as well as "politically insane."

Defenders of the controversial plan countered that without Olson's paid-for cooperation some of the bodies might never have been recovered. They added that if there had been no deal, there might not have been enough evidence to convict Olson of more than a single second-degree–murder count. He could conceivably have gotten away with a mere ten-year prison sentence after fatally stabbing, strangling, or bludgeoning eleven youngsters.

Federal Solicitor General Robert Kaplan, however,

claimed in an Associated Press article that police had sufficient evidence to convict Olson without agreeing to the ransom payments for the bodies. But he added, "There was no attempt to purchase a plea of guilty. What they were buying was peace of mind for those families who didn't know whether their children were dead or alive."

Walter Baker, one of the most vociferously outspoken critics of the Olson payoff and a Progressive Conservative MP, railed in Parliament: "To set up a kind of criminal entrepreneurship as a substitute for police investigation is something that cannot be tolerated."

There were other criticisms of the investigative agencies as well. How, it was asked, could Olson be picked up four times in four months, twice for sexual assaults, without police realizing he was the most likely suspect in the agonizing string of child murders?

The debate continued to rage after Olson, jealously guarding a fat scrapbook filled with clippings about his gruesome crimes, was transported to the Kingston Penitentiary to begin serving his life sentences. A confidential RCMP report was disclosed, revealing that the Mounties had at one time considered taking back the money after the bodies were recovered. The plan, however, had been abandoned because of legal considerations.

The controversy eventually landed in the courts when the parents of some of the victims filed suit to have the money recovered and distributed among the families. Justice William Trainor of the British Columbia Supreme Court issued a judgement upholding the petitioners. The judgement was overruled by the British Columbia Court of Appeals, however, and as of this writing attorneys for the petitioning families of the victims were planning to continue the fight in the federal courts.

CHAPTER 12

THE KING OF THE ONE-NIGHT STANDS

DOUGLAS DANIEL CLARK AND CAROL BUNDY

(1980)

Douglas Clark liked to call himself "The King of the One-Night Stands." And because he was drawn to matronly, overweight, and lonely women for his long-term relationships, he never ran out of willing females.

For shorter, more violent affairs, he liked the teenaged prostitutes and runaways with slender, still developing bodies whom he found along Hollywood's notorious Sunset Strip.

When Clark met Carol Bundy, the skinny, fast-talking lothario with the winning ways swept the plump, middle-aged vocational nurse off her feet. It seemed like a match that had been arranged in Hell.

A lonely diabetic, on the rebound from a torrid romance that had gone sour, Carol was an easy conquest.

Ironically, she and Doug met in a country-music bar where her old flame sang in a tenor voice that betrayed the Down Under accent he had brought with him from his Australian home.

Known as "The Australian Cowboy," John Robert

Murray was blessed with curly hair and rawboned good looks that made him no slouch in the romance department. A former Australian Army officer who came to the United States with hopes of becoming a new Tom Jones, Murray quickly learned that he was going to have to settle for much less. He did his singing on a part-time basis at the Little Nashville roadhouse in North Hollywood, and took a full-time job as an apartment-building manager.

It was at the apartments that he met Carol. She had just packed a suitcase, picked up her five- and eight-year-old sons and moved into the apartment complex to get away from a husband who, she complained, beat her. She suffered from cataracts that were so severe, she had to walk with a white cane. And almost from the first moment she met the Australian Cowboy, she knew she had to have him for her own.

She began deliberately clogging her kitchen sink, stuffing tissue into her toilet, doing anything she could think of to provide an excuse to lure the handsome building manager to her apartment. The ploys worked, and it wasn't long before the plump nurse and the curly-haired Australian were lovers.

He even took her to the local Social Security Office, where she was declared legally blind, and became eligible for $620 monthly Social Security checks. Then he took her to an eye doctor who fitted her with contact lenses that improved her sight so much she was able to discard the cane and function almost normally.

Carol was mesmerized by the charming Australian. The only fly in the ointment was the fact that he was married. When she tried to change that by offering to pay his wife to agree to a divorce, her world came tumbling down. Murray had no intention of getting a divorce, and by approaching his wife, Carol had ruined any chance of keeping their backstreet relationship going. He suggested that Carol move out of the building.

Devastated by the collapse of her romance with the handsome Murray, she found another apartment a few miles from her old home. She was still grieving over her loss three months later when she met Doug Clark at the Little Nashville. Clark, who worked as a boiler-room engineer at a Burbank soap factory to finance his bar-hopping and womanizing, moved in with her the same night.

Carol quickly found herself buying and cooking his food, washing his clothes, and providing transportation when he chose to use her car instead of his motorcycle. But the extra work was worth it for the nights she spent with Doug in a dizzy whirl of romance and passion.

If Murray hadn't been any slouch in the romance department, Doug was unbelievable, according to the bedazzled matron who bragged about her new lover's talents in the bedroom.

He had acquired plenty of practice. The son of a retired U.S. Navy admiral, Clark had romanced a succession of frowzy, desperate females whom he lived off. He was never very concerned about the physical appearances of his women, so long as they cared for his needs. And the sexual needs of the young man, who had been secretly wearing women's underclothes since childhood, were growing increasingly demanding — and weird. Even Carol's enthusiastic response to his frenzied lovemaking wasn't enough to satisfy all his twisted sexual desires. She grudgingly learned to accept his outrageous behavior when he took off every night or so, tom-catting along Sunset Boulevard in Hollywood, or trolling for young prostitutes.

She listened patiently as he talked animatedly of his bizarre fantasies about sex with the bodies of freshly murdered girls.

Fighting her rising jealousy, she dutifully snapped photographs when he brought home compliant teenaged girls who performed oral sex with him. On one occasion he brought home an eleven-year-old girl he found roller skating in a parking lot, and the thirty-seven–year–old mother meekly accepted his sexual activity with a girl young enough to be her own child.

And finally, she showed the same loyal acceptance of her boyfriend's kinky ways, when he proudly exhibited the bodies of two female hitchhikers he said he had just killed. He boasted that he had already had sex with the corpses.

Not only a sexual satyr who couldn't get enough of women, Clark was also a necrophile who gloried in having sex with dead bodies. In Hollywood, where an army of pimps, pornographers, and degenerates prey on the youngsters who have congregated on the streets desperately seeking adventure, fame, or love, casual violence, gross sexual abuse, and murder are not uncommon occurrences.

Every year troubled teenagers show up on the squalid streets, become known to a small circle of acquaintances who share their misery and degradation, then drop from sight. Many are never seen alive again. And every year the broken bodies of young runaways and prostitutes are found in the hills and gullies surrounding Hollywood, where they have been abandoned as carelessly as garbage.

Peopled by gawking tourists by day, the glittering Sunset Strip metamorphoses at night into a cesspool where child-whores of both sexes are repeatedly bought and sold for a few dollars each. Just about anything is available for a price, and degenerates flock there from all over the country to take advantage of the fleshly delights. But murder and necrophilia are unacceptable behavior, even on the Strip.

Police first became aware that they had a murderous sexual sadist on the loose when the bodies of two young step-sisters were found. Pretty fifteen-year-old Gina Marano, and Cynthia Chandler, a pixyish blue-eyed blonde who was a year older, were the victims. The teenagers were discovered on June 12, 1980, sprawled alongside a freeway off-ramp near Hollywood. Both girls had been shot — Gina in the head, Cindy through the heart.

The girls were identified two days later when a detective telephoned Los Angeles police with information about two teenagers who were missing from their Huntington Beach home. They had left without permission approximately two weeks earlier, shown up on the Strip, and quickly developed reputations among their peers as swinging party girls.

In the early pre-dawn hours of June 24, the corpse of a chunky young woman was found slumped behind a steakhouse in Burbank. Nearby residents told investigators that less than an hour earlier they had heard a woman screaming.

About 9:30 the same morning, a man found another female body in an alley as he was emptying his garbage. The grisly cadaver had no head. It wasn't until three days later that a resident of the same neighborhood stopped his car at the entrance to his driveway because an ornate wooden box was sitting in front of his garage. Irked at the idea of someone using his drive to dispose of their trash, he climbed out of his car, walked to the box, peered inside — and gasped. A severed human head was inside, carelessly wrapped in a pair of girl's bluejeans. A bullet was imbedded in the skull.

As if a decapitated head were not ghastly enough, the grisly trophy looked as if it had been scrubbed with a detergent after it was cut off. The pale flesh had been made up with lipstick, eye shadow, and other cosmetics, and it had been frozen solid, possibly by placing it in a refrigerator or freezer. The baffling case was becoming more macabre by the hour.

Careful comparison of severed bones, muscles, and flesh by skilled pathologists with the Los Angeles County Medical Examiner's Office disclosed that the head matched the body found earlier.

Homicide investigators fanned out along Sunset Boulevard and other areas frequented by street people, talking to pimps, whores, runaways, and shopkeepers. It wasn't long before they located a pimp who told them that two of his girls were missing, and he hadn't seen them since the night of June 23 when they were working the Sunset Strip. Their real names weren't learned until about a week later when the FBI provided an official report.

The decapitation victim was Exxie Wilson, a pretty, slim twenty-one–year–old streetwalker. The girl found in the alley was twenty-year-old Karen Jones, also an experienced prostitute. The women had found their way to Hollywood from Little Rock, Arkansas, after a vice crackdown in the southern city. The more attractive of the two friends, Exxie had been picked up more than twenty times for loitering and other prostitution-related offenses.

Ballistics tests showed that the bullets taken from the corpses of all four of the victims were apparently fired from the same small-caliber gun. The evidence was a clear indication to police that the same mad killer was responsible for all the deaths.

The Hillside Strangler killings (see Chapter 15) that raged through the Hollywood-Glendale area had ended less than two years before, and police and private citizens became suddenly aware that another madman was loose in their midst.

And like the Hillside Strangler horror, elements of the killer's behavior led police to briefly wonder if one of their own men could be mixed up in the slaughter.

A Hollywood woman contacted police a couple of weeks after the double slaying of the Huntington Beach teenagers and reported that she had met and befriended the girls at a party in Laurel Canyon in April. She said she felt sorry for Gina because she was so young, and gave her phone number to the girl so she could call if she ever needed help.

In June, she said, a man telephoned her late one night and identified himself as a Lieutenant Douglas Clark of the Los Angeles Police Department. He coolly advised her that he had killed the two girls, as well as some teenaged hookers he picked up on the Strip and shot in the head as they performed oral sex on him. He told the horrified woman that she was next on his death list.

Quick scrutiny of police records in Los Angeles and surrounding communities failed to turn up any Douglas Clark on their personnel rosters.

Area newspaper reporters, television commentators, and radio broadcasters were already talking of a vicious new killer they had nicknamed the "Sunset Slayer," when the next body turned up. The dead girl was identified as Marnette Comer, an adventurous seventeen-year-old runaway from Sacramento. She had last been seen by friends in Hollywood on June 1, when she had simply vanished from the streets. A band of snake-hunters stumbled across her mummified remains in an isolated ravine in the San Fernando Valley.

Marnette had been shot four times in the head with a small-caliber gun, and her stomach was slit open in what homicide investigators perceived to be an effort to hasten decomposition.

The ladies' man was on a sex-and-murder binge and his dumpy girlfriend was hopelessly caught up with him in the crazed round of lust, slaughter, and necrophilia. Doug drove Carol to the freeway off-ramp where he had dumped Gina and Cindy, and proudly showed her the bodies.

One afternoon while her boys were away visiting relatives, Carol returned home and found a woman's severed head on the kitchen counter. Her kinky lover had just taken it out of the refrigerator.

"Doug just laughed," she later recalled. He instructed her to play with it and to put fresh cosmetics on the cold lips and eyes.

"We had a lot of fun with her," Carol admitted. "I was making her up like a Barbie with makeup."

After they tired of playing with the cosmetics, Doug took the grisly trophy into the shower with him, and used it for sex.

But his favorite game was to pay a prostitute for oral sex in the front seat of his car, and just as he was reaching a sexual climax, shoot her in the head. He always stripped off the victim's underwear later to save as a trophy of the kill. Usually, he had sexual intercourse with the cadaver.

Doug bragged to Carol about killing and decapitating Exxie, then running Karen down and shooting her to death on a Burbank street. He thought it was amusing that Exxie's head was rolling around in the car trunk while he pursued her frightened girlfriend.

He boasted to Carol that he despised whores and loved killing them. To make the job easier and convenient, he kept a killing bag in his car, which contained a knife, rubber gloves, and plastic sacks. The murders, he confided, were merely a matter of "taking care of business."

And just in case Carol might ever entertain thoughts of betrayal, Doug threatened to kill her boys if she ever testified or provided evidence against him.

Carol was still head over heels in love, however, and in July she willingly began riding with him while he patrolled the Strip in his car, looking for unwary prostitutes or naive runaways to sexually abuse and kill. On one occasion they picked up a girl, and Carol handed Doug a gun which he used to shoot the teenager through the head. Months later a body was recovered near Tuna Canyon. Street sources informed police that the victim was apparently a girl they had known briefly as "Kathy." Acquaintances on the Strip can be vague and fleeting, and no one could — or would — provide a last name.

On another occasion Carol was cruising with Doug when they enticed a girl into his car at a shopping-center parking lot. Moments later the shrieking teenager pulled free of them and plunged to the pavement, writhing in pain and fear. Although she was bleeding from twenty-seven stab and slash wounds, somehow she lived. The car screeched out of the parking lot as shocked shoppers ran to the girl's assistance.

Sometimes when Doug was prowling the Strip, however, Carol took off on her own and stopped in at Little Nashville to have a beer with her old flame. She apparently talked too freely at one of those cozy get-togethers, because Murray told her he thought her new live-in beau might be tied to the Sunset Slayings everyone was discussing, and he was thinking about taking his suspicions to the police. Still deeply in love with Doug, Carol couldn't stand for that. So she arranged a midnight meeting outside the club with the loose-lipped singing cowboy.

A few minutes after midnight Carol, who was carrying a boning knife and a gun, slid into the passenger seat of Murray's van, and he drove away from the darkened parking lot outside the club.

Four days later the decomposing corpse of the Australian Cowboy was found inside his van, which was parked on a street only two blocks from Little Nashville. He had been stabbed in the chest, his buttocks laid open with deep slashes, and he'd been decapitated. Carol later said she had tossed his head into a ravine, but despite a search, it was never found.

All the sordid sex, violence, and gore was beginning to tell on the nurse, however. She had been trained in a career that focused on saving or prolonging lives, and easing pain. But since meeting Clark, her life had become twisted, and she now found herself dealing in violent death.

While on a coffee break at a convalescent hospital in Burbank where she worked, Carol suddenly burst into tears, turned to her nursing supervisor and screeched: "I can't take it anymore. I'm supposed to save lives, not take them."

The floodgates had opened, and Carol continued to blubber on, becoming hysterical as she related the dreadful murders, told how she had killed for the man she loved, and bewailed the need to save the lives of innocent young girls. Her supervisor did her best to calm the hysterical woman, and suggested she take the rest of the day off. Then the supervisor notified the police.

That afternoon a detective knocked on Carol's door in suburban Van Nuys. He had barely stepped inside when she blurted out that the man police were looking for as the Sunset Slayer was her boyfriend, Douglas Clark. If the startled lawman had had any serious doubts about her statements, they were dispelled a few minutes later when she picked up a photo album and showed him pictures of her lover being fellated by teenaged girls.

Clark was arrested at his job in the soap factory where officers found a .22-caliber handgun hidden in the boiler room. Ballistics tests indicated that five of the Sunset Slayer victims were killed with bullets fired from the weapon. A search of his apartment also turned up bloodstains which were matched by laboratory technicians with Gina Marano's type O blood.

Clark stubbornly refused to submit to questioning about the Sunset slayings. But his remorseful girlfriend was continuing to talk, and providing important answers to questions that had been baffling police since the gruesome string of killings began.

Even case-hardened homicide investigators, who long ago had grudgingly accepted the sordid happenings in the seamy Hollywood sexual underground, shook their heads in disgust as she recounted the lurid tale.

At first Carol denied any active personal involvement in the slaying of the girls, but she did admit to the killing and beheading of her old boyfriend.

"I did it for Doug," she told investigators. "I loved him."

Carol was jailed on charges of murdering Murray. Later she was named on additional charges in the slaying of the young woman whose corpse was found near Tuna Canyon, and in the stabbing of the Hollywood woman in the supermarket parking lot. Clark was charged with counts of first-degree murder in the deaths of each of the six girls and young women considered to have been victims of the Sunset Slayer.

Even in prison, the curious charm of the self-proclaimed "King of the One-Night Stands" continued to attract women. A fifteen-year-old girl who had seen him during one of his court appearances began visiting him in jail, and writing lurid love letters to him. He wrote back to her and the bizarre courtship continued until Carol got wind of the romance and mailed her own letter to the love-smitten teenager. The girl stopped writing and visiting Clark, and dropped from sight.

But it was only a few months later that a new exchange of love letters began between the accused serial killer and a slim beauty who was, herself, behind bars for attempted murder. The press had nicknamed Veronica Lynn Compton "The Copycat Strangler," after she attempted to garrote a woman in a botched effort to prove that her jailed sweetheart could not be one of the notorious Hillside Stranglers who terrorized the Glendale-Hollywood area for nearly two years.

Clark read about Veronica's arrest and wrote an admiring letter to her, prompting a torrid romance by mail. The correspondence, which featured morbid references to necrophilia, blood, mutilation, and murder, had to be one of the strangest ever conceived by lovers anywhere.

By the time Clark came to trial he was ready with his own imaginative version of copycat killings. Acting as his own attorney until that privilege was withdrawn as a result of several bitter exchanges with Judge Ricardo A. Torres, Clark claimed that Carol and her old lover, Murray, had murdered the girls and patterned the slayings after those of the notorious serial killer Theodore Bundy. (Theodore "Ted" Bundy, who is no relation to Carol, was known as the "Love Bite Killer." He was sentenced to be executed in the electric chair at the Florida State Prison at Starke, after conviction in the first-degree murders of two college coeds at Florida State University in Tallahassee, and of a twelve-year-old Lake City junior–high-school girl. He is also a suspect in a string of murders of young women during the mid-1970s in Washington, Oregon, Utah, and Colorado.)

The jury wasn't that easily bamboozled by the fast-talking gigolo, however, and on January 28, 1983, returned verdicts of guilty to six counts of first-degree murder with special circumstances. Clark's former sweetheart, Carol, was the state's star witness against him.

During the penalty phase of the proceedings, the cocky killer was permitted to present his own opening statement. Strutting before the jury box, he arrogantly announced that he was appointing himself the thirteenth juror — and voting for death. "We have to vote for the death penalty in this case," he declared. "The evidence cries out for it."

The real twelve-member jury agreed, and on February 11, recommended that Clark be sentenced to death in the gas chamber at the California State Prison at San Quentin for the Sunset slayings.

Carol originally pleaded innocent by reason of insanity. But on the day jury selection was to begin for her trial, she changed her plea to guilty of murdering Murray and the unidentified prostitute. Carol said she was "sort of half-way in love" with Murray, and they had had sex in the back of his van before she shot him in the head. Then, she confessed, she decapitated him and hid the skull so the bullet wouldn't be found.

Lamely explaining that because she had fallen in love with the charming maniac who overwhelmed her with sex, the contrite murderess confirmed that she also had helped Clark kill the prostitute. She cried as Judge Torres imposed the maximum sentence of twenty-seven years to life on one count of murder and twenty-five years to life on the other. He ordered the sentences to be served consecutively.

CHAPTER 13

LIKE FATHER, LIKE SON

GERALD ARMAND GALLEGO, JR., AND CHARLENE GALLEGO

(1978-1980)

When Gerald Gallego, Sr., was twenty-six years old, he became the first man to die in Mississippi's new gas chamber for one of two slayings he was convicted of committing.

But when his son, Gerald, Jr., was sentenced to death following a series of grisly murders in California and Nevada, he had surpassed even his late father's notorious record.

Gerald, Jr., and his pregnant wife were the focus of a nationwide manhunt before they were captured and jailed as suspects in the savage slayings of nine teenaged girls and women, and of one young man — who was the escort of a pretty female the killer wanted for himself.

The elder Gallego was a hardened nineteen-year-old convict in California's San Quentin Prison when his son, Gerald, Jr., was born. After his release from San Quentin, he left California and made his way to Mississippi where he soon got into trouble again. While being booked into a local jail, he disarmed the turnkey, took him hostage, and killed him.

The brutal cop-killer was quickly recaptured but while behind bars once again, he and a companion engineered another breakout. He tossed lye in a guard's face, and then stomped the blinded correctional officer to death. Tracked down by bloodhounds and recaptured, the elder Gallego remained securely behind bars this time until his execution.

Gerald, Jr., was nine years old in 1955 when his father was led into the gas chamber to pay the supreme penalty for the guard's murder. The third-grade student had believed his father already dead, of injuries suffered in an accident, and was unaware that shortly before his father's execution he had written a contrite letter advising other young people to avoid the criminal life that had led him to the gas chamber.

Despite his father's last-minute regrets and advice, it was barely a year after his execution before his son was on his way down the same dead-end criminal trail. It almost appeared as if young Gerald was determined to prove he could be an even more vile and savage killer than his brutal father.

A series of minor scrapes with the law led to his incarceration at the age of thirteen when the California Youth Authority had him locked up for engaging in sex with a six-year-old neighbor girl. It was the beginning of Gallego Jr.'s almost non-stop troubles with the law, mostly caused by his unholy appetite for sex, sadism, and violence.

By the time he was thirty-two years old, he had been married seven times, twice to the same woman. Some of the unions were bigamous and his seventh wife, Charlene, was one of those whose claim to the title of Mrs. Gallego was muddied by a previous marital knot he had neglected to sever. Her background was almost the exact opposite of her husband's. She had grown up with a supportive, loving family and her parents were upright, honest citizens, respected by their neighbors and associates in Sacramento, California. Yet, despite her proper background, Charlene fell in love with the troubled ex-convict, who was the son of an executed cop-killer. And she accepted his favorite nickname for her, "Ding-A-Ling," and considered it a term of affection.

She also accepted her mate's macabre fantasy of obtaining a virginal young woman he could keep in a private hideaway as a sex slave forced to cater to his every twisted desire.

Such strange sexual compulsions would have been inconceivably foreign to seventeen-year-old Rhonda Scheffler and her sixteen-year-old school chum, Kippi Vaught, when, on September 11, 1978, they set out in the Scheffler family car for a Sacramento shopping mall — and vanished.

Neither of the girls had been having the type of family or school difficulties that often make unhappy teenagers run away. Both were well behaved and trustworthy, and when their car was found abandoned in the shopping-mall parking lot the fear that had initially surrounded their disappearance turned to dread.

Two days later, the bodies of the girls were discovered near the town of Baxter, about fifteen miles east of Sacramento. Rhonda and Kippi had been shot in the head with a .25-caliber pistol, and the heads of both victims had been badly beaten with a blunt object. Marks on their wrists indicated they had been bound with tape, and examination of the bodies by pathologists confirmed that each of the girls had been sexually abused. The examination also indicated that the instrument used to batter their heads could have been a tire iron.

Witnesses who had seen the girls at the shopping mall were located, several possible suspects were questioned but cleared, and the investigation bogged down.

Then, on June 24, 1979, about one hundred miles northeast of Sacramento, in Reno, Nevada, teenagers Brenda Judd and Sandra Kaye Colley disappeared from the crowded midway at the Washoe County Fairgrounds. Brenda, fifteen, and Sandra, fourteen, were from the nearby town of Sparks, and had been attending the annual county fair. Witnesses were located who reported seeing the girls near a van at the fairgrounds, but despite hundreds of manhours spent by tireless police investigators, efforts to track down the missing teenagers were fruitless and no solid suspects were found who could be linked to their disappearance.

On April 24, 1980, seventeen-year-old Stacy Ann Redican and Karen Chipman-Twiggs vanished from another Sacramento shopping mall. As in the case of the Scheffler and Vaught girls, police considered Stacy and Karen to be unlikely to have run away, and the case was treated as a suspected double abduction.

Their families' worst fears were confirmed a few short months later, in July, when picnickers in the badlands some eighty miles northeast of Reno stumbled across two shallow graves. The badly decomposed bodies of two young women were buried a few inches under the earth.

Postmortem examinations and medical records indicated the remains were those of Stacy and Karen. Their skulls had been crushed by savage beatings with a hammer or similar metallic object.

There were now two separate homicide cases involving four girls apparently abducted in mid-day from busy shopping centers, and viciously bludgeoned. But the Sacramento police had little else to connect the cases which were nine months apart and in totally different areas.

Then on June 6, 1980, Linda Teresa Aguilar was reported missing by her boyfriend. The five-months-pregnant twenty-one-year-old had been hitchhiking from Port Orford, Oregon, where she lived with her boyfriend, to Gold Beach, thirty-five miles south, along the rugged Pacific coast.

Miss Aguilar's badly decomposed remains were discovered in a shallow grave a few miles south of Gold Beach on June 22. The hands and feet of the corpse were still tightly bound with yellow nylon rope.

The postmortem examination revealed that her skull had been shattered in several places by heavy blows from a hammer-like object, possibly a crowbar. More shocking still, the sand found in her mouth, throat, and windpipe, indicated that the pregnant young woman had been buried alive.

There remained little reason, however, to connect the ghastly slaying of the young mother-to-be to the other abductions and murders. Only the bludgeoning of the victim's head, her disappearance during the daylight hours, and the careless disposal of her body in a hastily dug, shallow grave indicated any possible connection to the other cases. All the other victims had been teenagers, abducted in pairs from locations crowded with other people, and none of them had been pregnant.

The profile of the next victim in the three-state binge of sex and savagery was as bafflingly untypical as that of the last.

In the short space of time it would have taken thirty-four–year–old Virginia Mochel to walk from the door of the West Sacramento bar where she waitressed, to her parked car, the pretty mother of two vanished. She seemed to have disappeared into thin air, until her corpse was discovered three months later, a few miles outside Sacramento. She had been naked when she was buried, and her arms were still tied behind her back with fishing line.

Witnesses at the bar remembered seeing Mrs. Mochel talking for some time with a couple who behaved as if they were married. The man appeared to have been feeling his drinks and showing off. The woman with him, described as good-looking and quiet, had apparently been content to let her voluble companion do most of the talking. One witness recalled that the man had said something about being a bartender.

Police were still following up leads in the Mochel case three months later when pretty Mary Beth Sowers and her fiancé, Craig Raymond Miller, were kidnapped at gunpoint from a parking lot.

Both serious students, the engaging young couple attended California State University in Sacramento, where Craig had been named Man of the Year in 1979. On Saturday night, November 1, the couple attended a Sigma Phi Epsilon Founder's Day Dinner at the Carousel, a posh Sacramento restaurant. They had been looking forward to a bright future together. Instead, they found horror and violent death.

Mary Beth, radiantly beautiful in a formal gown, and Craig, at his handsome best in a gleaming tuxedo, walked out of the restaurant together a few minutes after midnight. They were in the parking lot when a grim-faced woman whose stomach bulged prominently approached them. Pointing a handgun at the young couple, she ordered them to climb into the back seat of a 1977 Oldsmobile. A scowling, dark-complexioned man was hunched in the gloom of the passenger side of the front seat.

A student friend of Craig's who had witnessed the ominous confrontation hurried to the car to ask the college students if they were all right. The man in the front seat growled a warning for the student to leave, but before the youth could react, the woman rushed at him and slapped him hard across the face. Then she ran awkwardly around to the driver's side, slid behind the wheel of the vehicle, and screeched the car out of the parking lot with the two terrified captives huddled together in the back seat. The shaken college student quickly memorized the car's license number, then ran for help.

Police fed the number obtained by the alert student into the California Motor Vehicle Registration computer bank system. A few minutes later, they had the name of the owner, twenty-four-year-old Charlene Gallego, of Sacramento.

Unknown to investigators at that time, after the car sped out of the parking lot, the driver headed onto Highway 50 and drove to nearby El Dorado County. There, after leaving the highway, the woman pulled the car to a stop in an area well hidden from passing traffic and secluded from homes and businesses. Her companion now ordered Craig to get out of the car and to lie face down on the road. As the man was holding a gun on him, the student had no choice but to comply, and obediently, the frightened youth stretched out on the road surface. A moment later, the gunman fired three shots point-blank into his head. The horror was now over for Craig, but it was just beginning for Mary Beth.

Sobbing, she huddled helplessly in the back seat, as the woman drove back to a Sacramento apartment. Mary Beth was harshly ordered out of the car at gunpoint and shoved inside. The gunman pushed the hysterical coed into a bedroom. Unmoved by the muffled cries and sobs that came from behind the door, his woman companion patiently waited in the front room as he raped the girl.

After he had finished with her, Mary Beth was returned to the car and driven to a cow pasture near Loomis, a few miles outside Sacramento. Still wearing the remnants of her torn evening gown, Mary Beth was dragged from the car, and roughly hurled to the ground. Gallego then fired three bullets into her head.

Because nearby residents had heard the gunfire, Craig's body was found at about 11:00 A.M. the day he was shot. Meanwhile, Sacramento police were interviewing Charlene Gallego at her residence. She conceded that she owned the car, but denied that she knew anything about the reputed abduction of two college students. She explained that because she had been drinking heavily the night before, she didn't remember anything she had done, nor, she claimed, did she recall being with a man.

Because the incident was being treated as a missing-persons complaint at that stage of the investigation, police left her at the house. A short time later, when they received word from authorities in El Dorado County that Craig's body had been found, they hurried back to Charlene's home, but both she and her Oldsmobile were gone.

Investigators learned that Mrs. Gallego was seven months pregnant, and although she had not been living with her husband for a while, she had been with him the previous evening. His name was Gerald Armand Gallego, Jr., and he worked as a bartender at a local nightspot. Police fed Gallego's name into a computer, and were rewarded a few minutes later with a rap sheet identifying him as a vicious, lifetime criminal who was a sexual deviant and who could be extremely dangerous. Among the long list of arrests and convictions on his record were the armed robbery of a motel, a jail escape, and various sex offenses. Authorities in California's Butte County were holding a warrant for his arrest on charges of child-molestation, rape, and incest.

Acting on the assumption that the fugitive couple had crossed state lines, the FBI now entered the case, and a nationwide manhunt was initiated. Meanwhile, unsure if the twenty-one–year–old coed was alive or dead, police were still searching desperately for Mary Beth Sowers.

As the manhunt continued, authorities found Charlene's Oldsmobile abandoned in Reno, and she was traced for a time to Salt Lake City, Utah. Then police were tipped off by people in Sacramento that she had contacted them and requested they send her $500 at a Western Union Office in Omaha, Nebraska. Both Charlene and her husband surrendered without a struggle when they were confronted by police as they walked into the office to pick up the money. The couple waived extradition, and a few days later they were returned to California where they were locked up in the El Dorado County Jail.

At their arraignment, the Gallegos pleaded innocent to charges of murder and abduction. They were ordered held for trial, without bail. The next day, exactly three weeks after she was kidnapped, Mary Beth Sowers' remains were found in the cow pasture by a couple of boys. Earlier, searchers had just missed finding the body when a psychic had led them very near the location.

Charlene loyally stood by her husband. In January 1981, while still in jail, she gave birth to a son, whom she named Gerald, Jr., and he was turned over to relatives to raise.

But as the investigation and court hearings dragged on and Charlene remained locked away from her domineering mate, she finally agreed to testify against him. Even though the law protects confidentiality between husband and wife, she qualified to take the stand against him because she was not legally married. The union was not valid because he had not divorced his sixth wife when she became the seventh Mrs. Gallego.

A plea-bargain agreement was arranged between Charlene's attorneys and law-enforcement officers in three states. It provided that she plead guilty in the murders of the college sweethearts and testify against Gallego in any and all trials that might be scheduled for crimes he was suspected of committing and that she had knowledge of. In return, she would receive a fixed prison sentence of sixteen years and eight months in the Miller-Sowers case, and a concurrent term of sixteen years and eight months on second-degree murder charges in Nevada—and immunity from further prosecution.

Once Charlene agreed to talk, she unfolded an odyssey of horror that authorities say helped clear up ten baffling murders in three states.

Charlene described herself as a willing lure used by her husband to entice young women into his van whenever he decided that it was time to hunt for a new victim, a pretty girl who would be so frightened and intimidated by him that she would agree to become his sex slave.

Usually, said Charlene, she enticed the girls with offers of marijuana to get them close enough to the van so that Gallego could show his pistol and force them inside. She explained that the vehicle had a bed in the rear compartment, where Gallego, using his physical strength and the gun, forced the girls to give in to his perverse demands. Charlene said she would sit quietly in the front seat while the women and girls were raped, sodomized, forced to perform oral sex — and sometimes killed.

She described in graphic detail the kidnapping, sexual abuse, and murders of Kippi Vaught and Rhonda Scheffler, as well as the murders of Sandra Colley and Brenda Judd. But despite several trips into the desert near Lovelock, Nevada, to look for the bodies of Sandra and Brenda, she was unable to lead police to the shallow graves she said her husband had buried them in.

Charlene went with investigators to the site where the remains of Stacy Ann Redican and Karen Chipman-Twiggs were hidden, and admitted holding a pistol on the horrified teenagers while her husband sexually abused them. Detectives and prosecutors also listened in grim silence as she described the horrid murder of Linda Aguilar, who was buried alive in a grave that she said Gallego scooped out for her with a hubcap.

While Charlene was providing investigators with lurid details of the sex-murders Gallego was accused of committing, he was reportedly planning to bust out of the Sacramento County Jail. Authorities said the scheme collapsed when jailers discovered two homemade knives he planned to use in the escape.

Gallego's trial for the murders of Craig Miller and Mary Beth Sowers began in December 1982, and lasted three and one-half months. He represented himself as his own defense attorney. Now contrite, and angry at her former lover, Charlene, who was on the stand eleven days, sometimes broke into tears under his brutal cross-examination. But she stuck to her story about his obsessive search for the perfect love slave.

She testified that Gallego preferred petite, pretty girls with light hair like hers and had a fantasy about establishing a hideaway in a cellar or woods where he could keep young women to use sexually whenever he pleased.

The jury deliberated four days before returning verdicts of guilty to two counts of first-degree murder under special circumstances, and two kidnapping counts. The penalty phase of the sensational trial took almost another month to conclude, but the jury required only two hours of deliberation before recommending that the defendant die in California's gas chamber.

During the penalty phase of the proceeding, Charlene told the jury that Gallego killed Linda Aguilar and the woman bartender in West Sacramento. Gallego was not prosecuted in those murders, however, and he was not prosecuted in the slayings of Kippi Vaught and Rhonda Scheffler. Authorities decided to avoid unnecessary and expensive multiple prosecutions and to try only the strongest cases in states which provided for capital punishment. Oregon, where Linda Aguilar was murdered, has no death penalty.

Despite being the location of some of the most blood-curdling murders in the United States, however,

California has not carried out a death sentence since 1967, thanks largely to the state's liberal higher courts which consistently sided on appeals with death-row prisoners. Authorities in more conservative Nevada, where Gallego was accused of slaughtering four young girls, had no reason to believe that the wheels of justice would move any faster or more surely for him than they had for other notorious killers languishing on death row at San Quentin Penitentiary. So they extradited him to stand trial on murder charges in Nevada where the latest execution had been carried out in 1979.

After careful study, authorities decided not to put him on trial for the Sandra Colley–Brenda Judd murders because failure to recover the bodies seriously weakened the case.

But when prosecutors prepared for Gallego's trial in the murders of Stacy Ann Redican and Karen Chipman-Twiggs, one of the most curious situations in the history of American jurisprudence resulted.

Pershing County, Nevada, where the bodies of the girls were recovered and where they were presumed to have been slain, is sparsely populated and the cost of a long drawn-out murder trial could be a devastating burden to taxpayers. A series of Nevada newspaper editorials criticized California's liberal higher courts, and in a blistering column Stan Gilliam of the *Sacramento Bee* wrote: "Residents of Nevada's Pershing County are understandably concerned that the $60,000 projected cost of the trial will wipe out a third of the county's annual budget. There must be 59,999 other Californians besides me happy enough to see Gallego in the clutches of no-nonsense Nevada to send a dollar to help the cause," he wrote.

More than $23,000 was donated to help with the trial cost, most of it from Californians disgusted with their own court system which they were convinced was too easy on vicious killers.

In Orangevale, California, a father of three mailed $20 and a note. "If you have any funds left over, you might consider sending a Nevada judge to California for the purpose of teaching our addle-pated Appellate and Supreme Court justices enough law to try a chicken thief," he suggested.

Another thoughtful donor sent two $5 chips from a Lake Tahoe, Nevada, gambling casino.

"Keep him in Nevada. Hang him by his toes and everyone take a shot. I'm surprised and disgusted with lawyers in California. Kill him good and done," said another note from a contributor who sent $5.

"I hope this will help hang that SOB (not very ladylike) to the first and nearest tree," wrote a furious Sacramento woman who contributed $2. "Happy Valentine Day from an old lady who still believes in frontier justice."

Again, Charlene Gallego took the stand against her husband, and recited the sordid details of ten grisly murders she insisted were committed by her husband in his ugly sex-slave quest. Testimony about the eight other murders, in addition to those of the two Sacramento girls, was permitted by the court in order to establish that there was a distinct pattern in the sexually motivated slayings.

Charlene told the jury that she had lured the two girls to the van with the promise of marijuana, and that she had watched while Gallego raped them. She then related how he had taken them into the desert west of Reno and beat them to death with a hammer he had bought expressly to use as a murder tool.

The jury returned double verdicts of guilty to first-degree murder in each of the slayings, and of guilty to kidnapping of each of the girls. The same jury decided that the penalty for the murders should be execution by lethal injection and ordered life terms without parole for the kidnappings.

A California judge dismissed the charges against Charlene for the Sowers and Miller slayings. In a thirteen-page decision, he said he considered her plea to be invalid because the plea-bargaining agreement had been rejected by the state Board of Prison Terms.

The agreement in Nevada was accepted as valid, however, and she is serving her sentence there at a prison in Carson City for her part in the slaying of the Chipman and Redican girls.

CHAPTER 14

THE "RIPPER"

RICHARD COTTINGHAM

(1977-1980)

Someone was terrorizing and slaughtering the hookers along the seedy Times Square vice strip.

Forlorn young prostitutes who walk or ride away with strange men they have never seen before have always been easy prey for killers with a deep-seated hatred of women. But the depraved butcher who was prowling Manhattan's notorious open-air cesspool of sex and crime was committing murders so savage that even the hardened whores and pimps who populated its garish neon-lit streets were horrified.

It was firemen who were called to battle a blaze in a West 42nd Street hotel in December 1979, who discovered two of the madman's most gruesomely mutilated victims.

The first fireman into the smoke-filled room crawled across the floor toward a vaguely visible figure lying on a bed, pulled it down bedside him, and laboriously dragged it back to the hallway. He was preparing to give the victim, a nude young woman, mouth-to-mouth resuscitation, when he realized that she had no head. The hands had also been severed.

After the fire was extinguished, the nude body of another young woman was found on a second bed. Like the first victim, she had been decapitated and her hands neatly removed. Both bodies had been stretched out on the beds and a flammable liquid, possibly lighter fluid, poured between their legs, then set on fire. The buttocks of the women were severely burned, but the flesh on their bare torsos and arms and legs was untouched by the flames.

The missing body parts were never found, but the clothing apparently worn by the women when they entered the death room was found neatly stacked in a bathtub.

Eventually one of the victims was identified through x-rays as a known prostitute, twenty-two–year–old Deedah Goodarzi, a beautiful, dark-eyed Long Island high-school graduate, who was born in the Mideastern nation of Kuwait.

The mother of an infant, Deedah was known to her customers as Sabina or Jacqueline. She had been named on criminal charges of prostitution and theft in upstate New York and in California, had worked in a massage parlor in Atlantic City, and had walked the streets of Times Square for her pimp.

The second victim, who appeared to be younger, was never identified.

Word of the grisly discovery quickly spread through the streets of the west-side meat rack, and hookers hugging the doorways of the massage parlors, fleabag hotels, and sex arcades conversed about the murders in frightened whispers. They talked apprehensively about the well-dressed, sadistic johns who lured girls to motels, gave them drinks or dope, then became nasty and violent. And rumors flashed through the vice area about freaks who tied or handcuffed girls, then beat and cut them, or abused them with a variety of devices ranging from matches to pliers and electric shock. Pimps muttered ominously but helplessly about what they would do to the lunatic who was scaring and butchering their women. Some of the girls resolved to use only hotels where they were well known, and others vowed to study their tricks more carefully or to work in pairs.

Most of the girls and their pimps believed there was an almost certain tie between the shocking new killings and the gruesome slaying of the popular red-haired streetwalker they had known as "Bouncey." Bouncey, whose real name was Helen Sikes, was a pathetic product of foster homes, a teenaged runaway from California who had found her way to Times Square and become a prostitute. Until she had disappeared from the streets the previous January, she worked an area of Eighth Avenue near the hotel where the two decapitated bodies were later discovered.

Her horribly mutilated remains had been dumped in the nearby borough of Queens. The nineteen-year-old girl's legs had been chopped off and carried about a block away where they were neatly laid out, as if the body was still attached. Her head had been nearly severed from her body by someone using the same surgeon-like skill as that used to decapitate the two later victims.

Detectives from Manhattan and Queens were also comparing notes on the grisly prostitute killings. All three girls were white, about the same age, and at least two, and possibly all three, were prostitutes who worked the Times Square area. And fine straight lines scratched into the flesh of their backs indicated they could have been tortured prior to their deaths. Eventually, it was determined that the victims of the grisly twin killing had been strangled.

Despite the fear spread by the killer, whom journalists and street people were beginning to refer to as a new Jack the Ripper, there was no noticeable slowdown in the busy sex-for-sale trade in Times Square. And months after the shocking crime, hardworking investigators had no suspects lined up.

Then, on May 15, police were confronted with the mutilated body of another prostitute. Mary Ann Reyner, a beautiful veteran hooker, was found slashed and stabbed to death a few blocks from Times Square in a 29th Street hotel that she frequently used. Her breasts had been severed by someone whom investigators said had slowly and skilfully sliced them off. Then the killer set her body on fire. But Mary Ann Reyner wasn't the only prostitute from the Manhattan vice area who had met up with a deadly trick since the double slaying of Deedah Goodarzi and the unidentified girl. It was just that Manhattan police were not yet aware of it.

A teenaged hooker known as Shelly Dudley had been found strangled to death in a motel room in Hasbrouck Heights, New Jersey, across the George Washington Bridge from the area of Manhattan where she had climbed into a stranger's car. On May 4, a horrified motel employee had found the naked and brutally battered body of the girl stuffed under a bed.

The pieces of the baffling series of prostitute murders didn't begin to fall into place until about 9:00 A.M. on May 22 when a police patrolman was summoned to investigate a report of a woman screaming at the same New Jersey motel.

Several people were frantically gesturing as the officer pulled his squad car into the parking lot. Reaching for his shotgun, he pulled to a stop and leaped out. Hurrying to the rear entrance to the motel, he pushed open the door. Moments later a man carrying what appeared to be a small black handgun almost ran into him. Faced with the grim policeman holding a shotgun levelled at his chest, the stranger meekly gave up his weapon and permitted himself to be handcuffed.

Inside the motel room, a maid was already trying to

comfort a hysterical teenaged girl in handcuffs who was huddled on the bed, covered only by a sheet.

She blurted out a tearful story. She had arrived in New York only a few days before from the West Coast and was immediately picked up by a sweet-talking black pimp who lured her to an apartment and then forced her to become a prostitute, she sobbed. She said she had been on the street less than a week when she met a trick who wined her, dined her, and drove her to the New Jersey motel.

They were barely inside the room, when the john dropped his guise of friendly concern and turned into a sadistic monster. The man, who only a few minutes before had been promising that after they had sex he would help her to escape from her brutal pimp, hand-cuffed her, slashed her with a knife, bit her breasts until they bled, beat her with a belt, raped and sodomized her, and forced her to perform oral sex.

After enduring hours of agonizing pain and helpless terror, she managed to grab his pistol. When she threatened him with it, she related, he merely snarled and kept advancing toward her. She pulled the trigger, but the gun refused to fire, and a moment later her assailant had thrown the shrieking girl on the bed and began assaulting her. It was then that her screams were heard by a motel maid.

The bondage, torture, and perverse sexual assaults the sobbing girl had been submitted to were startlingly similar to the obscene abuse that had been meted out to the girl murdered at the motel only three weeks earlier.

The dead prostitute had also been brutally beaten, and her breasts had been bitten so savagely that one nipple was nearly ripped off. When her bruised and naked body was found, she was still handcuffed and her mouth was taped shut. Laboratory tests of seminal fluid disclosed that she had been used vaginally, anally, and orally a short time before she died.

The gruesome death of the young hooker, however,

hadn't been the first unsolved murder to take place at the motel. In December 1977, a guest at the motel had discovered the dead body of a local woman, a lovely twenty-six-year-old nurse named Maryann Carr.

The attractive onetime high-school cheerleader worked for a physician and had been married to her business-man husband only fifteen months when she was apparently abducted. Her hands and feet had been tied, and her lungs had collapsed when she had been either smothered or choked to death.

It now appeared that the police could have a hot suspect for more than one slaying. But no one realized just how many killings would eventually be solved as a direct result of the startling developments that occurred at the motel on that eventful May 22 morning.

The myopic and sullen suspect was identified as Richard Cottingham, a thirty-three-year-old husband, and the father of two small boys and an infant daughter. Residents who lived near the white Cape Cod-style house in Lodi, New Jersey, where he resided with his family considered him to be a model neighbor who, although courteous, appeared to place a high value on his privacy.

He was equally respected at his workplace in Manhattan, where he was a computer operator with Blue Cross-Blue Shield of Greater New York. During his thirteen years with the company he had compiled an unblemished work record.

But beneath all the surface respectability there was an air of mystery to Cottingham's life, and investigators were soon unraveling some of his darkest, most jealously kept secrets.

When he was apprehended at the motel he was carrying a damning collection of implements in a leather briefcase. Three sets of handcuffs, a black leather mouth gag, two black leather slave collars with chrome studs, and several vials of pills were among the contents. The pistol which he had tossed away turned out to be a non-working replica of a real handgun. A search of his pockets turned up a switchblade knife, and a key to the motel room that held the frightened, sobbing girl.

Armed with a search warrant, detectives entered his home and retrieved a treasure trove of evidence: female clothing, purses, cosmetics, and jewelry were found in Cottingham's private bedroom, which some investigators referred to as the suspect's trophy room. Pimps for some of the dead prostitutes identified clothing and other items that had belonged to their women. A rich store of pornography featuring young women being tortured and held in bondage was also confiscated from the hideaway.

Police and the press learned that the month before Cottingham's arrest, his wife had filed for a divorce. She accused her husband of spending almost no time or money on his family, of "extreme cruelty" toward her since their wedding in May 1970, and of discontinuing sexual activity with her at the end of 1976.

The divorce papers indicated that he was known to frequent Plato's Retreat in Manhattan, a well known sex club for mate swappers. "The . . . attraction of Plato's Retreat is the potential for sexual activities and the potential for changing of sexual partners," it was claimed in the divorce papers. A short time after Cottingham's arrest, his wife withdrew the divorce proceedings.

Court records were also turned up by police and newspaper reporters, disclosing that Cottingham had been arrested twice in the early 1970s for alleged offenses involving prostitutes. Both cases were dismissed, and the records sealed.

A few hours after Cottingham had been arrested and placed in a cell in Hasbrouck Heights, he smashed his glasses and used one of the razor-sharp slivers to cut a deep gash in his left wrist. He was treated at a local hospital and transferred to the larger Bergen County Jail.

The next day he was arraigned on a charge of the attempted murder of the fledgling hooker whose screams had brought the world crashing down on him. Bail was set at $250,000.

Soon, Cottingham was facing a staggering series of charges ranging from murder and kidnapping to various sexual assaults and drug offenses. And journalists were describing him as a strong suspect in the baffling Times Square torso slayings. Sensational news stories painted him as a depraved Jekyll-and-Hyde character who spent his days as a decent citizen, and his nights stalking prostitutes whom he would torture and mutilate to fulfil his sick sexual fantasies.

Among the most serious charges were the first-degree murders of: Valerie Street, the real identity of the nineteen-year-old prostitute tortured and strangled in the Hasbrouck Heights motel, and whom authorities had previously known by her street name, Shelly Dudley. She had gotten in trouble for a prostitution-related offense in Miami and moved to Manhattan only a few days before she was murdered; Deedah Goodarzi and the unidentified woman who were the twin victims of the torso slayings in Manhattan; Mary Ann Reyner, who was strangled and had her breasts cut off, before her body was set on fire; Maryann Carr, the vivacious and pretty nurse whose puzzling slaying had stymied police for nearly two and a half years.

Cottingham was never officially linked to the equally baffling torso slaying of the unfortunate Manhattan prostitute known as "Bouncey." As of this writing, that case is still unsolved.

He was, however, tied to other serious assaults on women, including two prostitutes and a housewife, who escaped with their lives only after enduring nights of sheer horror and agonizing torture.

Charges of kidnapping, sodomy, rape, robbery, and assault were filed against Cottingham for an attack on a four-months-pregnant, nineteen-year-old Manhattan streetwalker who had been brutalized by a crazed sexual sadist in October 1978. The girl told investigators that she had a few drinks with a john she had met on the street, and the next thing she remembered was woozily regaining consciousness as he beat her with a rubber hose. She again lapsed into unconsciousness and the next time she revived, he was gone. Her jewelry, purse, and clothing had been stolen, and she was crumpled naked on the floor of a South Hackensack, New Jersey, motel room bleeding from the breasts, mouth, vagina, and rectum.

Cottingham was also charged with the abduction and vicious assault and rape during the previous month of a pregnant twenty-two-year-old housewife and waitress. She said she had stopped in a bar for a drink when a stranger sat down beside her and began to chat. A short time later, after he had bought her a drink, she began to get woozy and the man enticed her into his car, drove her to New Jersey, burned her breasts, robbed her, and finally threw her from the moving vehicle. She was found unconscious and was hospitalized for several days.

Cottingham was also charged with kidnapping a twenty-seven-year-old prostitute who told police she was picked up, drugged, and brutalized before she was tossed unconscious into a vacant lot in Teaneck, New Jersey. The woman said she was robbed of her purse and jewelry, and her breasts were bitten until they bled.

The sandy-haired suspect wasn't taking his incarceration at all well, and before the criminal cases pending against him were disposed of, he made three more apparent suicide attempts. The most sensational of the suicide capers occurred in a packed Manhattan criminal courtroom when he suddenly jumped to his feet, pulled a razor from beneath a bandage worn since slicing a wrist the previous week, and slashed wildly at his other wrist while shrieking, "I'm innocent! I'm innocent! It's wrong!"

A day earlier the boyfriend of one of the murdered women had punched Cottingham in a hallway before startled guards could push the furious man away from their prisoner.

Cottingham also made a spectacular break for freedom during an earlier court appearance, pulling away from guards as he was being led unfettered into a Bergen County courtroom and leading them on a mad footrace down three flights of stairs, out a door and into the street. He was surrounded by officers and recaptured without a struggle minutes later.

Despite his disruptive shenanigans the fiendish killer remained securely behind bars for more than four years while an exhausting series of motions and trials proceeded resolutely through the courts of two states.

During the investigation and trials, Cottingham's ugly secret life was traced by former girlfriends and co-workers, by investigators, and by victims who had suffered through his dreadful assaults — and lived.

Two nurses testified that they had dated him, but neither indicated that she had been abused or ever put in fear of her life. One of the women told of love trysts with Cottingham at the same Hasbrouck Heights motel where the two young prostitutes had been tortured, and one killed. And a former co-worker told of remarks by the defendant, claiming that nurses were especially free with their sexual favors. Cottingham, it appeared, equated nurses with prostitutes.

The accused "ripper" slayer appeared for his first trial on twenty separate charges related to offenses allegedly occurring in New Jersey. A jury convicted him of fifteen of the twenty counts, including the murder of Valerie Street, and a variety of other charges of kidnapping, sex crimes, and drug or controlled-substances offenses. Not guilty findings were returned on attempted murder and aggravated assault charges tied to the non-fatal attack on the prostitute in the Hasbrouck Heights motel room. He was also found not guilty of kidnapping the twenty-seven-year-old prostitute who said she was brutalized and dumped in Teaneck, New Jersey, and not guilty of anal sodomy of the pregnant street-walker. The judge dismissed a charge of raping the same woman, because of lack of evidence.

Approximately six weeks after the verdict was returned, Cottingham was sentenced to from 173 to 197 years in a New Jersey state penitentiary.

A year later when he was tried in Bergen County for the slaying of Maryann Carr, he was found guilty of second-degree murder and sentenced to from twenty-five years to life in prison.

Cottingham was brought from the maximum-security New Jersey State Prison, at Trenton, to New York to be put on trial again in 1984, this time for the decapitation slayings of the three hookers killed in Manhattan. At the conclusion of the five-week trial, the jury deliberated only seventy minutes before returning verdicts of second-degree murder in each of the deaths. He was sentenced to serve another seventy-five years to life in prison.

During the lurid proceedings, the prosecutor described the defendant as a Jekyll-and-Hyde, and as an angel of death who had a lust to kill prostitutes and turned their hotel rooms into "chambers of horror and torture."

CHAPTER 15

THE KILLING COUSINS

KENNETH A. BIANCHI AND ANGELO BUONO

(1977-1979)

Despite their youthful zest for living, neither Diane
Wilder nor Karen Mandic was the kind of girl who
would ignore her responsibilities and slip away for a
spur-of-the-moment weekend. Nor would the Western
Washington University students have failed to confide
their weekend plans to their friends or employers.

Twenty-seven–year–old Diane had taught handi-
capped children in the Seattle school system until she
left to return to university and pursue an interest she
had developed about the Arab world.

Five years younger than her roommate, Karen was
also an independent and industrious young woman who
worked in the Fred Meyers Department Store in Bellingham, Washington, to help pay for her education.
Although her dinner break at 7:00 P.M. was usually only
an hour long, on the night of January 11, 1979, her boss
agreed to give her two hours off so that she could drive
to a house in the wealthy Edgemoor section of town.

Karen had explained that she and Diane were planning

to housesit the luxurious home for the absentee owners while the burglar alarm was being repaired, and would be paid $200 for the job. But when Karen hadn't returned to work, or telephoned by 11:00 P.M., the worried store manager called one of her friends, a security officer at the university, and asked him to check out the situation.

The security man drove to the house in Edgemoor, and then to the home the two women normally shared. Unable to locate them at either address, the security man then telephoned the Bellingham police.

Even though both women were adults and had been missing for only a few hours, Bellingham was still small enough for the police department to move quickly on a missing persons report. Before daylight the next morning, police were already deeply immersed in the investigation.

They quickly learned that Karen had been hired for the housesitting job by an engaging young man she had met when he worked at the department store as a security guard. His name was Kenneth Bianchi, and he had left the department store job to become a supervisor at the Coastal Security Agency.

When investigators contacted the owner of Coastal Security, he was mystified. He hadn't heard anything about a broken security alarm, or a housesitting assignment for the two young women. Bianchi's name repeatedly surfaced, as detectives combed the vacant Edgemoor house and followed up other leads.

Then the bodies of the two women were found. After hearing a radio report about the search, an alert citizen had noticed Karen's Mercury Bobcat abandoned in a cul-de-sac near her house. The missing coeds were inside. They were fully clothed, but both had been raped, and marks on their flesh indicated they had been bound and gagged before they were murdered.

Inconsistencies in Bianchi's statements, and his apparent tie to Karen, made him a prime suspect. Police authorities ordered his arrest, and he was taken peacefully into custody. A search of the security-company truck he was driving turned up a company card with the address of the empty house in Edgemoor and a key to the door. A woman's scarf was also found, and although the owner could not be immediately identified, friends of Diane told investigators that she collected and owned dozens of scarves.

At first glance, Bianchi seemed an unlikely murder suspect. He was living with Kelli Boyd, a young Bellingham woman, by whom he had fathered a son, and in the few months he'd been a member of the community he had developed a reputation as a likeable, industrious, and dependable family man. He was friendly, talkative, and his dark good looks had attracted the attention of more than one interested young woman. If he had wished to stray from Kelli, it was obvious that he could have found plenty of willing partners without resorting to kidnap and murder.

Although horrified by the ugly accusations against the father of her child, Kelli, nevertheless, provided her full cooperation to detectives investigating the slayings. She agreed to have the house she shared with Bianchi and their son searched, and turned over all the clothing he had worn on Thursday night to the officers. Semen stains matching spots on the clothing of the victims were found on his underwear, and his undershorts were also smeared with menstrual blood, a factor that took on special significance after an autopsy disclosed that Diane was having her period when she was killed. One of Bianchi's business cards was found in Karen's room, and her telephone number was found in his house.

After a warrant signed by a district-court judge allowed the police to conduct a search of Bianchi's home, some telephone equipment and a chainsaw were found in the basement and confiscated. The equipment had been reported missing from locations where Bianchi had been assigned as a security guard. Bianchi was charged with theft, and bail was set at $150,000. The theft count and high bail ensured the suspect would remain safely in custody while investigators continued to collect and analyze evidence, until there was enough to support the filing of charges against him for the slayings.

Pubic hairs were among the more important bits of evidence collected in the early stages of the investigation. One was recovered when it dropped from Diane's body onto a sterile sheet spread over the ground as the victims were being removed from the Mercury Bobcat. Two others were found on the basement staircase of the Edgemoor house where the women had apparently been lured. Suspicious carpet fibers were also found on the bodies of the victims, and on the soles of their shoes, but the investigators worried that the analysis of the hairs and fibers at the FBI Crime Laboratory in Quantico, Virginia, would take days.

Despite the fast-growing amount of circumstantial evidence piling up against him Bianchi stubbornly continued to insist that he was innocent in the rape and murder of the women. His friends stuck by him, convinced that the gentle young man they thought they knew so well could never have sadistically killed two helpless women.

Investigators learned that the suspected sex-killer and his girlfriend had lived in Los Angeles until a few months earlier when first Kelli and her baby, then Bianchi, moved back to Kelli's hometown.

The young couple had moved to the more peaceful solitude of the Great Northwest at just about the time a wave of sex-and-torture murders that had terrified Los Angeles residents for five terrible months, had mysteriously come to a sudden end.

Most of the victims of the elusive serial killer had been snatched from the Hollywood-Glendale area.

Their broken bodies, naked, raped, sodomized, and sometimes showing evidence of torture, were dumped along little-frequented hills and ravines in an area around Glendale of roughly six miles. With their usual eye for a dramatic phrase, journalists quickly labeled the crazed killer "The Hillside Strangler."

The first apparent victim was Yolanda Washington, a streetwise nineteen-year-old prostitute and part-time waitress with a two-year-old daughter. She was the only Negro among the ten California females whose deaths would eventually be officially attributed to the Hillside slayings. Yolanda had been picked up in Hollywood at about 11:00 P.M., on October 17, 1977. Her nude body was dumped near Universal City the next day.

Judith Lynn Miller, a fifteen-year-old runaway and Hollywood prostitute, was the next to die. She was picked up outside a diner on Sunset Boulevard, and her naked body was found grotesquely sprawled in a La Crescenta flowerbed a few hours later.

Then, Elissa Teresa Kastin, a twenty-one-year-old Hollywood waitress, was abducted, sexually tortured, and strangled before her body was tossed down an embankment in Glendale.

Jane Evelyn King, a twenty-eight-year-old blonde who was an aspiring model and actress, was suffocated and strangled. Her body was dumped along an off-ramp on the Golden State Freeway.

Fourteen-year-old Sonja Johnson and her twelve-year-old school chum, Dolores Cepeda, were abducted from a bus stop, then raped and murdered. Their bodies were found a week later near Elysian Park.

The same day the two schoolgirls were found, the body of Christine Weckler, a talented twenty-year-old student at the Pasadena Art Center of Design, was discovered on a quiet street in Highland Park. She had once lived in the same apartment complex as Bianchi.

Young women and girls in the Los Angeles area were

terrified. Although the press had stressed that the first two victims were prostitutes, it had become clear to police and to a nervous public that any young female could be the potential prey of the crazed killer.

Women flocked to self-defense classes, and sales of police-type whistles and disabling chemical sprays boomed. Business executives and college authorities established escort services to protect their female employees and students who had to travel at night. Women, young and old, bought shriek alarms for their cars and extra locks for their doors. Alarmed by the public's growing hysteria, the Los Angeles Police Department founded a massive Hillside Strangler Task Force that at one point included nearly one hundred officers and civilians, to follow up on clues and what would eventually amount to 10,000 tips from the public received over a twenty-four-hour telephone hotline. Investigators tracking down the leads fanned out across the United States, and traveled as far as London, England, to check out one suspect.

The Los Angeles County Sheriff's Department put together a smaller task force, and the Glendale Police Department assigned some of their most skilful homicide investigators to the baffling case.

And still the killings continued!

Lauren Rae Wagner, an eighteen-year-old business college student who was studying to become a paralegal assistant, was kidnapped virtually in front of her parents' San Fernando Valley home as she was returning alone in her car after spending an afternoon with her boyfriend. A neighbor later said she thought she saw two men leading her to their vehicle. Lauren's body was found the next day. The beautiful red-haired teenager had been raped, burned by electrical wire taped to her palms and plugged into an outlet, and then strangled.

Kimberly Diane Martin, an eighteen-year-old prostitute with a Hollywood nude-modeling service, answered a summons to a Glendale apartment building. Her naked body was found obscenely spreadeagled along an Echo Park hillside the next day.

The last strangler victim to die in California was Cindy Lee Hudspeth, a pretty, churchgoing strawberry blonde, who worked as a bank clerk, attended Glendale College, and spent every evening she could spare disco dancing with friends. Her naked body was found on February 17, 1978, crammed into the trunk of her Datsun, which had been pushed over a steep cliff in an isolated area of the Angeles National Forest. The wreckage was spotted by a private helicopter pilot. The twenty-year-old had lived across the street from the apartment building where Bianchi and Miss Weckler had once resided.

Then, as mysteriously as it had begun, the ghastly bloodletting that had raged through the hills and valleys surrounding the Southern California metropolis stopped. When that sometimes happens during a series of murders, the killer is usually never brought to justice for the crimes. Law-enforcement officials, mental-health authorities, and other experts generally discount the possibility that the killer has merely become frightened or tired of his behavior. It is more likely, they usually conclude, that he has been imprisoned for other unrelated offenses, has been confined to a mental institution, or died. Although puzzled police had no way of knowing it at the time, none of those explanations applied to the abrupt cessation of the Hillside slayings.

Instead, the slaughter stopped at about the time that Kenneth Bianchi followed Kelli and their infant son, Sean, two thousand miles north, up the Pacific coastline nearly to the Canadian border.

It was eleven months after the death of Cindy Hudspeth when Bianchi was taken into custody as a suspect in the double-slaying of the Bellingham coeds.

Bellingham police notified the Strangler Task Force

in Los Angeles and the Los Angeles County Sheriff's Department of Bianchi's arrest, and of the apparent similarity in the manner of death between the two Washington coeds and the California victims. Police were also notified in Rochester, New York, where Bianchi had lived before moving to Los Angeles. They were given a detailed rundown on the charges in Washington and asked for background information on the suspect's early life in Rochester.

Homicide detectives from both cities flew to Bellingham to question the curly-haired young man. Police from Rochester were especially interested in talking to Bianchi about a trio of slayings in 1971, 1972, and 1973 which had become popularly known as the "Alphabet Killings" because each of the little-girl–victims had had the same first and last initials. The perplexing slayings of Carmen Colon and Wanda Walkowicz, both eleven, and of Michelle Maenza, ten, were unsolved. Bianchi had been living in Rochester at the time the girls were abducted off the street, each while she was on an errand. When the bodies of the children were found, they had been raped and strangled.

Investigators were particularly outraged when they learned that about one hour after Carmen left home to pick up a medical prescription for her mother, a partially nude little girl was seen running from a car on a nearby highway. Although approximately a hundred motorists had passed the scene, craning to watch as the car backed up and the screaming and wildly struggling youngster was dragged back inside, none stopped. Inexplicably, the little-girl murders stopped after Michelle's death, and it was not until five years later that investigators learned that the vehicle belatedly described by witnesses to the disturbing roadside tableau was the same color and model as the car driven by Bianchi in Rochester at that time.

Bianchi appeared to have a normal interest in women

near his own age, to those who knew him as a teenager and young man in Rochester. He was eighteen when he married a practical nurse he had known most of his life. But a few months later the union was annulled, and he was dating again. Sometimes Bianchi, who was good-looking and articulate, dated three or four girls at a time. Women found him attractive, and often responded to his chronic lying, fitful laziness, occasional thievery, and sexual dallying with excessive mothering, believing that he merely needed time to mature.

However, according to records compiled by Rochester-area social agencies, the important women in Bianchi's infancy hadn't always been so caring and protective. His natural mother was a teenager with a reputation for heavy drinking and promiscuity. As soon as he was brought home from the hospital, she passed him on to a foster mother, who in turn handed him off to a succession of neighbors.

However, when he was three months old, Nicholas and Frances Bianchi adopted him, and his new mother lavished him with affection and loving care.

The young man studied police science and psychology at Monroe Community College in Rochester, planning to land a job with the Monroe County Sheriff's Department. But he was rejected for the position, and settled for a job as a security guard. He changed employment often, holding several different security jobs, but too many pieces of jewelry and other items were found to be missing after he had been on duty for him to keep the security jobs long. He also worked for a time as an ambulance emergency technician, but he disliked the night hours he had to work on the ambulance crew.

In January 1976, he moved to the Los Angeles area, where an older cousin, Angelo Buono, Jr., who operated a thriving car-upholstery business in suburban Glendale agreed to take him in until he was able to find a job and an apartment of his own.

Police in Rochester had never considered Bianchi to be a suspect in the little-girl murders while he was living there. And they never filed charges against him, not even years later after investigators flew to Bellingham to talk with the young man being held as a suspect in a double sex-slaying there. There was no strong evidence linking him to the Rochester crimes.

Members of Los Angeles' Hillside Strangler Task Force had better luck. A few weeks after Bianchi pleaded not guilty to the Bellingham murders, by reason of insanity, authorities in Los Angeles announced that he would be indicted in the Hillside Strangler slayings.

While he was locked in the Whatcom County Jail in Bellingham, the former security guard had been kept busy. He had not only been talking with homicide investigators from other jurisdictions, but with a steady stream of psychiatrists, hypnotists, and other mental-health professionals as well. And he had decided that he was not merely one individual, but that his confused mind harbored a whole host of personalities, all fighting for control. He was suddenly perceived in some medical quarters to be suffering from a multiple-personality disorder. And one of Bianchi's alternate personalities, a vicious, foul-mouthed, amoral character named Steve, was a depraved, woman-hating sex killer.

The deadly serious game continued for months, with Bianchi struggling to escape justice by convincing authorities that he had been in the helpless grip of a sick runaway personality when the coeds were slain. He eventually starred in an intriguing PBS television documentary, "The Mind of a Murderer," which focused on him as the possible reluctant victim of a mental aberration that permits alternate personalities to control the thoughts and behavior of afflicted individuals. The remarkable documentary was pieced together from sixty-five hours of videotape made by police while psychiatrists were studying Bianchi.

Despite the suspect's inspired posturing and impressive showing of psychiatric gobbledygook, in June, it was Kenneth Bianchi, not the mysterious Steve, who was formally charged with five of the Hillside Strangler slayings.

The following October the former security guard stood in the courtroom of Judge Jack Kurtz in the Whatcom County Courthouse in Bellingham, and tearfully agreed to abandon his insanity defense and plead guilty to the double murder. His claims to be suffering from the multiple-personality disorder were being rapidly chipped away and the circumstantial evidence of his guilt in the sadistic killings was overwhelming. Later, another judge in California would rule that he had faked his mysterious memory loss and put on a phony multiple-personality act.

Investigation and questioning by law-enforcement and mental-health experts had revealed that Bianchi had lured the two unsuspecting Washington women to the vacant house and pulled a gun on them. Then he had forced his prisoners into separate rooms, stripped and raped them. After the sexual assaults, he garroted them with articles of their own clothing.

Terms of an agreement worked out the night before the hearing called for sparing Bianchi the death penalty in Washington state and sentencing him to two consecutive life terms in prison without the possibility of parole. Other elements of the agreement were even more startling.

He had agreed to plead guilty to five of the Hillside Strangler slayings in Los Angeles. And he promised to testify that his cousin, Angelo Buono, had played a leading role in the slaughter. In return for his guilty pleas he was to be given five more consecutive life sentences. If he kept his word and testified truthfully against his cousin it was agreed that he would be permitted to serve his time in California where he believed the prisons to be more humane and easier to endure than those in Washington.

Wearing a three-piece suit over a bulletproof vest, and with tears welling in his eyes, the seemingly contrite defendant stood before Judge Kurtz in the heavily guarded courtroom and blubbered: "To begin to live with myself, I must do everything I can to get Angelo and to give my life *C*for study*c* so that someone won't follow in my footsteps."

The forty-nine–year–old Buono was arrested the next day. He vehemently denied involvement in the slayings, insisting that Bianchi was a liar. It would take more than four years, and cost Los Angeles County taxpayers more than $2 million to pay for the longest criminal trial in the nation's history before the conflicting stories of the two cousins could be sorted out. And an almost unbelievable tale of lust, hate, and horror would be forever etched in the minds of all those who followed the case.

Bianchi's statements and evidence presented during the two-year trial that began in November 1981 and ended in November 1983, revealed a depraved experiment that began with sexual abuse and exploitation by the deadly cousins and accelerated into rape, torture, and murder.

Divorced and the father of several children, Buono had already surrounded himself with young girls whom he used sexually, when his cousin arrived from Rochester. Bianchi had barely settled in when the two men began forcing teenagers to go out on calls to private homes as prostitutes.

When two of the girls ran away, the outraged pimps began to kill other women. Bianchi confessed to strangling Yolanda Washington after Buono had picked her up. Judith Miller was next. Then the killing cousins, posing as policemen, began cruising the streets of Hollywood and Glendale. Bianchi, who had been turned down twice for police work since arriving in Los Angeles, nevertheless knew enough about the profession that he and his cousin looked and sounded convincing in their roles.

Dolores Cepeda and Sonja Johnson were victims of the bogus-policeman ruse. The killers followed the girls from a shopping center, then confronted them at a bus stop. They told the girls that they were investigating a burglary and ordered them to climb inside their car to be driven to a nearby police station for questioning as potential witnesses. Once the youngsters were inside the car their fate was sealed. That night their nude bodies were dumped into a trash-filled ravine near Dodger Stadium.

During a psychiatric interview at the Los Angeles County Men's Central Jail, Bianchi revealed that Catherine Lorre, the only daughter of the late, Hungarian-born film actor Peter Lorre, nearly became the first victim of the masquerade.

She was walking in Hollywood when a car stopped at the curb next to her, and Bianchi stepped out. He flashed a badge, told her he was an undercover vice-squad officer and demanded to see her identification. He realized who she was when he came across a prized photograph of her as a baby, sitting on the lap of her famous father.

Buono, still sitting in the car, signaled to Bianchi to leave her alone. He was worried that her late father's fame would attract too much attention to the crime if they kidnapped and murdered her. She was permitted to walk away, unaware of her close brush with death.

It was never made clear if the same ruse was used on Kristina Weckler. But the art student was somehow lured from her apartment by Bianchi, taken to the parking lot where Buono was waiting, and driven to his house at gunpoint.

Kristina's death was the most horrible of all. After she was raped by both men, they decided to try a different method of murder. They injected her with air and cleaning solvent, but although the agonized girl went into convulsions, she remained alive. So they tied a plastic bag around her neck and attached it to a gas pipe from a stove. Kristina finally died of asphyxiation.

Although the police masquerade was used in most of the abductions and murders, Cindy Hudspeth was one of the exceptions. Buono had given her a business card at the restaurant where she worked, and the part-time waitress made the fatal mistake of stopping at his shop to order two floor mats for her car. On the pretense of giving her a list of part-time jobs, Buono and Bianchi lured her inside the house where they stripped her, tied her spread-eagled to the bed, raped and strangled her.

With the meeting of Bianchi and Veronica Lynn Compton, the bizarre murder case took on grotesque new dimensions. When the dark-haired Latin beauty wrote a fan letter to Bianchi, she appeared to be just another befuddled prison groupie — a member of that perplexing breed of unfortunate females who become infatuated with men who are locked up for highly publicized multiple murders or other especially grisly crimes.

A torrid correspondence quickly developed between the prisoner and the divorcee. Soon the shapely, if definitely wiffy, twenty-three-year-old poet, aspiring actress, and playwright whose creative writing dwelled heavily on sadomasochism and gore, was visiting the notorious serial killer twice a day at the jail.

It was during those romantic meetings that they reputedly hatched a harebrained scheme intended to demonstrate Bianchi's innocence of the Washington double murder. It would eventually earn Veronica recognition in newspapers around the country as the "Copycat Strangler."

She later related that they also agreed she would testify in court that Bianchi was with her in her suburban house trailer on the nights each of the Hillside

Strangler victims was killed. Bianchi would then be cleared and his cousin would be left holding the bag for the Los Angeles killings, the lovers reasoned.

As part of the cockeyed plot, Veronica smuggled a sample of Bianchi's semen out of the jail. The plan called for her to plant the semen on, or inside, the body of a new Washington victim so authorities would believe that a man with Bianchi's physical characteristics had committed the murder while he was in jail.

Her head filled with thoughts of romance and murder, the love-smitten woman flew to Bellingham to put the first half of the plan into action. Although she and Bianchi had considered murdering a Western Washington University coed, instead she struck up a conversation with a part-time cocktail waitress at a local lounge and lured her to a motel room.

Fortunately for the intended victim, she was stronger than her murderous hostess. When Mrs. Compton walked up behind her chair, suddenly looped a length of strong cord around her neck, and pulled, nothing went as expected.

The startled victim of the attack tried to scream but choking, reached desperately behind her, dug her fingernails into Veronica's arms, and lurched forward. Veronica catapulted over the woman's head, crashed into a piece of furniture, and collapsed on the floor, stunned. In moments the waitress was outside the door, inside her car, and speeding away.

Police arrested Veronica at her trailer home in a Los Angeles suburb several days later. In early 1981, she was sentenced to a life term in a Washington state prison for attempted premeditated murder. The sentence carried no possibility of parole until 1994.

Shortly after her arrest, Veronica announced during a jailhouse press interview that she and Bianchi were planning to marry and eventually become parents of a daughter, but the prison Romeo was no longer interested in her. The bizarre romance died with the collapse of the even more bizarre murder plot.

Anxious to avoid a long trial and to skirt the dangers of losing a complex case, state authorities offered the gaunt, closed-mouthed Buono an opportunity to escape execution in California's gas chamber at San Quentin. The deal included terms that were somewhat similar to those arranged with his cousin: life in prison with the possibility of parole, in return for a guilty plea. He refused.

The marathon trial on charges of murdering ten females ranging in age from twelve to twenty-eight began. Despite a maddeningly fitful performance on the stand where he told contradictory stories, Bianchi was the star witness. The two-hundredth witness in the trial, he testified for four months. Buono exercised his right not to testify.

Mrs. Compton, who claimed that she had regained her reason after treatment by prison doctors, took the stand and testified that Bianchi had admitted to her that he committed the Hillside Strangler killings alone. She insisted that she plotted with him to frame Buono, but decided to tell the truth because she didn't want to "see a potentially innocent man get convicted of a crime he didn't commit."

The exhausting court action that had already eaten up ten months of preliminary hearings and six months of pre-trial motions, dragged through another two full years of trial, before ending with jury verdicts of guilty to nine counts of first-degree murder. The panel of seven women and five men returned a verdict of innocent in the slaying of Yolanda Washington, who had been considered the first victim of the ghastly serial killings.

Prosecutors conceded that they weren't surprised at Buono's acquittal in the Yolanda Washington murder because it was thought to be the weakest of the ten cases against Buono. Deputy Attorney General Michael Nash said jurors apparently rejected the testimony of a prostitute who said she took the victim to Buono's home two weeks before the slaying. She testified that she accompanied Yolanda and two other women to sell Buono a trick list of customers for prostitution.

The jury recommended life in prison without the possibility of parole in each of the convictions. Courtroom observers blamed the jury's failure to recommend the death penalty on the life sentences already meted out to Bianchi. Defense attorneys had argued that the life sentences ordered for Bianchi in exchange for his testimony against his cousin should be the jury's guide in deciding Buono's fate.

Because California law prohibits a judge from changing a jury's recommendation for a life sentence to the death penalty, Superior Court Judge Ronald George was left with no alternative. Expressing his disappointment, the judge declared:

"I do not believe that life in prison for Kenneth Bianchi and Angelo Buono will accomplish anything worthwhile for society or them."

The judge said he expected that the two killers would gain only pleasure from reflecting on the torture of their victims, and that they were incapable of remorse. "In view of the jury's mercy," he concluded however, ". . . I am without authority to set the punishment at death." He reluctantly ordered life sentences on each of the nine counts of first-degree murder for the defendant.

Because Buono was already assured of spending the rest of his life behind bars, Judge George dismissed eleven other felony counts of rape and pandering. The jurist also granted a motion by the State to have Bianchi transferred to Washington to begin serving his life terms, because his rambling, flip-flop performance during the trial had breached his plea agreement to testify truthfully and fully against Buono.

"I think Mr. Bianchi did everything he could to sabotage this case," Judge George declared.

In Washington, corrections-department authorities assigned Bianchi to special protective-custody status to protect him from other prisoners. In 1984, after unconfirmed reports reached officials of threats within the prison on Bianchi's life, he was granted permission to legally change his name to Anthony A. D'Amato. Later he again changed his name to Nicholas Fontana.

Buono is serving his life sentences in California.

BESTSELLING
SELF-HELP TITLES
from
PaperJacks

___ **BOUNCING BACK** — Andrew J. DuBrin Ph.D.

                                            7701-03189/$2.95

How to handle setbacks in your work and personal life.

___ **BREAKING THE SECRETARY BARRIER** — Janet Dight

                                            7701-0602-1/$3.95

How to get out from behind the typewriter and into a management job.

___ **CRY ANGER** — Jack Birnbaum M.D.   7701-04428/$3.50

A common-sense do-it-yourself approach to fighting the biggest epidemic of our times — DEPRESSION.

___ **IN THE CENTER OF THE NIGHT** — Jayne Blankenship

                                            7701-04002/$3.95

A story of survival against the despair of her husband's death, and the gradual healing of herself and, in the process, others.

___ **WHAT DID I DO WRONG?** — Lynn Caine   7701-04185/$3.95

Mothering and guilt.

Available at your local bookstore or return this coupon to:

BOOKS BY MAIL

320 Steelcase Rd. E.   **210 5th Ave., 7th Floor**
Markham, Ont., L3R 2M1   **New York, N.Y. 10010**

Please send me the books I have checked above. I am enclosing a total of $_____ (Please add 1.00 for one book and 50 cents for each additional book.) My cheque or money order is enclosed. (No cash or C.O.D.'s please.)

Name _____

Address _____ Apt. _____

City _____

Prov./State _____ P.C./Zip _____

Prices subject to change without notice   (SH/2)

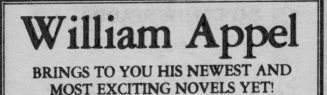

FREE!!
BOOKS BY MAIL
CATALOGUE

BOOKS BY MAIL will share with you our current bestselling books as well as hard to find specialty titles in areas that will match your interests. You will be updated on what's new in books at no cost to you. Just fill in the coupon below and discover the convenience of having books delivered to your home.

PLEASE ADD $1.00 TO COVER THE COST OF POSTAGE & HANDLING.

- -

BOOKS BY MAIL
320 Steelcase Road E.,
Markham, Ontario L3R 2M1

IN THE U.S. -
210 5th Ave., 7th Floor
New York, N.Y., 10010

Please send Books By Mail catalogue to:

Name _____
(please print)

Address _____

City _____

Prov./State _____ P.C./Zip _____

(BBM1)